THE VOICE OF ISIS

TEACHINGS OF
THE ORDER OF CHRISTIAN MYSTICS

THE VOICE OF ISIS

TEACHINGS OF THE ORDER OF CHRISTIAN MYSTICS

THE "CURTISS BOOKS" FREELY AVAILABLE AT

WWW.ORDEROFCHRISTIANMYSTICS.CO.ZA

THE VOICE OF ISIS

By the Teacher of

The Order of Christian Mystics

Transcribed by
HARRIETTE AUGUSTA CURTISS
and
F. HOMER CURTISS, B.S., M.D.
Founders of
THE ORDER OF CHRISTIAN MYSTICS
and
AUTHORS OF THE "CURTISS BOOKS"

2010 EDITION

REPUBLISHED FOR THE ORDER BY
MOUNT LINDEN PUBLISHING
JOHANNESBURG, SOUTH AFRICA
ISBN: 978-1-920483-13-5

Dedication

This edition is lovingly dedicated to the Memory

of the Founders of

The Order of Christian Mystics

Pyrahmos and Rahmea

and to

The Teacher of the Order

who on earth was called

Helena Petrovna Blavatsky

"Ministers of Christ and Stewards of the Mysteries of God."
1 Corinthians 4 vs. 1

Contents

TABLE OF CONTENTS

CHAPTER I

LIFE'S DUTIES

CHAPTER II

THE CYCLE OF FULFILLMENT

Contents

CHAPTER III

DEGREES AND ORDERS

PAGE 50

The seven-fold division of the cosmos—the geometry of Nature—geometrical law in the mental world—the Great White Lodge, how constituted—what is a Master?—Masters affinitized to all stages of evolution and classes of thought—the seven Degrees of Humanity—seven Orders in each Degree—the great Fourth Degree—it includes all advanced movements—its Orders—how the Orders are formed—positive and negative Orders—the Order of the 36—the Order of the 28—the Order of the 21—*The Order of the 15*—its former manifestations—the Holy Grail—the Order of the 10—the higher Orders as yet unmanifested—the great Third Degree, Divinity.

CHAPTER IV

THE WISDOM RELIGION

PAGE 66

Originally given to all mankind—existed many centuries before Christianity—the esoteric doctrines—the reasons for esoterism—the Wisdom still preserved—how to seek—fearlessness required—"when the pupil is ready the Teacher appears"—how to come close—disciples must be proved—compassion the result—the union with the Divine, how accomplished—the Path of Attainment—realization in the flesh.

CHAPTER V

CONCERNING THE DOCTRINE OF HELL FIRE

PAGE 75

The *Bible* an allegory—scriptures universally true—teachings of the Johannites—use of myths—the Path of At-one-ment—Hebrew symbols—journey of the awakened Soul—the Master Jesus, a historical personage—Our Lord

CHAPTER VI

THE ELEVENTH COMMANDMENT

PAGE 86

CHAPTER VII

NARCOTICS, ALCOHOL AND PSYCHISM

PAGE 98

Contents

CHAPTER X

THE DOCTRINE OF AVATARA

PAGE 137

Definition—Jesus an Avatar—not a mortal—method of appearance—advent determined by humanity—necessity for an inspired priesthood—sacrament of marriage—lesser manifestations—Avesha Avatars—each movement to have an Avesha—qualifications and limitations of an Avesha—an Avatar comes to humanity not to any one sect—*Bible* references—time of His coming—law of cycles—cycles of the century—signs of His coming—the 144,000—mission of *The Order of the 15*.

CHAPTER XI

A STUDY OF REINCARNATION OR REBIRTH

PAGE 155

A world-old teaching—proof acceptable to all impossible—illustrated by actor in *Hamlet*—what happens after death—definition of the astral-plane—Soul chooses to reincarnate—incarnates among old associates—how the "why" is forgotten—more Souls excarnate than incarnate—many wait for special stages of civilization—incarnate under their own sub-ray—time between incarnations—change of sex in incarnation—reasons for change of sex—possibility of attaining androgynous condition—incarnation to work for humanity—voluntary incarnation of a Great Teacher—complex personality of H.P.B.

CHAPTER XII

POWER

PAGE 164

The image of God—"All power is given unto me"—cosmic centers of power—only man correlates all powers—Eastern teachings—the seven mystic powers—the supreme power—power of intellect—power of will—power of thought—power

CHAPTER XIII

A BRIEF OUTLINE OF EVOLUTION.

DETAILS OF THE RELATION OF THE MASTERS TO HUMANITY

CHAPTER XIV

THE LAW

Contents

CHAPTER XV

WORLD CHAINS

CHAPTER XVI

PURITY

Contents

CHAPTER XVII

THE ORIGIN OF MAN

CHAPTER XVIII

THE SYMBOL OF THE SERPENT

Contents

CHAPTER XIX

PURIFICATION VERSUS DEIFICATION

PAGE 256

The need of this lesson—the forbidden fruit—purity and modesty must be preserved—the "queen of this world"—misleading astral entities—creating sickness and disease—meaning of Peer Gynt—the Ancient One— pre-Adamite races symbolized by Lillith—truth back of the world's conventions—the twain who are one flesh— forming the Trinity—absolute privacy required—misled through flattery—excuses for license impurity—reverses the triangle—apply the test of common-sense—add something to the world's standards—the woman in purple and scarlet— marriage a symbol of the Divine marriage—Divine Love overlaps human love—attainment not a dream—lessons of the unmarried—spread thoughts of purity—re-entering Eden.

CHAPTER XX

THE MEMORY OF PAST LIVES

PAGE 269

Destiny of each Soul—warnings by memory of past mistakes—why memory of past lives is not more common— memory of trials of one life enough—live in the present—other reason—show the memory is awakened—illustration of Abraham Lincoln—psychics told they were the Virgin Mary, Moses, Solomon, etc. how to distinguish the true—innate qualities will manifest—law of reasonality—example of an Egyptian priestess—object of re-birth—those who are told of their great mission—the preparation necessary—false astral teachings—how to guard against—blind obedience never required by the Masters.

Contents

CHAPTER XXI

THE CYCLE OF NECESSITY

PAGE 284

The Higher Self—chooses environment—personality has free-will—all experiences in the One Life—animals lack free-will—each Soul has a special work—may learn by experience of others—how Soul gains control—spiritualization of the centers—danger of opening psychic centers—rules for psychic protection how to test psychic messages—masters of evil and their methods—flattery a feature—how the Masters contact a pupil—temptations in the wilderness—fasting forty days—first temptation, power—second temptation, self-righteousness—third temptation, ambition—judge leniently—cultivate the fruits of the Spirit.

CHAPTER XXII

THE PATH

PAGE 295

Reality of the Path of Discipleship—renunciation—the four Gates—First Gate, charity and tolerance—Second Gate, harmony, conquering of fear—Third Gate, patience—Fourth Gate, mastery of thought—the Silent Thinker—three classes of dreams—how to control dreams—how to remodel your life—contacting thought-currents from above—the goal of attainment.

CHAPTER XXIII

EARTH'S FINER FORCES

PAGE 308

The foot esteemed in the Orient—use of silk on feet—earth-forces contacted through feet—how the earth breathes—effect of locality on character—masculine force from mountains, feminine from sea—Kundalini force and Tree of Life—allegory of Moses and the burning bush—crops without rain—magnetic action of sun and moon—reason for having largest meal at noon—use of shoes.

Contents

CHAPTER XXIV

THE LIGHT

PAGE 320

Four days of creation—same for the student—first day the light—second day, the firmament—third day, dry land—period of transmutation—descent of Spirit into matter—the end seen from the beginning—creeping things of the darkness—the Star of Initiation—light of Divine Love—effect in your life—do not be surprised at trials and tests—never say "I cannot"—courage necessary—Jewel of Great Price—"Let there be Light."

CHAPTER XXV

THE TWO TABLES OF STONE

PAGE 331

Law of spiritual evolution—guided by the Elohim—force of Saturn the first to emanate—the Law written on two tables of stone—Moses is Mikael-Jehova—the Philosopher's Stone—law heretofore read from the positive stone—markings on the negative stone covered up—stone rejected by the builders—humanity facing its initiation—children of earth making mock—a new cycle, an advanced step—man's boasted supremacy unsatisfying—the woman-question a burning one—man positive on physical-plane, woman on spiritual-plane—male Souls in feminine bodies—feminine equalities must balance masculine—the two tables of stone equal—both needed.

CHAPTER XXVI

HEALING PRAYER

PAGE 341

Office of the Master, Jesus—power of a name—effects on higher planes—the angels draw near—angels complementary to humanity—prayer like a projectile—the rationale of healing—the One Life

Contents

CHAPTER XXVII

THE SILENCE

PAGE 346

The Law of Growth—distinctions between concentration, meditation, prayer and the Silence—How to meditate—concentration required—importance of breathing—rhythmic breathing—the complete breath—directions—rules for inhalation and exhalation—thought to be held while breathing—you are but a channel for the Divine—entering the Silence—Dare, Do, Keep Silent—the Voice of the Silence.

CHAPTER XXVIII

NATURE'S MYSTIC ALPHABET

PAGE 356

Relations of sound, number, color, form—God geometrizes—law of correspondence—Nature-shapes geometrical—sound the first letter—how to find your key-note—selecting your color—sorrow the base clef in the Psalm of Life—primary colors, red, yellow, blue—others supplementary—colors born of white—no pure white—red the key-note of man—yellow the Soul-color—blue is feminine, color of the auric envelope—orange the color of prana—orange foods—green the Nature-color—why Nature is green—indigo, spiritual mind—violet not an earthly color—1 is unity—2 separation—3 the trinity—4 the earth-plane—5 humanity—6 The Christ-force—7 Divine Wisdom—8 evolution—9 initiation—10 unity—the One Law.

CHAPTER XXIX

THE WORD

PAGE 370

Esoteric teaching—*Bible* not literally true—the Word is the Voice of the Higher Self—a Ray from the Divine—sunbeam imprisoned in the fruit—"as an Ape in the World-forest"—the Guardian Angel—fruit imprisoned

Contents

the Augean stables—cruelty of the Hindus—sacrifice human life to insects—killing vermin—killing animals for food—spiritual growth does not depend upon the stomach—does vegetarianism produce greater tolerance and love—vegetarian races not more spiritual—meat does not contain the desire—body-passions must be controlled not starved—perfect man must have all functions at fullest power—Masters who ate meat—the thought-force most important—when thinking continually of food you dwell in the stomach—each kingdom sacrifices its life to the higher—a change in the form only in which the life-force expresses—this is the scheme of evolution—perverted by man's selfishness—their commercial value perfects the animals—the cruelty of Nature—effect on butchers—killing flies and mosquitoes—killing for sport or vanity—man's responsibility to the lower kingdoms—decide the question for yourself.

CHAPTER XXXIII

PRAYER OF CONSECRATION. CONCENTRATION HOURS

PAGE 408

Power of mantra—the prayer of consecration—comprehension of self necessary—the key to the mysteries—concentrating at noon—correlating with the Heart Center of the Order—realization of personal communion with the Teacher—special healing services.

CHAPTER XXXIV

THE MEANING OF THE SYMBOL

PAGE 413

A symbol tells the source and object of its teachings—the meaning of the circle—the Open Eye—the meaning of the triangle—the five-pointed stars—the meaning of 15—the Motto—meaning of DARE—meaning of DO—meaning of KEEP SILENT.

Contents

APPENDIX.

PREFACE TO THE SECOND EDITION

The first edition of *The Voice of Isis* was put forth in the nature of an experiment to determine whether or not occult students of today would appreciate a new interpretation of the world-old esoteric principles of the Wisdom Religion couched in simple language, recognizing the occult and mystical side of the Christian scriptures and embracing the scientific advances of the twentieth century.

The speedy sale of that edition answered the above question in a most positive manner. It also supported our claim that the Wisdom Religion is the one World religion back of all and, being a systematized expression of cosmic verities, can be interpreted in terms of the most advanced thought, and meet the spiritual needs, of any age; for it comprehends and anticipates in the principles of its philosophy all the discoveries, advances and attainments of which man is capable in this world-period.

The hearty reception accorded this volume of spiritual philosophy, among all classes of readers also shows that in spite of the scientific, materialistic, and godless education of the day, there is a great spiritual and psychic awakening taking place; that the human heart is as hungry as ever for direct communion with the super-physical planes of consciousness as a personal experience, and that the human mind is as unsatisfied as ever with purely mechanistic and materialistic conceptions of the universe, and reaches out as eagerly for, and is more than ever ready to accept, a spiritual philosophy which includes all that materialistic science can reveal, and which is presented in a rational and common sense manner.

Los Angeles, California, September, 1914.

PREFACE

The Path to Mastery is marked by the severest self discipline, absolute obedience and unswerving allegiance to the chosen Teacher or Guru. Throughout the ages this training has been administered most rigorously by various teachers, societies and brotherhoods, so much so that the neophyte, once having pledged himself to any one occult school or teacher, was dominated as to what he should eat, wear, do, think and believe, having almost no freedom of body or mind. Such training was necessary in the past—and still is for some. The helpfulness of that method consisted in bringing the student to a realization of the greatness of his calling, the littleness of the personal self, the emptiness of the pleasures of sense and the barrenness of physical life as compared with the fullness and glory of spiritual attainment.

While *The Order of the 15* recognizes that the occult law back of the outer observances required by former movements is as true today as ever, and that discipline, obedience and faithfulness are as requisite today as of old, still being an *advanced Order* it must employ *advanced methods* for attaining the same ends.

OBJECTS OF THE ORDER OF THE 15

OBJECT 1. COMPLETE INDIVIDUALITY THROUGH UNION WITH THE HIGHER SELF.

The Order of the 15 is put forth to gather together those who are willing to face themselves and who are sufficiently advanced to consciously take into their own hands the responsibility for the disciplining of their lives. Those Souls who are earnestly attracted to its teachings and will ultimately be drawn into its ranks are those who in former lives have passed through the severe disciplining and personal training mentioned above and hence should be ready to recognize the necessity for discipline and desire the conscious realization of the higher life so sincerely as to be willing to make its attainment their chief aim in life. They must give the same implicit obedience—not blind, but that which is born of perfect confidence—and the same unswerving allegiance to their Teacher as of old, this time not because of vows to an earthly teacher or Brotherhood enforced by penalty, but voluntarily and gladly, with no human voice to command and no great personality to follow. For in this case the Teacher whom they must learn to recognize and obey is their own divine Father-in-heaven, their Higher Self, who speaks to them in the sanctuary of their own hearts.

The ideal put forth by this Order is therefore one of constant self-mastery in obedience to the personal guidance *from within* and prompted by the earnest desire for spiritual growth and the ability to help humanity to a greater realization of The Christ-consciousness. The teachings of this Order are entirely constructive, for if only the true is persistently put forth the false will disappear of itself. This teaching is the acme of individualism-Mastery, the manifestation of the Real Self for the individual, and the acme of oneness for the Race. Necessarily the fundamental assumption of this teaching is the possibility of each Soul coming into conscious personal touch not only with his own Father-in-heaven but also with those Great Souls, the Masters of Love and Wisdom, who are the Elder Brothers and Guardians of the Race. *The Order of the 15 is one* of the avenues through which those Great Souls are working to lead their followers into personal relationship. It is a testing ground for those who have passed the tests of enforced discipline, an opportunity for them to prove their ability and willingness to follow the guidance that comes from within.

Naturally many are called but few are chosen, for only those are finally chosen and admitted to full membership who have proved their ability to stand firm and be trained to work unselfishly for humanity along the special lines laid down by this Order through its agents. It is a far more advanced step to voluntarily give love, fidelity and obedience to a teacher because your own Soul recognizes the source of the teachings, the objects of the movement and the sacrifice necessarily made by the agents that you may receive the teachings, than to give such allegiance because of any form of compulsion.

OBJECT 2. PERSONAL TRAINING IN THE PHILOSOPHY OF LIFE.

The personal training of each pupil is carried on partly on the inner planes and partly by correspondence with the Teacher of the Order through the Secretary. Such correspondence is open to all who need personal help with the problems of their Soul life. The answers will contain explanations of the spiritual laws which apply to the individual needs of the pupil. Definite commands will not be given, for the training is designed to foster in the individual perfect freedom of choice and to develop the strength of will necessary voluntarily to apply the Law to his own problems. The letters are signed by the Secretary merely as the Agent of the Teacher, and only if the intuition of the pupil can grasp the fact that the instruction given is more than the human wisdom of the agents can its real significance be appreciated. Necessarily such letters are more or less cryptic and hence require meditation that the light of intuition may reveal their true meaning. The method of teaching employed by the Teacher of this Order is one in which praise and flattery of the pupil plays little part, rather the Teacher points out the stumbling blocks in the pupil's Path to Realization and tests both his intuition, his sincerity and his humility. Only the determined and the courageous can win final victory.

OBJECT 3. A HIGHER STANDARD OF PURITY ON ALL PLANES.

It is comparatively easy for one who is determined to lead The Christ-life to curb his grosser passions, refrain from acts of impurity and injustice and lead what the world calls an upright life. But the requirements for entering the Mysteries are far more exacting. Ere he can safely enter the more advanced stages of occultism he must learn to control the currents of his thoughts, as well as his words and acts. Hence *The Order of the 15* helps its pupils to gain a higher conception of purity on all planes, especially in their ideas in regard to the use of the Great Creative Force.

OBJECT 4. THE ESOTERIC INTERPRETATION OF THE BIBLE.

While many orders, societies and organizations base their teachings upon various Eastern scriptures or medieval teachings, this Order teaches that the Christian *Bible* contains the same spiritual teachings and the same occult philosophy found in the older scriptures. Furthermore, it is couched in terms which appeal to the Western type of mind, once the esoteric key to its symbology and mysticism is known. This key *The Order of the 15* gives to its students, thus enabling them to apply the underlying laws of every parable, allegory and miracle to their own spiritual growth.

OBJECT 5. TRAINING THE SENSES TO RESPOND TO VIBRATIONS FROM ALL PLANES.

This Order offers no formulas or exercises for developing psychic powers, teaching that all such faculties should evolve gradually *as a natural result* of normal spiritual growth, hence they should not be sought for or forced through special forms of concentration, "sitting for development," etc. But as the Soul evolves the senses must respond to higher notes of vibration and awaken to higher states of consciousness. When this occurs the pupil must be taught both how to protect himself from the many dangers of the psychic realm and also how to make the best use of the newly acquired powers in furthering his spiritual growth. Perhaps the earliest recognition the pupil has of the divine guidance of his Father-in-heaven is through symbolic dreams and visions. The Teacher of the Order aids the pupil in interpreting such spiritual lessons until he is sufficiently versed in the language of symbology and methods of interpretation to grasp the lesson for himself. This work is a part of the personal correspondence with the Teacher of the Order.

OBJECT 6. PREPARATION FOR THE COMING WORLD TEACHER, THE AVATAR.

Like nearly all advanced thinkers along spiritual lines and all advanced spiritual movements of today, *The Order of the 15* expects a great spiritual Teacher to appear on earth during the early years of this century. Hence one of the main objects of this Order is so to train its pupils that, through their own intuitions they may learn to recognize and respond to the influence of that Great Teacher upon the higher planes so that when the days of the famine come, "not a famine of bread, nor a thirst for water, but of hearing the words of the Lord," the days when "they shall run to and fro to seek the word of the Lord," the days which precede the coming of the Avatar, they shall not be deceived but shall find and know. Only by a recognition of that Great Teacher upon the higher planes or by recognizing Him through His teachings can humanity hope to know Him when He appears in the flesh.

OBJECT 7. SPECIAL TRAINING IN RECOGNIZING THE ONENESS OF TRUTH WHEREVER FOUND.

While we have heard much of Universal Brotherhood and its various methods of attainment, from the Reign of Terror to the present day, still this Order teaches a new conception of this much to be desired state. Since the human race reflects Truth, like a diamond reflects light, through many facets, Universal Brotherhood can never be achieved by all men thinking alike. Nor do we believe such an achievement desirable, for in Nature we find perfect Brotherhood expressed in many forms, the oak and the violet at its root receive the life-force from the same soil, air, water and sunshine, yet each develop to perfection. In the same way *The Order of the 15* strives to send out the One Life and permits each Soul to assimilate it and grow to the perfection of his own individuality in perfect freedom. Hence our idea of Universal Brotherhood is universal recognition of the oneness of Truth in its various expressions or unity in diversity, thereby manifesting perfect tolerance toward all.

INTRODUCTION.

"How often would I have gathered thy children
together, as a hen doth gather her brood under
her wings, and ye would not!" *St. Luke* XIII, 34.

The Egyptians recognized and adored the Productive
Principle, both in Nature and in man, under the symbol of
Isis, the Universal Mother, the power of bringing forth in
humanity the Divine Child or The Christ. The title of this
volume indicates that its teachings are designed to bring forth
in humanity a new conception of the spiritual life through
the development of the Mother-love, that divine feminine-
principle of the Soul which brings forth in the daily life.

Isis was also called the "Mother of God," the "Celestial
Virgin" and the "Queen of Heaven," just as her counterpart,
the Virgin Mary, is among Christian peoples, and was usually
represented carrying in her hand the *crux ansata*. It was none
other than Cyril, Bishop of Alexandria, who openly embraced
the cause of Isis and anthropomorphized her into Mary,
Mother of God.[1] While we do not worship Isis or Mary as
a personality, yet we recognize that which they symbolize.
For it is only by a recognition of the Mother-principle of
Love and Compassion that we can bring forth The Christ-
child individually in our hearts and lives, and collectively
in humanity.

---

1   *Isis Unveiled*, Blavatsky, Vol. II, 41.

Heretofore most teachings of a religio-philosophic character have been given out as from the intellectual or Father aspect of Truth, and have in a measure appalled humanity by a sense of the great gulfs to be crossed and the great heights to be attained ere the Father's house is reached. But in this volume the teachings are presented as from the lips of a loving, tender mother taking her children into her arms, weak, sinful and disobedient though they be, and helping them over the hard places by teaching them at her knee how, by the mastery of the little things of daily life, they shall, step by step, attain to the status of the Divine Manhood exemplified in the Father.

This volume is composed of the monthly lessons sent out by *The Order of the 15*, considerably elaborated and enlarged. The lessons in this volume will no longer be issued separately in pamphlet form. These teachings are presented in Love and Compassion with the earnest desire to sympathize with and help upward and onward the Mother's struggling sons and daughters. The Great Mother holds out her arms to all her children, be they Pagan, Jew, Christian or non-Christian, recognizing that each child must feed at its Mother's breast and partake of the milk of her love and sympathy no matter what the circumstances of his or her physical life, or what their religious training.

These teachings will appeal most strongly to those whose hearts can recognize the great Mother-love now being poured out upon the world to prepare it for the coming of the great spiritual Teacher or Avatar who is soon to appear and who will promulgate the teachings for the coming sixth sub-race and prepare a nucleus for the Sixth Great Race.

THE VOICE OF ISIS

CHAPTER I

LIFE'S DUTIES

"Whatsoever thy hand findeth to do, do it with thy might." *Ecclesiastes*, IX, 10.

"Believe thou not that sitting in dark forests, in proud seclusion and apart from men; believe thou not that life on roots and plants, that thirst assuaged with the snow from the great Range—believe thou not, O Devotee, that this will lead thee to the goal of final Liberation." *The Voice of the Silence*, Blavatsky, Fragment I.

Many students of the higher life find themselves surrounded by conditions which absolutely preclude their devoting themselves to study and to the observances which seem necessary for self-development. Life often seems to press so heavily upon them that both body and mind are wearied to the point of exhaustion, and both men and women are reduced to a state of beasts of burden. Yet even here let us seek a remedy.

There are two classes of duties, the real duties which must be performed and the mere superfluities of life which we are wont to call duties but which we voluntarily impose upon ourselves. No real duty is given you which you have not the strength to perform or without a purpose to be gained by its performance. Real duties do not exhaust you, for "as thy days, so shall thy strength be." Instead of letting any duty arouse in your mind the thought that it can by any possibility separate you from the Inner

Light or from your spiritual development or your real
advance along the Path or prevent you from drawing
close and learning Wisdom at the Master's feet, realize
that *it would be impossible for you to take one step onward while you were leaving any real duty undone.* "But
to attain true renunciation of action without devotion
through action is difficult, O thou of mighty arms; while
the devotee who is engaged in the right practice of his
duties approacheth the Supreme Spirit in no long time."[1]

The second class are imaginary duties, or self imposed
tasks, which cater only to superfluities and are fulfilled
simply to propitiate the world's opinion. The first duty
of each student of the higher life is to make a careful
analysis and decide what are real and what are superficial
duties, then to so order his life that the real, vital and first
duty of caring for his Immortal Soul will not be crowded
out. To do this he must look upon duty in a new light.
Many persons, recognizing the false light in which duty
has been presented, strive to do away with it altogether,
saying that nothing should be done that is not a joyful
service. While we agree with this view for a certain stage
of development, still it is often necessary to require children to perform duties which later in life they find to be
joyful service. All real duties confront you because in
your evolution you have set up conditions which make
just these tasks necessary to build into your Soul certain
qualities in which you are lacking. In short, they are the
result of the great Law of Karma, and without the lessons they teach your character is incomplete. Hence, they
are the things which, when they are performed and the
qualities they are meant to develop are incorporated into

---

1 *Bhagavad Gita*, Chapter V.

your being, will give you the strength and ability to take your next step. We hear many say that household cares or business duties occupy so much of their time that they cannot find time to enter the Silence, hence, there is no use trying to live the higher life, since the many interruptions make it impossible. Instead of taking such an attitude of mind, realize that such duties and interruptions are your task and make them yield you their lesson. Every morning select some text or thought and fix your mind upon it during the day, making every task, be it ever so trifling, yield something toward the main idea. If you are seeking poise, take for your daily meditation the thought of Divine Love. Think of this expressing itself as calmness, unchanged and unmoved by anything. If constant interruptions occur, realize that perhaps they furnish just the lesson you need *i.e.*, the power to remain calm interiorly in the face of outward activity. Since all real duties are your task in them lies your opportunity and in their proper performance lies your victory. Not in the performance merely, but in the attitude *of mind* you hold toward them and *the manner* of their performance. If you perform a duty because you are compelled to and fail to incorporate its lesson in your heart, at your next step you will find yourself confronted by another duty of the same general character but far more difficult of performance, and this will continue until you not only perform the duty but gain the lacking quality of Soul this duty is intended to inculcate. If business cares seem to hold you in a net of sordid money getting, learn from them the lesson of persistence; that just as no complication in business life can daunt you, so in your spiritual life nothing shall prevent you from obtaining spiritual gold. Teach your subconscious mind to know and realize that only that which can be brought to The Christ for His blessing is legitimate. Learn to have faith that you shall achieve if you learn this lesson.

There is one real duty which confronts all students of the higher life that cannot be ignored, *i.e.*, to decide just what avenue of help is most beneficial, not only to their own advancement, but also the one which brings the greatest amount of practical help to humanity. It is not enough to say that you can gain good from all sources, for while that may be true, still your personal development is not the first duty that confronts you, for that comes *as a result* of living The Christ-life and trying to help humanity. While you should do the individual duties presented to you, you should also lend your forces to increase the power of the organized movements put forth by the Masters of Wisdom for the help of humanity. Such organized movements are like great rivers which although they depend upon tiny springs and streamlets for volume, yet unite these into something far different from and of far greater usefulness than the individual springs and streamlets contributing to them. Hence, your first duty is conscientiously, prayerfully and earnestly to seek for the special channel through which you desire to help humanity, and when found throw into that channel all you have to give, whether it be money—the easiest of all things to give—or love, devotion and thought, or service. Fear not to seek. "The pilgrim who would cool his weary limbs in running waters, yet dares not plunge for terror of the stream, risks to succumb from heat. Inaction based on selfish fear can bear but evil fruit." No Soul can consciously advance who is not helping in the uplifting of all.

If you cannot find time to enter the Silence, still no power in heaven or earth can keep the Silence from entering into you if you will let it, for the Silence is the peace of God that passeth understanding. While doing the duties of the day your mind need not be chained to them. It is not what your hands are doing, but *what your heart is worshiping* that determines your growth. If you make business or household cares your God, you will, of necessity, retard your more rapid spiritual advance; for as long as you are worshiping a false God your spiritual evolution is being retarded. "Thou shalt have no other gods before Me." If, on the contrary, you make of your duties stepping-stones to the real worship of your heart, you will find them a great help. Hands and mind may both be occupied, but while using them, and in the very performance of the task, and because it is hampering, you must dive deep into the Divine and seek in your own heart for the sustaining power and not depend upon earthly surroundings to bring it to you, just as a tree which finds itself planted in a crevice of a rock must send its roots down deep to seek the streams that are hidden from sight ere it can maintain its growth. Under such circumstances, the tree often attains greater perfection than one planted on the plain, for the streams that run deep are refreshing and uncontaminated, and are unfailing. If you are persistent and determined in this seeking you will gain more growth from meeting everything as it comes to you than one who can sit for hours in silence, yet who has not learned to control the children of his own brain. *There is no duty higher than the one which lies nearest*, provided it be a real duty. It is not a real duty to try to relieve another from doing his plain duty, for "It is better to do one's own duty, even though it be devoid of excellence, than to perform another's duty well. It is better to perish in the performance of one's own duty; the duty of another is full of danger."[1] Like the children of Israel who had each to gather manna for himself alone and could gather only enough for one day, so is each one given strength to perform all the real duties of each day. But if this strength is wasted in assumed duties or is used up in doing for another that which it is necessary for his development that he do for himself, then you are depleted and your duties, like the manna gathered in excess,[2] become a menace to your growth rather than a help.

The object of evolution is to gain Wisdom out of every condition. Whatever the condition that confronts you, know well that it will never leave you until you have gained the Wisdom it is intended to teach. Everything that comes to you in the way of trouble and sorrow is simply the result of your own shortcomings, or a lack of some Soul-quality which only such experiences can teach you. In fact, this is the underlying idea of Karma; not that it is a punishment or even an inevitable law of suffering which you must endure to the end, but that in the course of your evolution your Higher Self finds that you lack certain Soul qualities, hence chooses to incarnate in certain families and under certain conditions which will bring out the Soul-qualities which are lacking. If you refuse to recognize the lesson, or run away from the conditions ere they are conquered, you will have to meet them again and again in various forms in this and other lives until the victory is gained. Remember, that the hard conditions of the environment are deliberately chosen

---

1 *The Bhagavad Gita*, Chapter III.
2 "But some of them left of it until the morning and it bred worms, and stank." *Exodus*, XVI, 20.

by the Soul that it may quickly gain the qualities needed. The instant this is done the Law is fulfilled, hence there is no Karma or anything else that can hold you to those conditions.

Only thus can you find self-poise, for self-poise is the result of self-knowledge. The instant you begin to see that it is yourself who is responsible for all the disturbing influences that are around you and that it rests with you to correct them, then you have begun in the right way to gain self-poise. The first thing to be gained is self-recognition. When buffeted by circumstances you are apt to blame your sufferings upon your conditions or upon others, or to think some Divine Power is punishing you, for it is most difficult to face yourself and recognize that the trouble lies in you. But while this is difficult to realize, still it is comforting to know that if the fault is within, the remedy also lies within. Once recognize this and really learn the lesson—not only mentally but intuitively—and you no longer have to experience the adverse conditions.

When an earthen vessel is to be used, only a certain amount of fire is needed to harden and prepare the clay. But if it is a golden vessel to be placed upon the King's table it must pass through a seven-times heated furnace and be hammered and tested and purified until the gold is without a flaw; then it must be fashioned into the shape best adapted to its purpose. So is it with the vessel of clay which we call our personality. There must be all kinds of vessels and each must have the preparation best adapted to its uses.

All Wisdom gained from earthly experience is meant to help unfold your dormant faculties and make the personality one with its Father-in-heaven. There is nothing that confronts you that is not a step in this great journey called the "Cycle of Necessity." Therefore, realize that it is not your tasks or duties that weary you or retard your evolution, *but your attitude of mind toward them*, the permitting of everyday trifles to so occupy your mind that you never let them go.

The little joys of life are just as satisfying as the little cares are annoying. While you are facing the little cares watch out for the little joys. Many little joys wake the heart until like a glorious blossom it opens to the sun. If you dwell in the little joys they run together and soon break out into a mighty soul satisfying happiness which will be like a strong, deep undercurrent of joy bearing you through all the cares and sorrows of life. Remember this and begin at once to look for every ripple of sunshine—open the doors and let it in.

In every heart there is a well so deep and still that it can reflect only one star at a time, and this star, whatever it be, is, for the time it is reflected there, the guiding star of your destiny. Just as a great telescope can sweep the heavens and focus upon any star desired, so can you have for your ruling star anything you determine to focus upon. If your star be household worries, a desire to live in the same style as your neighbors, to expand your business, or the love and worship of money, or any other condition, even the worship of a personality, while it reigns it shuts out the light from all other stars. "Ye cannot serve God and mammon." Whatever it is that is reflected in this deep well of your inmost heart is the God you are worshiping; for worship is constant thought of the thing worshiped, a constant filling of the undercurrents of your mind with it, laying upon the shrine and offering to that which you worship of your best efforts and thoughts. Whatever it is that occupies these deep undercurrents, whatever is poured into the deep places of your nature, even subconsciously—something that is always there no matter how busy you may be on the surface—that is what you are worshiping, for it is that for which you are giving your life and thought-force to create. By these currents of force you are literally molding the atoms of your bodies into vehicles through which that which you worship can manifest. You also create around yourself an auric world in which your dominant thought will be king and all else subservient, no matter how much lip-service is given to other things.

There is only one thing that you can rightly place in the Holy Sanctuary and hope that it will dwell there forever, and that is The Christ. Let The Christ be king over all your thoughts, aspirations and desires and all things shall be cared for. "He who seeth me in all things and all things in me looseneth not his hold on me and I forsake him not. And whosoever, believing in spiritual unity, worshippeth me who am in all things, dwelleth with me in whatsoever condition he may be."[1]

The little things of life may occupy the surface of your thoughts, but underneath all, in the Holy Sanctuary, The Christ dwelleth, and The Christ careth for all things. Your home, your children, your business, your petty cares are all but ripples on the surface, while deep down in the shrine of your heart dwells The Christ. Once having found this Holy of Holies and placed therein the One who alone is worthy of your worship, no matter how busy you are or how occupied with worldly cares, in an instant your consciousness can enter that sacred place and find rest and peace and communion. Then nothing can really fret you, for you carry the Silence within you. The

---

1 *The Bhagavad Gita*, Chapter VI.

winds and tempests of earth only ripple the surface. In the deep places all is peace and calm. You have no fear, for you have entered the Silence and have felt the strength and comfort and power of The Christ within. You know that His love pervades your life and all are safe in His keeping. All things are safe and sure. The trials of your business and your home do not upset you now, for you know how to keep calm, where to find peace.

The moment you find yourself getting disturbed, slip back into this calm, quiet interior place and find refreshment. Let the radiance of this center fill your life. The Christ is there, and no matter how the storm rages on the surface or how you rock in the little boat of your personality on the storm-tossed sea of life, still you know that at the first call for help you will see The Christ walking on the water and will hear the command. "Peace, be still."

CHAPTER II

"And then shall appear the sign of the Son of man
in heaven: and then shall all the tribes of the earth
mourn, and they shall see the Son of man coming in
the clouds of heaven with power and great glory."
St. Matthew XXIV, 30.

The year 1912 marks the beginning of a most important era in the history of the world. As the earth, in its
yearly journey around the sun, passes through a sign of
the zodiac each month, so does our solar system during
its great journey around the central sun of this universe
(Alcyone), pass through each sign of the zodiac; but in
this greater cycle, instead of a month, our solar system
requires approximately 2170 years to traverse each sign.
In this great journey our solar system has reached and
is now entering the sign Aquarius, the Man from the
East, one of the four sacred animals of *Ezekiel* and the
Apocalypse, also one of the four great divisions of the
mundane cross. On February seventh, 1912, the mystic planet Uranus also entered this sign, its own house,
where it will remain about seven years. Hence the year
1912 marks the beginning of the *first period* of the Cycle
of Fulfillment for this present sub-race.

The word fulfillment sends a thrill of joy through
the heart, but let us consider a wider meaning of the
word. A fulfillment is a just compensation for that
which has been accomplished or attempted, a reaping of that which has been sown, both good and evil.
A fulfillment is not a recompense for mere suffering endured, for suffering of itself has no purifying or

uplifting power, it is uplifting only when the lesson which necessitated it has been learned and the lacking Soul-quality has been built into the character. This planet has passed through much suffering and has had its lessons to learn, both as a living entity (the informing principle of the planet) and through its inhabitants.

Moses the great law-giver commanded the Lord's chosen people that, after the completion of every seventh sabbath of years, they should celebrate the following year as a Year of Jubilee. This mystic cycle observed literally every fiftieth year has the same significance as the Cycle of Fulfillment. During the Year of Jubilee all debtors were released from prison and all slaves set free, and in this Cycle of Fulfillment all the forces, powers and capacities within the individual, the Race and the planet, which have been imprisoned for indebtedness to the Law, will be released. This does not mean, however, that any will be exempted from paying karmic debts, but that those who were in prison to the Law for debts will be released or given an opportunity to work them out during this period.

The lower aspects of all these powers and forces must first be reaped and the adjustment made upon the lower planes ere the higher phases of the fulfillment can be brought about. The reaping of the harvest has already begun, but ere it can be garnered into the great granary it must pass through the winnowing; the chaff and dirt must be blown away and only the golden grain remain. The elements have been cast into the crucible and the fires must burn until all the baser elements rise to the surface and are removed ere the gold can be purified for the King's use.

The influence of Uranus in Aquarius will bring to the world many great and sudden changes, both in the physical conditions of the planet and in the mental and psychic realms of its inhabitants. "A partial cataclysm occurs at the close of every 'age' of the world, they say, which does not destroy the latter, but only changes its general appearance. New races of men and animals and a new flora evolve from the dissolution of the precedent ones."[1] The earth will have to endure not only changes in climate, terrible storms and disasters of every sort, but also cataclysmic changes in its crust ere the adjustment to the new vibration is accomplished and the earth is prepared as a dwelling place for the New Humanity.

The great Law of Divine Harmony[2] is forever working in a seven-fold manner, as (1) order, (2) compensation, (3) karma, (4) vibration, (5) cycles, (6) polarity and (7) balance. It will be noted that vibration stands in the center of these manifestations of the Law. It is Fohat, the Breath of Eternal Motion or Thor's Hammer, the Swastika, by the action of which the sparks of life are thrown off. The seven aspects are like separate ingredients put into a vessel that bread may be made. Until the motion of mixing (vibration) brings about an amalgamation and change of conditions in the ingredients they do not become dough but remain flour, yeast, salt, water, etc. Thus through vibration must the Law in its entirety bring about the fulfillment of all earth conditions. Everything, from the planets to the tiniest grain of sand or microscopic bacterium, has its rate of vibration (keynote) and its cyclic motion. The orbits of the planets may be called their cycles of vibration, the wavelength of their oscillation, but within those great oscillations there are many, many lesser vibrations (cycles) as the minute and the second vibrate within the hour.

---

1   *Isis Unveiled*, Blavatsky, Vol II, 424.
2   See Chapter XIV.

A wind storm has its rate of vibration or key-note, and everything within its path, while vibrating to its own key-note, must vibrate in harmony with the dominant note of the storm or be swept away. This planet in fulfilling the Law as vibration and cycles has reached a point in the zodiac where it is entering into new conditions; where it must respond to a new key-note, its Cycle of Fulfillment, and fulfill the Law in its entirety or be swept away. As it responds to this new vibration everything upon it must accommodate itself to the new conditions. The failure of certain factors to adapt themselves will bring about the storms and cataclysmic changes which will adjust conditions to the new note with startling suddenness, just as a tree which remains rigid and refuses to adapt itself to the storm will be suddenly broken off or uprooted.

Every planet in its course of development has to meet the forces sent forth from all the starry worlds and systems. Those which are in advance of it will send to it overwhelming force, almost greater than it can bear, while those which are less advanced will draw from it with a grasping force. But there comes a time in the life of every planet, as well as in the life of every individual, when a crisis is reached. In the case of a planet this point is generally reached toward the close of the Fifth or the beginning of the Sixth Great Race. Then every effort is made to tear it to pieces; all the forces, both within and without, are exerted in an attempt at disruption, an attempt to tear the planet or individual into separate fragments. Only those who can endure this great cosmic testing and come out of the fiery ordeal alive can survive and continue their evolution. The heavens are full of wandering comets, asteroids and fragments of planets, all that is left of worlds which have gone to pieces under this great test. These fragments are destined to spend eons of time wandering in space ere they can once more be gathered together and obtain the force necessary to become a planet, or until they are drawn into some evolving planet whose vibrations are in harmony with theirs.

Great alchemical changes are transpiring within and around the earth that will terminate in cataclysms of periodic activity. These are not altogether malign influences, for among the stars astronomy and astrology agree that there are no malign and no beneficent planets, in the ordinarily accepted meaning of the terms; all is Cosmic Law. The peculiar force exerted by every star in the firmament upon every other star is just that force which is needed for each particular star's well being at the time. The earth today, in entering the first period of its Cycle of Fulfillment, is meeting the influence of stars whose force and light have been traveling for ages and ages, but which are only just now beginning to penetrate its atmosphere. Some of these forces might be called malign and some beneficent, but the influence of each is necessary to the earth's evolution. The coming of these forces is not accidental, nor are they coming in a haphazard manner. Millions and millions of eons ago, ere this earth was reborn, ere the Sons of Mind breathed into the evolution of this planet the Breath of Divine Life, those distant firmaments were set in their particular and appointed places and the influences sent out from their centers were so timed as to reach the newborn earth at the exact period when those particular forces would be needed to push it on toward its fulfillment. Conceive of a constant pressure exerted upon the earth's surface from all the planets and stars, and at the same time a pressure from within, a force going outward to impinge upon all the stars. As long as these forces are evenly distributed the result is that the earth's crust becomes more and more consolidated and at the same time purified. Because of this pressure many alchemical changes are taking place. Liquids are being transformed into solids; solids are being transmuted into gases and gases are becoming luminous ether and so forth. Thus the earth is slowly being prepared to become a sun. In its present state, were the earth subjected to the forces which operate through a sun, it would be instantly volatilized into a cloud of gaseous matter. It must be tested and tried; not as a punishment, but as a necessary preparation for its work as a sun. No planet can become a shining, burning sun until it has passed this crucial test, until the without and the within are perfectly balanced and have compacted it into a state that nothing can destroy or, in occult parlance, until it has become the "Diamond Heart." Only when a planet has obtained at-one-ment or has assimilated all the forces of the stars and planets and all the inter-stellar spaces, can it be said to have conquered and become a sun, ready to take its place in the grand procession around the Central Sun. The sun of this solar system is such a conqueror and all the planets and stars of our cosmos are in varying stages or degrees of development toward this great end.

So must it be with you. The pressure from without cannot harm you if the within be properly balanced. When the forces from within are balanced the outer pressure will only strengthen the individuality and make you better fitted to become Sons of God. Keep the within balanced and, like the needle to the pole, steadily polarized to The Christ-force, so that nothing can move you. Gather the forces that are sent against you, recognize them as necessary for your evolution, and turn them to your advantage.

The influence which each star exerts is determined by the thought-force generated by its inhabitants, just as the influence of each individual is the sum total of the thoughts he continually harbors; for the aura of a man or a planet is the sum total of the thought-atmosphere created by or attracted to it. The influence of the earth upon the cosmos is said to be malign. The struggle for supremacy, the selfishness, the greed for gold and the vileness into which the misuse of the serpent-power has plunged its inhabitants naturally emanate a malign influence; but nevertheless the earth has a great potency for good, owing to the wonderful possibilities residing in a characteristic that is only just beginning to be comprehended, i.e., the result of the great test which the humanity of this globe must pass through. The earth is said to be malefic because upon her bosom is fought out the great struggle between good and evil. It is here that the Great Initiator (Saturn) stands. This is his plane of manifestation. Here it is that humanity is confronted with the great problem of the creative power of sex and its higher possibilities, together with its temptations and its power to degrade and debase. But through the lessons learned by its terrible suffering humanity is raised to a higher state. The overcoming and the learning of the lessons of the creative power will give not only to man, but also to the planet upon which this battle is waged, a glorious place in the cosmos. Therefore, instead of the earth being malign, the influence it sends out is one of patient endurance and determined victory. Victory over discouragement is one of the greatest victories man can win. For this reason this planet sends out into space the most wonderful melody of all the planets, for only here is the chord of suffering endured and discouragement conquered blended with the key-note of the globe, the earth being the only planet that has a bass clef of suffering to complete its chord.

The earth is the eighth note in the celestial scale, and like the eighth note in music, while it completes one octave it becomes the first note in a new and higher octave. Ultimately the earth will stand forth as the brightest sun in this system, in fact it will become a Pole Star and reach into an advanced system. It will send forth an influence without which the perfect evolution of all the other planetary bodies would be incomplete. This earth is the stage upon which is to be enacted a new and grander drama of life, and today the characters in the drama are being assembled and the stage is being set.

The year 1912 is therefore but the dawn of the Cycle of Fulfillment, the time prophesied in the text quoted at the head of this lesson; the Sign of the Son of Man. This sign is none other than the celestial sign Aquarius into which we are now entering. The Son of Man comes in the heavens because our solar system, for the next 2170 years will be passing through this sign, during which the forces symbolized by Aquarius will be focused upon it. And only after the purification, when all "the tribes of the earth mourn" can come the "power and great glory" of the fulfillment or the attainment of the Wisdom of the Divine Man. This sign is represented by a man pouring water upon the earth, symbolic of the fulfillment which comes as a result of the pouring out of the Mother-force (water). In Nature water is the chief factor which makes the earth bring forth, while in man that which is symbolized by water—the great Mother-principle—brings forth spiritual fruits.

Since this is the Cycle of Fulfillment for the planet, the same conditions must necessarily affect its inhabitants. As man is the microcosm of the macrocosm he has within himself centers which should respond to every vibration of the planet. Hence as the earth strikes its new key-note man must vibrate or attune himself to it or be storm swept by his failure, just as the fruit and leaves of certain trees are stripped from the branches by a storm which only strengthens other trees.

All nations are today feeling the necessity of adjusting themselves to the new conditions upon which humanity as a whole is entering. This is especially noticeable in the political conditions in China, Persia, Turkey, Portugal and Mexico and in the industrial conditions in England, Germany, France and America. We may expect such turbulent conditions to continue until every nation makes the necessary adjustment to the note of the Brotherhood of Man or is swept away, as the ancient government of China has been.

Within the nations every organization and movement, whether political, economic, philanthropic, philosophical, religious, mystical or whatnot, must be shaken to its foundations, must have all the dead leaves of old ideas and conditions stripped from it and prove whether it be founded upon the eternal principles of truth, justice, unselfishness, love and brotherhood or upon the dictates of selfishness, ambition, injustice and greed.[1] And within the ranks of all organized efforts of mankind each individual will have to face similar testings and adjustments, modified by his or her Karma, to prove the nature and worth of the

---

1   Since the first publication of this lesson (January, 1912) this prediction has been remarkably fulfilled in many directions.

principles of life he or she is following. But above all, the new conditions will affect all those who have devoted themselves to the study of the occult, who are delving into the deeper mysteries of Being, who are trying to live The Chist-life. For out of these must be gathered the mystic hundred and forty and four thousand who shall have the Father's name written in their foreheads (opening of the Third Eye).

Many individuals find themselves suffering from poverty, sickness or persistent adversities until hope seems dead. This is because they have turned their backs upon the world and hence find all the world against them. They no longer serve the world and it no longer rewards them. They suffer because, having turned from the world, they have not yet sounded the key-note of the new life by which alone they can enter into its rewards. They are passing over the interval between the two notes, and it will be longer or shorter according to their ability to awaken to the new vibration. This period is symbolized in occult literature by the Great Abyss. There is, however, a narrow bridge over this Abyss builded of naked swords, which leads to the Eternal City, over which all must walk with bleeding feet. But there is a Hand to guide and a Voice to cheer you if you but seek them in the darkness. It is always darkest just before the dawn. All old karmic conditions must be swept away ere the new era can manifest. Let no earnest seeker after Wisdom grow discouraged, but hold fast to the guiding Hand and trust to the Power which shall bring him safely through.

The earth could no more bear the whole force of a sun without being consumed than you, as individuals or this Movement today as a unit, could express that which you are destined to express. Nor could you now stand in the fires of spiritual force which you must ultimately transmit any more than the inhabitants of the earth could live upon it were it suddenly to take its place as a sun. At some period you must be Sons of Righteousness, but you must grow into it. You must be brave to endure the growing pains; for you will never find the Place of Peace which will balance and hold all the forces under perfect control if you cannot endure the testing, learn the Wisdom and gain the blessings that every battle holds for you. Find the Place of Peace. Make the pressure within evenly and perfectly balanced that the pressure from without may strengthen you. Be calm and rest in the midst of the storm. Realize the absolute calm and rest which dwells in the midst of a vortex. Repeat constantly: "I am strong. I can conquer. My forces are not scattered because they are evenly balanced and under perfect control." Then will the forces that come against you form a protecting aura of strength and power which nothing harmful can enter. Let this be your watchword: "I am balanced. I am calm. If the Law be with me who can be against me?" If you can gain this realization, have no fear for the result.

Once let your consciousness realize, if only for a moment, the peace and power of Divine Love, and you have donned a shield and buckler which shall preserve you in the day of trial. Some day you will find our consciousness functioning within that radiant center where Love is all-creative, and Power is omnipotent, and Glory is unspeakable. There you shall meet the Great Mother face to face.

CHAPTER III

DEGREES OF EVOLUTION

Before taking up the spiritual aspects of the teachings of *The Order of the 15*, it is necessary to give a brief summary of its philosophical and geometrical basis.

This chapter is necessarily somewhat mathematical and technical and hence will be more or less difficult for some minds, but if any who find it so will carefully re-read it after studying the chapters which follow they will have little trouble in grasping its details. Its importance at the beginning of the book is that in it is set forth an outline of *The Order of the 15*, the reasons for its existence and its name, its relations to other Orders and its special work in the Grand Plan.

It is said that "God geometrizes." This is a truth founded on the fact, already well demonstrated by science, that all forces flow and act along geometrical lines. This is as true of the forces which create a world as of those which create a snow crystal. The cosmos — the known universe — is composed of seven degrees or states of matter. These states of matter correspond to the seven states of consciousness into which all manifestations of the One Life are divided, — etheric, mineral, vegetable, animal, human, superhuman and Divine.

This seven-fold division of the cosmos is illustrated by a plant. It first exists as a seed, in which are latent all the powers and possibilities of the mature plant.

As a seed (its 7th degree) it has only the power to imbibe two kinds of food, water (1st kind) and heat (2nd kind). These it assimilates and builds into growth which bursts the confining shell and permits the sprout to be born into the earth (its 6th degree) outside its shell. With the development of the sprout and roots it is able to select various classes of a new food (3rd kind), earth, and develops the strength and stability that enables it to be born into the new world of air (its 5th degree). Here it puts forth special organs, the leaves, to assimilate the new food (4th kind), the gases of the air. It thus acquires the strength and ability to put forth a bud which soon unfolds into a blossom. This blossom opens its heart to another world (4th degree), the light, where it assimilates still another food (5th kind), the emanations from the sun. This enables the plant to replace its beautiful blossom by the fruit and be born into a still higher degree (the 3rd). The fruit now absorbs a new food (6th kind) life-essence, which gives it the power to sustain life when eaten and thus enter a higher degree (the 2nd). As it ripens it absorbs still another food (7th kind), the creative power of the One Life, which enables it to enter the First Degree, manifest the intelligence necessary to register every step of its growth and development within the seed, store up the potency and create after its kind.

The matter composing a stone manifests the geometrical forms of the crystals composing it; the matter composing a daisy will manifest in the geometrical form of a daisy; the matter composing an animal follows the lines of that particular species, etc. In the expression of these various geometrical forms, states of matter and consciousness, each has its own numerical value. A crystal has a certain characteristic number of sides and angles, a daisy a certain number of petals, an animal a certain number of tissues, organs, senses, etc. The expression of the geometrical law of the universe can thus be traced in all the kingdoms, for all nature-forms can be analyzed into a few single geometrical figures and their combinations. Every plant that grows follows certain geometrical lines, sending its roots in one direction, its trunk in another and its branches in diverse other directions, yet all combining to make the perfect tree.

All growth must be along these lines; for there is but one law of growth behind all manifested forms of the One Life. The above illustrates perfectly the stages of your own growth; so, study it carefully when you are inclined to be impatient at your progress, and realize that all advance is but a growth resulting from the assimilation of such food as you are able to digest.

Man the thinker carries this same law into the mental world and we find mankind separated into seven great classes called Degrees, their sub-divisions being called Orders. But it must be remembered that these are but convenient terms used to represent the conditions under which, and the lines along which, evolution takes place just as a daisy is divided into root, stalk, leaf and blossom according to its stage of growth or degree of evolution, yet all are but parts of the one plant.

Those great spiritual Beings—our Elder Brothers—who have evolved through the Orders of the four lower great divisions or Degrees and have attained all the wisdom to be gained there-from are now evolving in the Orders of the Degrees above the human and hence are called Initiates, Adepts, Mahatmas or Masters of Wisdom according to Their stage of spiritual evolution.

The Great White Lodge—which is the aggregate of all these Great Souls who, through repeated experiences and determined effort through many earth lives, have obtained Mastery, firstly, over the passions, appetites and desires of the personal self, and secondly, over the forces of their bodies and the life-currents of the cosmos—is working back of and within every movement in any way benefiting mankind, and is constantly manipulating currents of force for the advancement of evolution. This body of Masters is called a Lodge because, like a lodge, it is divided into Degrees and Orders corresponding to and directly connected with the various Degrees and Orders of humanity. Every Order in each Degree is thoroughly organized for its particular work. The Lodge must work in humanity through Degrees and Orders corresponding to the lines of its own divisions and each Master must work through the Degree and Order which corresponds to the one in which He finds Himself in the Great White Lodge, for such is the geometrical plan of the universe, and evolution can advance only along these general lines. Every avenue for aiding humanity is taken advantage of and every channel is utilized to the extent to which it makes its use possible, for there is an Order of Mastery affinitized to every stage of human evolution. Therefore every movement, whether spiritual, ethical, social or political, that is working toward the betterment of mankind receives inspiration and help from the great Spiritual Beings who are affinitized to that particular avenue of helpfulness. No matter what lines of constructive thought you may be interested in it will be possible for you to receive divine inspiration from these Great Teachers couched in terms comprehensible to you. In *Revela-*

tion we read that there were twelve thousand sealed out of every tribe. This symbol illustrates the above mentioned law, namely, that it is possible to reach the heights of spiritual attainment (Mastery) out of every condition of life, for the twelve tribes of Israel symbolize the twelve classes of humanity born under the twelve signs of the zodiac.

Each great Degree of humanity is divided into seven steps or Orders, which correspond to the seven notes of the musical scale, and the seven color rays of the solar spectrum, hence manifest perfect harmony or the pure white light of the sun. They are determined mathematically and arranged geometrically in accordance with the One Law, i.e., Divine Harmony, which must necessarily act along geometrical lines. Every human being manifesting during the present cycle finds itself in its proper Order in one of these seven great divisions or Degrees.

THE SEVENTH DEGREE OF HUMANITY.

This Degree is composed of seven Orders and comprises all entities who have reached the self-conscious stage of evolution, but who have not yet progressed very far above the animal kingdom. It includes the lowest types of savages. The lower Orders of this 7th Degree are, as it were, the kindergarten of The Lodge, and are just as truly under its guidance and protection as are the higher Orders. In fact the lowest Order of this Degree overlaps the animal kingdom in that it embraces those anthropoid apes which, as the degenerate descendants of certain Lemeuro-Atlantean races, contain a spark of the Divine Fire. "Such anthropoids form an exception because they were not intended by Nature, but are the direct product and creation of 'senseless' man"[1] of those early races. "After the middle point of the Fourth Race in the Fourth Round on

1 *The Secret Doctrine*, Blavatsky Vol. 1, p. 207.

our globe—no more Monads can enter the human kingdom. The door is closed for this Cycle, and the balance struck."[1] Since every spark of the Divine Fire is an emanation from a great Master, all entities containing such a spark, no matter how obtained, must necessarily be a part of the body of their Parent-Master, and their evolution must be watched over and guided by Him until they are fitted to become one with Him. The higher Orders of this Degree include the more advanced members of the lower races and those members of the advanced races who may have made physical and intellectual progress but who still have only a low degree of spiritual development.

THE 6TH DEGREE.

The Sixth Degree, with its seven Orders, comprises all those in the position of teachers or leaders among the different races who are working consciously toward the betterment of humanity, but who have not yet realized their divine guidance or the assistance given them by the Masters of Wisdom, and who, perhaps, have never heard of The Lodge of Masters. Its lowest Orders are composed of those untutored savages who, nevertheless, are leading and guiding those under them toward their highest conception of Truth, while the highest Orders embrace those humanitarian or philanthropic workers among the more advanced races who are earnestly seeking the physical, moral, intellectual, or social betterment of the Race.

THE 5TH DEGREE.

The seven Orders of the Fifth Degree include those who are more or less interested in esoteric matters; who are not satisfied with the outer manifestations of life, but who are seeking for the Soul of things; who have some knowledge of The Lodge as

1 *Ibid*, p. 205.

a fact, and who are studying along general occult or mystical lines.

THE 4TH DEGREE.

This Degree is graded in sequence according to its Orders, and embraces all those earnest students and teachers who have taken their lower nature in hand and are deliberately striving to lead such a spiritual life as will bring them into *personal touch* with the Masters of The Lodge.

The Third, Second and First Degrees are most sacred and above our present comprehension, so it will be impossible to consider them at this time. For when one enters the Third Degree he has become more than human, he has entered the super-human. Yet this Degree overlaps the human (Fourth Degree) just as the human overlaps the animal.

THE ORDERS OF THE FOURTH DEGREE.

Since it is in the Fourth Degree that all who are drawn into this Movement are now functioning we will consider in some detail the seven steps or Orders into which it is divided. The highest Order of the lower (Fifth) Degree overlaps the lowest Order of the Fourth Degree, just as the eighth note in music is the completion of the lower octave and the beginning of the succeeding higher octave.

Admission to the organized work of these Orders does not rest with any organization save the Great White Lodge, and it alone can grant or withhold membership, and it does this upon the inner planes with often no outward recognition on the physical plane. The object of these Orders of Evolution is the spiritualization of matter after the crucifixion is completed.

The mathematical law for the formation of the Orders

is as follows, each Order taking its name from the sum
of the digits composing its number:

Fig. No. 1.	Fig. No. 2.

ORDERS — THE CROSS OF MATTER

ORDERS	Positive	Negative
1. 1=**1**		
2. 1+2=**3**	1	
3. 1+2+3=**6**	3	
4. 1+2+3+4=**10**		6
5. 1+2+3+4+5=**15**		10
6. 1+2+3+4+5+6=**21**	15	
7. 1+2+3+4+5+6+7=**28**	21	
8. 1+2+3+4+5+6+7+8=**36**		28
		36

The cross was not first introduced in the Christian Era,
but is the most primitive of all symbols, representing
the real crucifixion or involution or the descent of Spirit
into matter where it must be crucified upon the mundane
cross and pass along the geometrical lines of evolution.
The cross, being the fourth geometrical figure, represents
the completion of involution, the turning point where
evolution begins, or the Fourth Degree. This cross is
also the Tree of Life, planted in the midst of the Garden
when mankind fell into generation, by whose fruit, if ye
eat thereof, "ye shall become as Gods." We will therefore
begin at the foot of the cross with the Order of the 36
which may be said to be the root of the Tree of Life, or
the Guardian Wall around the foot of the cross.

NEGATIVE ORDERS

THE ORDER OF THE 36

This Order is the negative aspect of the highest Order (1) of this Degree or is the point where the
force of the 1 enters the earth-plane. Naturally the
persons composing this Order are those who through
their normal evolution have become aware of The

Christ-force working in them and in humanity as a whole and who have lifted up their eyes to the cross and realized something of the meaning of the crucifixion upon it. As long as Christendom worships The Christ crucified it is but driving the nails more firmly, for The Christ is crucified by being immersed in matter that matter may be redeemed; a voluntary sacrifice to which man's disobedience has added cruelty and suffering:

The Master Jesus is the great Hierarchical Ruler of the Order of the 1 and consequently must overshadow its negative expression, the Order of the 36. That which is known as the Christian religion is a manifestation of this Order on earth, but this Order also embraces all those, in whatever church, society or organization, who have recognized the divine Christ-force within them and are determinately seeking to balance this force in their lives.

This Order receives its name from the sum of the first eight numerals. Eight is the number of evolution and therefore, according to mathematical laws, evolution alone can admit a candidate to this Order. The promulgation of the Wisdom Religion in this country is an attempt to build up a strong Guardian Wall around the cross, by teaching the vital truths back of the symbols of Christianity; an attempt to cultivate and to water the tap-root of the Tree of Life in humanity.

Today the Order of the 36 includes all who have imbibed anything of the esoteric truths, and are endeavoring to both live and teach them, be they called Christians, Theosophists or by any other name. It is the preparatory school of the followers of The Christ. It also stands for the great Universal Church (not necessarily orthodox) and embraces all who are willing to sanctify themselves and work consciously for humanity. The Order of the 36 is the first Order in which the candidate consciously decides to enter "The Path" which leads to Mastery. All of its members have been acquainted with poverty and suffering, if not of body and estate, then of mind, through which they have gained such a realization of the difference between the Christ force and the man Jesus that they can recognize the universal Christ-principle working in humanity even when expressing itself through other avenues than the teachings of the Master Jesus. This realization is the first step up the Mount of Initiation.

THE ORDER OF THE 28

After candidates have entered the Order of the 36 and have proved themselves worthy to continue by the character of their subsequent lives, at once a new Order forms itself and grows naturally out of this Order, just as new lines are added to a crystal. This new Order is composed of those Souls who have advanced a little beyond their fellows, and would correspond to the inner section of any occult organization put forth previous to *The Order of the 15*.[1] It includes those in the orthodox churches who are no longer satisfied with the dead-letter interpretations of the Scriptures, but who have listened to the voice of their own Father-in-heaven and are willing to express a greater tolerance and accept broader ideas on spiritual matters.

This is the Order of the 28. It is the sum of the numerals of 7, the mystic feminine number. The end and aim of this Order is the unfolding of the teachings of Isis-the Mother side of the Godhead-and the evolution of the feminine nature or Soul-principle through the power of love, in contradistinction to intellectual attainments.

1   Jan. 1, 1908, at Philadelphia, Pa.

Isis represents the power to bring forth in humanity. Hence the geometrical figure symbolizing this Order is the square or the sacrificial stone on which the lower self is sacrificed that the power to bring forth The Christ-man may be attained.

It will be noticed that the Orders thus far considered are upon the negative side of the cross. (See Fig. 2.) They must therefore be developed and given to humanity by the negative action of natural development. In other words, a Soul will grow into these two Orders (36 and 28) unconsciously as it advances toward freedom, with very little individualized help; but both Orders are advanced collectively by the Masters of The Lodge.

Admission to these Orders depends upon natural law—the Law of Growth. A person enters them as soon as he becomes fit, either by the preparation afforded by life itself, or after the successful passing of well defined initiations upon the inner planes, often without the consciousness of the personality.

POSITIVE ORDERS

In accordance with the laws of evolution whenever Souls advance beyond the general development of an Order, naturally a new Order forms itself, just as a bud springs from a branch. In fact two new Orders (21 and 15) form themselves simultaneously, both being on the positive side of the cross.

THE ORDER OF THE 21

The Order of the 21 is the sum of the numerals of 6. The 6 is the number of The Christos-principle or the generative power of the Great Creative Force of the Father, manifesting in and through the universe, bringing forth all forms along geometrical lines. The 6 indicates the harmonizing of Nature, in its highest possibilities, through the operation of The Christos or the informing principle, the laws of which are taught in this Order. As Nature grows geometrically and in harmony, so this Order teaches man to evolve in harmony by a study of the laws of geometry and music as expressed through form, color and number, all of which are governed by the Law of Vibration. This, therefore, is pre-eminently the Order concerned with the laws of Nature and their bearing on the evolution of humanity. The persons drawn into this intellectual Order are those who have a natural trend toward geometry, music, color, or mathematical studies.

THE ORDER OF THE 15

Many Souls grow naturally from the Order of the 28 into the Order of the 21, while those who have specially developed their love-nature pass into *The Order of the 15*, it being the Order that reaches into the higher octave of love, *i.e.*, Divine Love, yet it is possible to be in both Orders at the same time.

These two Orders (21 and 15) are put forth simultaneously because they are closely interwoven, the one (21) representing the Head, or the development of the Intellect, and the other (15) representing the Heart or the development of Intuition; the one the masculine, the other the feminine force.

The Order of the 15 is the sum of the numerals of 5. The 5 is the great mystical number of humanity, and was held most sacred by the ancients. On their Temples where the numerals were carved in stone the number 5 was inlaid with pure gold. The numeral 5 stands for humanity, hence this Order ordains to help humanity to reach the highest state of evolution. Its teachings deal with the human every-day problems which must be mastered ere man becomes more than man.

This is the Order of Transmutation or Alchemy. And while geometry and music are touched upon, more attention is given to the transmutation of all the baser qualities, including the elements or inner forces of all life, into the spiritual gold of Regeneration through the power of Divine Love.

The Order of the 15 has always existed, and traces of its various manifestations can be found in ancient and medieval history. The Order of the Annunciation, held in such high esteem by royalty today, is said to have been founded by Count Amadeus of Savoy, but long before that, and all through the Middle Ages, the number 15 was celebrated with many religious ceremonies and observances, the Order of the Annunciation being but an adaptation to Romish ideas of the ancient *Order of the 15*. The emblem of the Order of the Annunciation is a star on which is represented the annunciation surrounded by fifteen love-knots. This also symbolizes *The Order of the 15*, for its mission has always been, even in the darkest periods of the world's history, to announce the possibility of bringing into manifestation (birth) The Christ-force, which is brought about by the spread of tolerance, liberty and brotherly love. The Masons, also, retain a degree of this Order, called the Degree of the Fifteen, its main objects being devoted to the spread of "Toleration and Liberty, against Fanaticism and Persecution, political and religious; and to that of Education, Instruction and Enlightenment against Error, Barbarism and Ignorance."[1] These instances all show that *The Order of the 15* has always been

---

1 *Morals and Dogma*, Pike, p. 160-171.

the Open Door through which the Light of the Great Law has reached humanity and shown it how to evolve above the light of any one candlestick, be it ever so golden or its light ever so brilliant, and how to behold the Divine Law which imparts the Light to all, giving to each as much as his candle is able to manifest in the world.

The Order of the 15 is the Order of the Holy Grail whose lessons prepare for the final Initiation into the *Order of the Flame*. It is an expression of the Mother-force, the power of bringing forth. It is not what you know or believe, but what you bring forth in your life that admits you into full membership in this Order.

The two Orders (21 and 15) have already been formed on the earth-plane, and as they are upon the positive side of the cross (Fig. 2) the members of these Orders must come into direct personal touch with the workers of the Great White Lodge. This has already been done and a personal contact has been established. Like all other Orders, however, membership does not depend upon recognition by any embodied teacher or teachers, but must be a conscious step taken voluntarily by each Soul alone.

Having taken this step alone, apparently in the darkness, the pupil will be brought to the initiation which his demand will surely bring about. He will meet this initiation either unconsciously through natural worldly events (events, however, which he will have no difficulty in connecting with this great step), or consciously in the higher astral. The experiences met with at this period will not consist of a few great Soul-stirring events, which when once passed entitle him to admission, but will consist of events which will bring to him a repetition of experiences which will force him to face himself and bring to his consciousness every secret and open fault; events which will force him to gaze into the eyes of the self that he has created out of the personality which his Real Self (or Ego) has created to train and function through; the self built up out of the thought-forms he has created. It therefore contains the essence of the desires, ambitions, passions and aspirations of his personality. It is the Dweller on the Threshold that each must meet, recognize as his own creation, and conquer.

There can be no dodging the issue or turning back from these events, for it is a mathematical law that he cannot pass on until he has acquired strength to conquer these faults, one by one, as they are presented to him. If he refuses, or is unable to conquer, his Soul must wait and work in the lower Orders until it grows stronger, and until another cyclic opportunity for advance is afforded.

It is not a matter of pledges or words. He can never obtain membership in this Order until he is able to *live* the earlier teachings and *demonstrate to the world by his life* that he has at least passed the earlier tests, and has made some successful attempt to "Let your light shine before men," and that he has been "born again," and has been marked with the "New Name" given by his Father.

HIGHER ORDERS

The Order of the 10 has not yet been openly established upon the earth-plane, although its teachings have been given esoterically for many centuries. It was from a Master guiding this esoteric Order that the teachings of the Wisdom Religion were first given out to the Western world.

The Order of the 10 is the Order in which the teachings of The Christ receive their completion upon the earth-plane. It is necessarily composed only of those who can receive *direct teachings* from the Masters of Wisdom. These are the disciples who "sit at the feet of the Master."

The Order of the 6 is the sum of the numerals of 3 and will be brought to humanity by the coming Avatar.

The Order of the 3 and the 1. These perfected Orders are beyond the comprehension of man in his present state of spiritual development, the *Order of the 1* overlapping a new (Third) Great Degree, the Divine.

CHAPTER IV

THE WISDOM RELIGION

"Wisdom is the principal thing; therefore get
wisdom; and with all thy getting get understanding. .
. . She shall give to thine head an ornament of grace:
a crown of glory shall she deliver to thee." *Proverbs
IV, 7-9*

The Wisdom Religion is the one original religion
given to all mankind. The Greeks called it *Theophania*[1]
or "the science of the manifestation or appearance of the
gods to men." It is the heritage of the human race and no
one nation or people can claim it as theirs to the exclusion of others. All so-called religions which are racial
and limited are but the various human interpretations
of the one Wisdom Religion by various peoples, each
adapting it, according to their racial type of thought, to
their particular point of view, and limiting and overlay-
ing it with their human misconceptions. It is the one or
first and Supreme Wisdom. Pythagoras termed it, "The
Gnosis or Knowledge of things that are." This seems to
be the best definition, for it makes the great distinction
between the teachings of many modern so-called religions—which deal almost entirely with theories about
things which even the propounders thereof do not pretend
to *know*, but which they expect their followers to accept because these theories have been accepted by their
denomination for ages—and the One Religion which
was taught to man only by those who absolutely *knew*.

---

1   *Theos*, gods; *phaenomai*, appear.

Many centuries before the origin of the Christian religion, there existed in the ancient land of Atlantis, and later in Asia, a Wisdom Religion which spread over the then known world. Fragments of this religion, carved upon temples, pillars and tablets by the ancient Babylonians, Egyptians, Chinese and Hindus, also by the Persians and Mesopotamians, are still decipherable. In the beginning this one Wisdom Religion was taught by the Divine Instructors, the Sons of God mentioned in *Genesis*, and later by the Sages of India, the Magians of Babylonia and Persia, the Prophets of Israel, the Hierophants of Egypt and Arabia, the Seers and Philosophers of Greece, and by the Master Jesus and the initiated disciples of the early Christian Church, all of whom acquired this wisdom and knowledge through the regular channels, *i.e.*, through the mastery of the flesh and conscious communion and union with the Divine. Nor has it ever ceased to be taught by advanced Souls who gained their knowledge of this divine wisdom in the same way. Never, even during the darkest ages, has the world lacked the testimony of some Great Soul who attained to this divine knowledge in the one and only way, nor will the time ever come when this testimony is lacking. But "as usual, that which is and was from its beginning divine, pure and spiritual in its earliest unity, became—by reason of its differentiation through the distorted prism of man's conceptions—human and impure, as reflecting man's own sinful nature."[1] One application of the law "So the last shall be first, and the first last," is that the one Wisdom Religion shall prevail upon the earth during the last Races of humanity, as it did during the first. The great difference is that in the beginning humanity was like a child

---

1   *The Secret Doctrine*, Blavatsky, Vol. 1, p. 631.

learning the great truths from the Gods direct, much as a child learns to lisp its prayers at its mother's knee. Later, when humanity grew up and entered the world's arena, it had to put into practice the lessons inculcated in its childhood. And at the last, when humanity has reached the stage of manhood, we have the promise that the Race shall become once more pure and innocent, not, however, with the purity and innocence of ignorance, but of Wisdom. In other words, it will again practice the precepts of the Wisdom Religion given by the Father in the beginning, so that the condition at the last shall be as it was at the first, completing the old and becoming the first step of a new and grander dispensation as yet undreamt of by man.

"There was in every ancient country having claims to civilization, an Esoteric Doctrine, a system which was designated WISDOM, and those who were devoted to its prosecution were first denominated sages, or wise men."[1]

The Wisdom Religion has always been divided into two parts; that which-while essentially divine, pertained, nevertheless, to matters comprehensible even to the unenlightened and necessary for their progress and daily life-was called the Exoteric or Outer Doctrine, and that which was given only to initiated disciples, called the Esoteric or Inner Doctrine. The Wisdom Religion deals with "things that are," and hence is not a religion of ritual and dogma, although it gives to them their soul. It takes but little thought to realize that all "things that are" must have deep, underlying causes which produce the effects. These causes, naturally, can be known and understood only by the few. In every science, while much can be given to the world at large, still the

---

1   Quoted by *The Secret Doctrine*, Blavatsky, Vol. III, p. 55.

deep, mysterious workings of the science—be that science what it may—can be discovered only by one who has made it a life study, devoting all his time, thought and enthusiasm to its inner and less apparent causes. Unless there were some who could and did thus study, no true idea of that science could be given to the world. Every experiment must be proved in the laboratory ere it can be given to the world—the scientist must *know*. If the many confusing technicalities were laid before the general, untrained public, they would tend not only to confuse, but also to discourage, and perhaps work great harm. For instance, a poisonous drug, which in the hands of a trained physician may be wisely experimented with and its greatest potencies and powers to save life discovered—as well as its dangers—if given to the general public might prove disastrous.

Thus it is with the Wisdom Religion. It can reveal its inner truths only to those few who have devoted many lives to its study and who have thereby evolved to a point where it can be taught them direct from God, for it would be unwise and dangerous to give many of its mysteries to untrained disciples, be they ever so earnest and sincere. Hence the Esoteric or Inner has always gone hand in hand with the Exoteric Doctrine. The Esoteric when mentioned outwardly at all, is set forth in parables and symbols so that only those whose hearts are illumined by the light of The Christos can understand the deeper meanings, yet such parables always contain an obvious moral precept which is helpful to all who receive it.

Many ask, if the Wisdom Religion is so true and of such benefit to humanity, and is possessed in its fullness by the Masters of Wisdom, why is it hedged about by so many apparently insurmountable difficulties?

and why have the Masters permitted so much misunderstanding and error to be given to the world as truth? and many similar questions. We read, "Yet there must have been some very good reason for it, since from the very dawn of History such has been the policy of every Hierophant and 'Master.' . . . From the very day when the first mystic, taught by the first Instructor of the 'Divine Dynasties' of the early races, was taught the means of communication between this world and the worlds of the invisible host, between the sphere of matter and that of pure spirit, he concluded that to abandon this mysterious science to the desecration, willing or unwilling, of the profane rabble—was to lose it. An abuse of it might lead mankind to speedy destruction; it was like surrounding a group of children with explosive substances, and furnishing them with matches. The first Divine Instructor initiated but a select few, and these kept silence with the multitudes."[1] That is, only those were initiated who, of their own free-will and desire had shown a determination to penetrate into the hidden mysteries, and a capacity to use the knowledge gained for the good of all, under the direction of their Instructors. When, however, seekers whose motives are pure and selfless are determined to penetrate into the Inner Mysteries and earnestly ask for guidance, the way to the desired knowledge always opens. For while it is dangerous to reveal the Inner Mysteries to those whose hearts are unprepared, it is equally dangerous to withhold them from those whose hearts are ready.

There must be absolute fearlessness, for "the pathway to the Gods" leads through the horrors of the lower astral world, whose debasing influences and obsessing entities will and must wreck their will upon

---

1 *The Secret Doctrine*, Vol. III, p. 52.

the disciple who opens his doors to that world unless he has grown strong and fearless through a special training which has brought about an influx of sufficient divine Power and Wisdom to enable him understandingly to cope with such forces instead of being used by them. The allegory of Daniel cast into the lion's den, also the three prophets in the fiery furnace, are illustrations of this point. Each walked unharmed amidst his fearful surroundings because The Christ-force" — the Angel of the Lord"—protected him.

No matter how eagerly disciples desire these secrets it was, and still is, the duty of every Teacher of the Mysteries to withhold all esoteric instruction from them until, by the character of their lives, they have proved that they are ready to be entrusted with it. It is not enough for them to intend to do their best; it is absolutely necessary that they acquire Wisdom to cope, like Daniel, with all conditions and forces of life. Such Wisdom can only be acquired after many lives of experience and severe testing. Hence no mortal can tell when he or any other is ready for initiation into the Mysteries. Only those Divine Instructors who have watched him life after life, and have noted how he has borne himself in the various vicissitudes of mortal experience, can judge as to his attaining Mastery in a particular incarnation. Hence the occult axiom, which is literally true and has never failed, "When the pupil is ready the Teacher appears." The Teacher here referred to is usually not a superhuman Being, but is that person, teaching or thing which will give the seeker the knowledge needed for his next step. And only when no human being or accessible teaching can fulfill that need does a more than human Teacher appear. The pupil is not the judge of his readiness for this step, for he is not

ready until he has gained the ability to recognize his
Teacher on the inner planes. Until that time it is his duty
to take the steps, one by one, as life presents them, until
a next step brings him into the presence of his Teacher.
To come close to the Masters strive to do the works of
the Masters, for the more you strive to do those works
the closer you come. An apprentice works apart from
the Master-workman while learning the preliminaries,
but when he begins to do master-work he works under
the direct supervision of the Master-workman and becomes his helper.

Solomon, referring to this Esoteric Doctrine says,
"with all thy getting, get understanding," and David emphasizes this point when he says, "The fear of the Lord
(or the Law) is the beginning of Wisdom." For until we
gain a wholesome fear or, to speak more correctly—awe,
of the Great Law which the Wisdom Religion teaches,
the disciple is not ready even to set out consciously on
the Path of Attainment. The first conscious step upon
the Path is a comprehension of the sacredness and the
desirability of the spiritual Wisdom which is spoken of
in the *Bible* as the Pearl of Great Price, for the attainment of which the disciple gladly sells all that he—the
personal self—has. When he has thus gladly sacrificed
his all for it he will realize that it is not something to be
talked about idly or displayed before men, but something to be sought for in the inner sanctuary of the heart.

The disciple must be willing to be *proved* worthy ere he can hope to receive. Solomon says, "When
Wisdom entereth into thine heart, and knowledge is
pleasant unto thy soul; discretion shall preserve thee,
understanding shall keep thee." Every candidate for
initiation must feel within himself the Great Self, the
Mighty Lord and Protector. The I Am or *Ego Suum*

shows His full power to each one who can recognize the Still Small Voice, and *this recognition can only come through the cultivation of* *the spirit of Love*.

We attain to a knowledge of this Mighty Lord, our Father-in-heaven, when we do the works of our Father. First and foremost of these works are the manifesting in our lives of Divine Love and Compassion. He who says he has realized the Divine within himself, yet only as power for his own upliftment and who uses it only for his own advancement, has never even approached that realization. Such receive the condemnation of those who prophesied and did many wondrous works in His name: "I know you not whence ye are; depart from me, all ye workers of iniquity."[1] The first action of the Divine in the heart is to awaken Love and Compassion for the Race. God is Love, and the disciple cannot draw near to or have a realization of God without an awakening of that divine Love and Compassion which is not limited to individuals, but which is poured out for all the world—for God so loves the world that He continually gives His only begotten Son—the emanation from Himself, Love—that whosoever believeth on this Son shall have eternal life.

He who feels another's sorrow, who forgets self for others, has realized, in a measure at least, the Divine. And while the works of the Father are what the world would call magic, still the greatest miracle of all is the miracle of loving. How few there be who really and truly love their fellow man! How few there be who forget themselves, their own pleasures, their own so-called rights, their own happiness for another, for the meanest of God's "little ones," for perhaps even a dumb brute. He who feels another's sorrow has touched somewhere upon the Divine within. There-

1 *St. Luke*, XIII, 27.

fore when you would attain to this realization, empty out the personal and let the Divine Father overshadow you and shelter and feed you with the mystic Bread of which when ye eat thereof ye shall hunger no more, neither thirst.

The Wisdom Religion teaches the means of accomplishing this union of the human with the Divine; for there is no possibility of attaining Mastery or of entering the kingdom of heaven unless the human is indissolubly linked to the God within. It is the firm belief in the possibilities of such union that helps one to attain it. This is the only possible Path of Attainment. The more this truth grows upon the candidate the greater the power of the Immortal God to manifest through him. And as the manifestation of the God within grows and waxes strong the Man of Sin, or the mere animal man, dies or is literally consumed in the divine ardor. As St. Paul says: "The first man is of the earth, earthy: the second man is the Lord from heaven . . . . and as we have borne the image of the earthy, we shall also bear the image of the heavenly."[1] The Wisdom Religion not only teaches this, but the Esoteric Doctrine signifies much more, for it teaches the possibility of the recognition by initiated mortals, not only of the actual presence on earth of a God or Gods, but the actual blending of the Higher Self, the personal God, with man, His representative on earth. But to accomplish this, the candidate must feed his spiritual body on this divine realization just as the physical body is fed with mortal food; for the bread of God is that which cometh down from heaven and giveth life unto the world.

---

1   *I Corinthians*, XV, 47-50.

CHAPTER V

CONCERNING THE DOCTRINE OF HELL FIRE

"And the devil that deceived them was cast into
the lake of fire and brimstone, where the beast and
the false prophet are, and shall be tormented day and
night forever and ever." *Revelation*, XX, 10

The Christian *Bible*, like all great scriptures, is an
inspired setting forth of the one Divine Wisdom in
symbolic language. It deals with principles, not things.
It describes qualities, forces and spiritual events, not
historical men, places or physical events. It is "A reper-
tory of invented personages in its older Jewish portions,
and of dark sayings and parables in its later additions,
and thus quite misleading to anyone ignorant of its
Esotericism."[1] It is less understood than more ancient
scriptures, because all so-called study of it has pro-
ceeded upon the hypothesis that it is intended to present
historical facts. In reality, no great scripture is historically true, nor is it supposed to be by those who, having
been initiated into its mysteries,[2] understand something
of their inner meaning. It is time this fact is more widely
known.

All scriptures and myths are collections of allegories and parables, grouped and arranged to illustrate
symbolically some feature of the growth of the Soul.
Hence, while not historically true, as modern research
has abundantly shown, *they are universally true*, because they illustrate phases of experience through
which every Soul passes during its evolution toward
conscious union with the Divine. As far back as the
early Gnostic sect of the Johannites—the forerunners

---

1   *The Secret Doctrine*, Blavatsky, Vol. III, p. 81.
2   See *Matthew* XIII, 11.

of the Crusaders — who claimed to be the only true initiates into the secret mysteries of Jesus and who claimed direct apostolic descent from St. John, it was taught that the stories as narrated in the Gospels were but allegories. Whenever possible, familiar historical incidents, names and places are used to illustrate the points more clearly, and also to inculcate a moral lesson for "them that are without," *i.e.*, not initiated,[1] who are able to grasp only surface truths. Since scriptural stories and events do not agree with the proven facts of history (except incidentally, here and there), the *Bible* has either been accepted in a literal sense and slavishly followed, even against all common sense and justice, or it has been mutilated and only such parts as can, seemingly, be "proved" accepted, and the rest rejected or discredited. Bloody wars have been waged in efforts to harmonize its discrepancies, and sanction found in it for everything from debauchery to the buying and selling of brothers and sisters in slavery.

In studying the seemingly preposterous myths and legends of gods and goddesses found in more ancient scriptures, we have no difficulty in understanding that they are not supposed to have an accurate historical basis, even though referring to historical or astronomical events. We do not attempt to pin them down to actual facts, but seek for the hidden meaning pertaining to the spiritual development of mankind which we know they must contain. The *Bible*, instead of dealing with gods and goddesses, deals *in exactly the same way* with personages and places, some of which are taken from history, not because their use in this way pretends to be history, but because the his-

---

1 "And he said unto them, unto you it is given to know the mystery of the kingdom of God: but unto them that are without, all these things are done in parables" *Mark IV*, 11

torical facts readily lend themselves to the illustration of the lesson intended. Other names and places used are just as fictitious as those used in the ancient myths; but they all have their inner, occult significance—the numerical value of the very words themselves have a definite meaning—and are purposely selected to indicate steps in the Path of At-one-ment up which each Soul must journey.

The Old Testament, written for the purpose of teaching the Divine Truths to the Hebrews draws its symbology largely from Hebrew or Chaldean history, and expresses its symbols in terms of Hebrew thought. But like the scriptures given to other nations, while the symbols used are expressed in a particular race thought, nevertheless the true meaning or the hidden lesson applies to all mankind. The New Testament is the symbolic history of The Christ-force or principle[1] in each heart— the journey of the awakened Soul from the time of the birth of The Christ in the heart to the crucifixion on the cross[2] of material desires, the final victory of the spiritual over the physical and the resurrection and immortality of the flesh—all of which must be experienced in some incarnation by every redeemed Soul.

It makes very little difference, as far as the truth of the teachings is concerned, whether or not a man by the name of Jesus ever lived. It is the teaching that counts. The multitude see the beautiful story, which is filled with living truth, and those who are ready sense the inner meaning, thus each one gets exactly what he is ready to receive. As a matter of history, there was a Great Master by the name of Jesus—the greatest Avatar yet come to earth—who did

---

1   See *St.Matthew* XXII, 41-4.
2   See lesson on *"The Meaning of the Cross."*

pass through the experiences symbolized in the *Bible*
during the pilgrimage of His Soul toward Mastery. The
stories are woven about this great Initiate and historic
events and places are adapted to carry out the symbology. And His teachings remain today the most sublime
ever given to man. The Christian *Bible* is the deepest
treatise on esoteric or Divine Wisdom ever given to
man; for it contains all the accumulated wisdom of past
ages together with a prophecy of times to come. A passage characteristic of the esoteric meaning of the *Bible* is
found in *Revelation* XI, 3-8: "And I will give power unto
my two witnesses. . . . And when they have finished their
testimony, the beast that ascended out of the bottomless
pit shall make war against them, and shall overcome
them and kill them. And their dead bodies shall lie in
the streets of the great city, which spiritually is called
Sodom and Egypt, where also our Lord was crucified."[1]
This text alone should convince the most skeptical that
only a symbolic meaning is intended. It scarcely needs
to be pointed out that "our Lord" was crucified neither
in Sodom nor yet in Egypt, but that both names were
accepted symbols for that state of darkness in which
the unredeemed Soul wanders, and in which The Christ
(Higher Self) is daily crucified. Our Lord, or the Great
Law of Divine Love was and is today crucified both in
Sodom and Egypt, or in the states of impurity and darkness symbolized by those names.

There is no doctrine that has caused so much con-
troversy as the doctrine of hell-fire. As the Race
outgrows the repugnant idea of an everlasting physical
punishment, there is a tendency to sweep this whole
teaching into limbo as being a bogie used to scare
mankind in its childhood, but not to be dignified by seri-

---

1   See explanation in the lesson on *"The False Prophet,"* p. 2.

ous consideration in its mature years—a something that pertained to the age of superstition and the childhood of the Race. But back of the ignorant and repellant misconception of this doctrine there is a pertinent and deeply occult significance; for such a doctrine would not be given the prominent place it occupies unless it contained the germ of a vital truth necessary for the growth of the Soul. When hell is mentioned in the *Bible* it means one of three things, viz.: occasionally the suffering of earthly experience, but usually the unseen state, Sheol, the lower sub-planes of the astral, a state of consciousness or Hades. More correctly it refers to the Eighth Sphere, the place of transmutation where evil is transmuted into good. When hell-fire is mentioned it refers to the purifying fires of Karma. Hence, to say that the gates of hell shall not prevail against you means, firstly, that if your intuition is developed so that you can be guided by The Christ-consciousness neither the state of consciousness designated as hell nor the sufferings of earthly conditions nor the denizens of the lower astral can deceive or prevail against you; secondly, that by the creative power of The Christ within you create within yourself a Divine World so that there is nothing of you to be cast into the crucible of transmutation and be disintegrated, but that all shall be immortalized and rise with the Risen Lord, that where He is there ye may be also; thirdly, that your Intuition being centered in The Christ "no evil thing can come nigh thy dwelling," no falsehood can lead you astray, no astral entity can deceive you and no false teaching appeal to you. All of which things are gates of hell which cannot prevail against the Risen Christ-consciousness.

The devil, as explained in the lesson on *The False Prophet*, is the accumulated evil thought-force of the world seeking expression in humanity and deceiving all men. The inner meaning of the following passage: "Ye are of your father the devil, and the lusts of your father ye will do. . . . When he speaketh a lie, he speaketh of his own: for he is a liar, and the father of it,"[1] is that men are children of the devil in that they are born under the great delusion, the one great, paramount lie, that the physical body, together with material existence, is the great reality. Instead realize that the personality[2] is but a garment or mask assumed by the Real Self, and that material existence is but the stage upon which but a single scene in the drama of the Soul's life is enacted. Nothing is true that is not from eternity to eternity, hence the evil (the devil) which blinds the eyes of the personality and throws its illusive glamour over all mankind is the creator or father of all lies. This great lie, together with everything that tends to strengthen it and make it seem desirable, is like a mill-stone around the neck of everyone born into earth life. In occult parlance it is the world's Karma which all must bear. In this sense humanity is a child of the devil or, as Job expresses it, "man is born unto trouble, as the sparks fly upward." But in this very lament we see the remedy; for it is only by the hammering on the anvil of life, and the burning of the karmic fires, that the Divine Sparks are released to fly upward to unity in the Godhead.

The "lake which burneth with fire and brimstone," into which the False Prophet and the Beast are cast, is one of the seven manifestations of the Great Law (acting in its aspect of Karma)[3] which permits nothing to endure that is false, that cannot withstand the vibrations of Divine Truth. Its fires are the fires of pu-

---

1 *St. John* VIII, 44.
2 *Per*, through; *sonare*, to sound; personality, a mask to speak through.
3 See Chapter VIII.

rification and transmutation that consume all that is impure or false; all that maketh a lie. And that which maketh a lie is not limited to the utterance of a falsehood, but includes everything that tends to create a false impression; everything that represents itself to be that which it is not. Fire is the highest earthly element, and its action transforms or raises all substances to a higher condition. While the substances burned cease to exist on the physical-plane they still exist in a higher state, leaving behind only that which belongs to earth in the form of ashes.

Brimstone or sulphur is used in daily life for purifying, bleaching and subliming. Salt purifies and preserves, but brimstone sublimes and raises to a higher condition. It represents the earth-plane, also that stage in which the novice is cast into the flame to be sublimed; where he has the dross of earth consumed that his spiritual pneuma may he released and rise to a higher manifestation. The fires are the blazing fires of Karma that the personality itself has lit, and in which it must stand until all is transmuted into gold. Brimstone is the means by which the other elements cast into the burning are prepared for their next step in evolution. But in accomplishing this the brimstone must sacrifice its bodily form and be sublimed. This action is the foundation for, and the real meaning of the symbol of fire and brimstone used in our text. And like all such symbols it survives because it contains a germ of truth. The lake, of course, is not a physical lake of fire and brimstone any more than the so-called hell is a physical place; but it is an actual condition. It represents the earth-plane, also that stage must pass. The earth itself is passing through this same burning and purification that its substance may be prepared for the future and higher conditions which will prevail during the coming new Race. The gases generated by the subliming action of the sulphur are gathering in certain areas preparatory to the great explosions of the future, and the humanity that is to survive those great cataclysms must have passed through the burning and purifying flames of Karmic Law that they may be enabled to breathe the rarified atmosphere resulting from the changed physical conditions which will then exist.

Hell is separation from God. The Psalmist cries, "For thou wilt not leave my soul in hell; neither wilt thou suffer thine Holy One to see corruption."[1] The physical body is in hell and does see corruption; for hell is made up of the fermenting, corroding and corrupting influences which act upon the physical and mental bodies from birth until final dissolution. In the case of the mental body these influences may last through many incarnations, until all that is false in habits, ideas, beliefs and understandings is completely consumed and the mind illumined by spiritual understanding.

All must willingly stand in this burning, but they must also perform the much harder task of standing aside and permitting others, even their own loved ones to be sublimed; to stand in the burning and suffer through the conditions which Karma presents to them. How many would gladly attempt to bear the hardships and sufferings of their loved ones rather than stand aside and permit them to fulfill their karmic destiny in exact justice! But their loved ones cannot be purified and pass on to higher things if their burdens are borne for them and they are not allowed to meet their tests and stand in the fiery furnace which they in ages past have lighted, for only when they can

---

1 *Psalms*, XVI, 10.

enter this fiery furnace and find the Lord Christ walking with them—by this recognition the fires lose their
power to harm—are they ready to pass on. If sentimen-
tal reasons are permitted to interfere with the loved
ones' performance of duty, the time of the purification
is pushed back and more fuel is accumulated for the
burning. Stand aside then, and while giving all love,
sympathy and encouragement, allow all to meet their
tests and burnings that they may be purified and advance
to higher things. It is into this hell that The Christ-
principle descends after the crucifixion, and it is into
this hell that each Soul must descend that all that belongs
to the lower self (personality) may be consumed, leaving only the purified Spirit to rise to the heights beyond.
This is the meaning of the doctrine of hell-fire; and it
manifests on the four lower planes. The Soul, however,
as the Psalmist says, will not be left in hell, but will
garner from it the experience necessary to clothe itself in
immortality. Hell endures forever and ever, for there is
no end to eternity or evolution and there will always be
something to burn and be purified and transmuted. This
does not mean that any Soul will stand in hell forever,
but that each Soul must pass through it. No one remains
in it one moment longer than is required to transmute
the base metal of personality into the pure gold of spiritual attainment. For Karma is not a punishment or even
an inevitable law of suffering which we must endure
to the end; but rather in the course of evolution our
Higher Self finds that we lack certain Soul-qualities,
hence chooses to incarnate in certain families and under
certain conditions which will bring out the Soul-quality
which is lacking. Everything must pass through the
burning that it may be transmuted into love to lay at the

Master's feet, while selfishness and all earthly dross is left behind like ashes.

Every sincere seeker should gladly stand in the flames of the karmic hell, for only the faults, only that which is impure or false can burn. All the false teachings, false doctrines, false love, false living; all misunderstandings and misconceptions, being but transitory, will be consumed, but nothing that is real, that is immortal can burn; the true will emerge as pure gold. In that day we will know as we are known; for the coverings of falsehood and pretense will have disappeared in the burning.

Therefore, let this realization of the fire that burneth and the worm that dieth not, remain with you as the greatest comfort to your Soul. Realize that all you have to do is to wait and trust and pray that everything that holds you back from your true spiritual advance may be quickly consumed that the burning may come to an end. That which burns is mortal and transitory and has no part nor lot in your real life. Realize that the burning cannot last one moment longer than you give fuel to the flames. As soon as the dross is burned away the dawning of the resurrection morn will come. As soon as you cease to deceive, cease to lie, cease to be false, you cease to furnish fuel to the flames, hence the burning will last only until that which has been accumulated is consumed.

Stand still, then, in the burning that you may be purified. Weave for yourselves immortal garments of Purity and Truth. Lay up for yourselves treasures in immortal habitations, "where neither moth nor rust doth corrupt, and where thieves do not break through nor steal." And when the fires of hell have become the crown of glory that shall illumine the saints, then shall they walk the streets of the New Jerusalem (the puri-fled earth) in white raiment. "And there shall be no night there; and they need no candle, neither light of the sun; for the Lord God giveth them light; and they shall reign for ever and ever."[1] For these are they that have come out of great tribulation.

1　*Revelation*, XXII, 5.

CHAPTER VI

THE ELEVENTH COMMANDMENT

"But we beseech you, brethren, . . . that ye study to be quiet, and to do your own business." I *Thessalonians*, IV, 11.

"Wist ye not that I must be about my Father's business?" *St. Luke*, II, 49.

"Beware of fear that spreadeth, like the black and soundless wings of midnight bat, between the moonlight of thy Soul and thy great goal that loometh in the distance far away." *The Voice of the Silence*, Blavatsky, Fragment III.

In the life of every earnest seeker after Truth, after the first enthusiasm of the awakening to his spiritual possibilities and the wonder of his newly found joy, there comes a period of depression in which everything seems to fail him, and a shadow of discouragement, almost lack of faith, seems to spread over him. In his mind questionings arise at first fleeting, then growing more persistent. "After all, is this great change that has come into my life worth the effort I have made to give up old ideals and conditions and remodel my life? Are these new ideas practical or are they mere ephemeral sophistries which fail me in my hour of need? And the teachers to whom I have listened, are they not human beings, full of frailties like myself, with no higher wisdom for my guidance; with nothing to give me that I have not already of myself?" A great fear possesses him, lest conditions beat him back and compel him to resume the old treadmill of his former life, without hope and without being able to contact the spiritual power that sustained him at first. All his beautiful soul experiences, looked at from this Slough of Despond, now seem to have been but fantastic imaginings, and the cry goes forth: What is the use of all this struggling? At this point, unless some understanding of the Law is grasped, the seeker is apt to slip back, apt to repudiate all the good resolutions and vows he has made to his Higher Self and, like the man from out whom the unclean spirit was cast, he then takes unto himself seven other unclean spirits of worry, doubt, fear and discouragement, and his last state is worse than the first. If, however, it is pointed out to him at this time that this depression is but a natural phenomenon, through some phase of which most seekers pass and which is just as natural as a night of darkness after a day of sunshine, he will be able to take advantage of this night period of the Soul to strengthen his courage and faith.

If he turns to the *Bible* for comfort he will find it in the twenty-third *Psalm*. "Yea, though I walk through the valley of the shadow of death, I will fear no evil: for thou art with me; thy rod and thy staff they comfort me." The period of depression is indeed "the valley of the shadow of death," *i.e.*, the shadow of the death of his high ideals; a valley in that it is a depression between two heights. And just as surely as he has descended from one height into this valley, so must he, if he persevere, climb the height beyond. But if he insists on walking up and down the valley, for lack of courage to essay the height ahead, the shadow will descend and enwrap him. "Beware, Disciple, of that lethal shade. No light that shines from Spirit can dispel the darkness of the nether Soul, unless all selfish thought has fled there from. . . . It is the shadow of thyself outside the PATH, cast on the darkness of thy sins."[1] The rod and staff are

---

1 *The Voice of the Silence*, Blavatsky, Fragment III.

given to every disciple, not only to lean upon, but also as an alpen-stock with which to climb the Mountains of Attainment.

There is an old injunction often used in a spirit of impatience and anger or flippantly alluded to as the 11th commandment, yet which contains a deep occult significance, *i.e.*, "Mind your own business." The ten commandments given to Moses seem to cover all phases of mortal life so that he who keeps that decalog does his whole duty to God and man, yet while the 10 and the decimal system is accepted as perfection in worldly affairs; the duodecimal (12) is a system often used in the computation of occult periods. Hence, the seeker who is striving to live above mere worldly affairs, who is striving to shape his life in accord with the deeper mysteries of existence, has need of two more commandments to make up his duo-decalog. Whereas, the ten commandments were delivered on Mt. Sinai, amidst thunderings and lightnings, the eleventh and twelfth commandments are given by the Still Small Voice that speaks in the Silence. The eleventh commandment may sound irreverent, but in its occult significance it is far from being so, for if obeyed it covers the period of depression referred to above. The significance of the twelfth commandment can only be grasped when the eleventh has become a part of your life.

Each one of you who chooses, after due deliberation and meditation, to set for yourself a divine standard of life, has entered upon a new business, one which vitally concerns yourself. And at the very outset of this new business you must meet yourself face to face, take account of stock and find out what your real business is. To mind your own business does not mean merely negatively to refrain from interfering

with the business of others, although that is included. The deeper meaning is to find out what your
own business is, then actively to be about it. This applies particularly to you who have determined to live
the higher life, you who have passed through the ecstasy of the awakening and are now passing through the
natural reaction, the Slough of Despond, "the valley of
the shadow of death." The reason for the depression is
that the moment you say to your Higher Self that you
will henceforth live in accord with the will of that Self
working through you, you find yourself face to face with
your old personality. This personality is composite, the
aggregate of the factors and forces of the age in which
you live. That is, it is made up of elements from all the
lower kingdoms—mineral, vegetable, animal—as well as
the mental traits and tendencies that are the Karma, not
only of the Soul, but also of the age, the race, the nation,
the community and the family in which you live, all of
which are literally built into your physical, astral, desire
and mental bodies, a microcosm in very truth. Because
this personality and its traits are not altogether your
own, but are taken from the various kingdoms and other
sources, the instant you determine to break away from
the bonds of the flesh and express your Real Self, you
take all these varied factors out of their customary vibration and impose upon them the will of the higher Being,
your True Self. The new key-note is resisted by all the
elements in the personality as well as in the environment,
and the combined opposition of all is focused upon you.
There is aroused within you every sleeping tendency;
tendencies which heretofore you did not recognize nor
even suspect. Many of these are but the reflex effects of
the thought-currents of the community. Others are ten-

dencies stimulated by the influences of the zodiacal sign in which you were born acting in a negative way, also the negative aspect of your planetary influences, all acting upon the atoms of your personality through your subconscious mind uncontrolled by the human consciousness, to say nothing of inspiration from the Super-conscious Mind. You find yourself in the condition St. Paul speaks of: "I find then a law, that, when I would do good, evil is present with me."[1] And the more determined you are to do the will of the Divine Self the more unsuspected tendencies you find within you to transmute, tendencies which were quiescent or sleeping as long as you advanced passively with the current of the community, but which are now awakened and fighting for life.

Do not confuse the sub-conscious with the Super-conscious Mind as is so commonly done. The subconscious is the animal mind, that which is below the threshold of human waking consciousness, as sub means under or below. It is the sum total of the consciousness of all the cells, organs, ganglia and centers of consciousness in the animal body synthesized by the animal Soul. It controls all the vegetative functions such as respiration, circulation, digestion, reflex action, etc. It is also this mind that automatically reproduces that which is impressed upon it by human consciousness such as a harmonious or inharmonious attitude toward life, ideas of health or disease, weakness or power, etc. Hence it can be called upon to adjust only such conditions as come within its domain, for it is but the servant of man's human consciousness, just as man's human consciousness should be the servant of the higher or Super-consciousness.

The Super-conscious mind is the intelligence of the

1 *Romans*, VII, 21.

Real Self overshadowing its human personality. It is man's touch with the Divine. To come into touch with the Higher Consciousness the activities of the human consciousness must be stilled, for when the mind is controlled it becomes like a mirror to reflect and record that which comes to it from the Higher Self.

It is the awakening into activity of these unrecognized forces that makes the darkness of the night period so depressing and awful. Each Soul must face this darkness alone. Your attention is called to this because "scarce one passes through without bitter complaint . . . . your Teacher or your predecessor may hold your hand in his, and give you the utmost sympathy the human heart is capable of. But when the silence and the darkness come, you lose all knowledge of him; you are alone and he cannot help you, not because his power is gone, but because you have invoked your great enemy. By your great enemy I mean yourself. If you have the power to face your own Soul in the darkness and silence, you will have conquered the physical or animal self which dwells in sensation only."[1] When the light of The Christ has illumined your heart and has awakened a recognition of your divine possibilities it must also awaken all the latent propensities in your composite personality, for the same sun which causes the good seed to sprout in the garden of your heart will also stimulate in even greater profusion the growth of the weeds which, unless ruthlessly uprooted, will choke out the life of the good seed. The business then that you must mind is to pull up the weeds or conquer the foes within one by one as they appear. Make no compromise. You must conquer or be overcome. For the very rec-

---

1   Comments on *Light on the Path*.

ognition of your divine birthright lashes into fury all
those forces of the lower self which have held you in
bondage so long. However, while this step brings out
every latent fault it also awakens every latent power for
good. In fact, you never know what you really are until
the light of The Christ has illumined every corner of
your being. Ofttimes the unexpected beauty and strength
revealed is quite as overwhelming as the shortcomings.
The battle is not onesided. In fact, "He that is with you
(your Higher Self) is greater than he (the personality or
lower self) that is against you."

When you find this state of depression and lethargy
approaching, instead of trying to mind the business of
another, understand that it is never another's business
you are to mind nor outside conditions you are to fight,
but the very forces within that are bringing the doubts
upon you. The first temptation, when confronted by this
apparent disillusionment, is to pick flaws, first in the
teachings which have so greatly helped heretofore, then
in the personalities of others, hoping thereby to excuse
your own shortcomings. But you can never find truth or
happiness by dissecting it, only by turning your attention to yourself and finding out why you now doubt and
criticize that which brought you so much happiness and
satisfaction at first. Then set to work to conquer with a
full realization that every one of the awakened forces of
the lower self are fighting to overcome the manifestation
of the Real Self and make you sink back once more into
the passive condition in which you were but one of the
many and your life but the result of the ebb and flow of
the thought-currents common to your family and environment, a creature ruled by circumstances and a slave
to outward conditions. You never have to fight another's

battles, only your own. Because your personality is made up of atoms from the entire community and environment in which you dwell, as you overcome your own faults by creating their opposites you add strength to the power that is striving to conquer the same faults in the whole community. Moreover, you cannot thus sink back without lending your forces to swell the tide that will overwhelm you and all who are near and dear to you. Every time you mind another's business or waste force striving with enemies outside yourself you are adding strength to the things you would conquer.

The Christ, speaking through the Master Jesus, has said: "In my Father's house are many mansions: I go to prepare a place for you. And if I go and prepare a place for you, I will come again, and receive you unto myself; that where I am, there ye may be also."[1] The Christ-power is the creative power of Divine Love that has brought you up out of the darkness and set your feet upon a rock; that has literally gone before you to prepare your Path. The place The Christ is preparing for you is not some post-mortem heaven inhabited by beings suddenly perfected through the experience called death, but is the place, conditions and personality you are now in. If you have been called by The Christ to face these particular conditions rest assured that The Christ has gone before to prepare the place for you. But while the mansion or dwelling place is chosen and prepared by The Christ within, still it is you who must furnish and equip and dwell in it. This is the business which you must mind. All worldly dwelling places must be shared by all the elements of confusion which go to make up the personality—a confused and imperfect reflection of the Real Self. Your real mansion is prepared for you by The

1   *St. John.* XIV, 2,3.

Christ, but ere you can dwell in it The Christ must come again in your heart and life and receive you unto Himself. The first step must be to drive out the aliens who are now dwelling in your mansion. Since the great aim of physical existence is not personal salvation, but the redemption (spiritualization) of physical matter and the ultimate evolution of all humanity from its lower and merely human state of consciousness to oneness with The Christ-consciousness, each individual Soul finds itself confronted with a certain amount of matter from the various kingdoms which it is its business to spiritualize and redeem; a certain personality with particular traits, tendencies, passions and desires, out of which, as raw material, the Soul must fashion the furnishings of its mansion in the Father's house. How is this to be accomplished? Here you are concerned with the little physical inequalities and disquietudes of life, and you ask over and over again, "If The Christ has called me to this higher life, why do not conditions immediately change? why is there anything for me to do but open my heart and receive the blessings promised by the Father?" One reason is that if your Father-in-heaven gave you all the conditions you now deem so necessary—wealth to use for good, leisure to study, opportunity to teach, etc.—you would either find that when obtained they did not satisfy your Soul hunger or that you would sit down exactly as you are today with all your faults and deficiencies nicely covered over and would never recognize them, grow or advance, and be about your Father's business the redemption of the world. Hence you must mind your own business; must empty, cleanse, purify and refurnish your mansion or "temple of the living God,"[1]

---

1   "Know ye not that ye are the temple of God, and that the Spirit of God dwelleth in you?" I *Cor*. III, 16.

that "where I am ye may be also." In other words to so prepare your mansion that the Father shall dwell with you and The Christ shall be the light thereof. Why then waste time and force striving for the things of the outer world? Why fret and fume over the little difficulties you meet in preparing your mansion? why weep and ask for this or that thing? Why not just rest in the thought that The Christ has prepared this place for you and that you must be about your business, *i.e.*, using the materials found in your personality and environment to furnish the dwelling place for Him when He returns to take you unto Himself. For your Father's business is the redemption of the world and each apparently separated individuality has a special part of that business to perform.

Each of you have your own problems, and each problem brings you up against your own lower self and forces you to recognize just what it is that keeps your mansion in an unfinished state. Like Hamlet, so many feel "The time is out of joint;—O cursed spite! That ever I was born to set it right !"[1] If you study Hamlet you will find that in his attempt to set the world aright he only brought sorrow and suffering to himself and those he loved, and sacrificed not only his own personality but also the personality of others in his misguided attempt. No person has ever been born to set the world aright except so much of it as he finds expressed in his own personality. If you mind your own business and let the faults of others go, trusting to the Law to straighten them out, and confine yourself to straightening out your own faults, you will realize the joy that comes from such conquering. When you cease to worry over the faults of others, it will be like a physical burden rolling from

---

1   *Hamlet*, end of Act I.

your shoulders. If you have never done this, try it merely as a physical experiment for your own happiness, and the results will prove its truth.

The world can never be redeemed by preaching, talking or even by ministering to the sorrows of others, relieving their distress, building model tenements or libraries or by changing economic conditions. While all these things are necessary factors they are only really helpful as they are the result of a true minding of the business of the Father, recognizing the absolute oneness of all, not only in a metaphysical sense, but also in the personality and the elements composing it. When mankind realizes this, Universal Brotherhood will be an accomplished fact. You will then realize in a practical way that everything you do to or for another will react upon yourself. Then the injunction, Do unto others as you would they should do unto you, will become the law of life, for you will realize that as you do unto others you literally do unto yourself; that you must share the sorrows and joys, the privations and honors of even your most distant brothers and sisters. This will not be fighting another's battles or minding another's business, except as your own conquering helps all. It is as though a great building were being erected in which each worker by strictly minding his own business—which is his part of the great plan, whether he be bricklayer or architect—is making the work of all easier and advancing the completion of the entire structure. Each must share the results of the success or failure of any one to mind his own business.

These results can be attained only by elevating to a higher rate of vibration first the thought-forces and then the physical conditions of the self, the family, the community. This must be accomplished accord-

ing to the natural law of harmony. If you were in a con-
gregation which was singing out of tune, the best way
to bring about harmony would be not to stop the singing and talk about it, but to sing steadily and firmly in
perfect tune yourself. Those next to you would catch
and spread the harmony until all were singing in tune.
It will be only the working out of this law of harmony
that will ultimately redeem "the round world and all
that dwell thereon."

Only the manifestation of The Christ in your heart
and life can bring peace on earth, goodwill toward men.
Any line of conduct that really brings peace and goodwill is therefore an expression of The Christ or Divine
Harmony.

CHAPTER VII

NARCOTICS, ALCOHOL AND PSYCHISM

The human body is the Temple of the Living God.[1]
Within it are certain vital centers comparable to doors[2]
which open into inner shrines. Using these centers as
points of contact, the life forces from the higher planes
flow into the physical body through them as an electrical current flows through a wire. And it is through these
centers that The Christ-force must flow to reach and
spiritualize man's various bodies before their redemption or resurrection can take place. By resurrection we
mean the ultimate building up of a spiritual body within
the physical by a process of gradually raising the vibrations of its particles to respond to the key-note sounded
by the Divine or Higher Self.

These centers or doors are normally protected by nature with oily coverings or sheaths (composed of both
astral and physical matter) which permit the flow of the
normal life-forces and protect them from all others. These
doors should be opened only by a gradual purification
and development of the protecting sheaths. Normally
this takes place as a natural growth resulting from a life
of mental and bodily purity, and intense spiritual aspiration. It should not be a forced or hothouse growth,
for each door must be opened and closed under the
absolute control of the will. Each individual has been
given these doors to guard, and is held responsible for

---

1   I *Corinthians* VI, 19.
2   In ancient times a door meant a passage way leading into a chamber and was
    not used as commonly as now to mean that which closed the passage way.

their keeping. Only as he can master them, and in full knowledge open them to the knock of The Christ, and close them to His enemies, can he hope to conquer. It is only after long training and great spiritual growth that the entities of the astral world can be mastered and held at bay when the doors are opened. In fact the first and most important work of the advanced disciple is to stand faithful watch over these doors. "Keep thou the door of thine heart."

The Holy Ghost is the Mother-principle or the power of bringing forth, hence, the destruction of the sheaths prevents the bringing forth or manifesting of The Christ-force within you. The sin against the Holy Ghost, the "unpardonable sin," (unpardonable only because ir-reparable) is the separation of the personality from the guidance of the Higher Self through the destruction of the means of contact. This takes place through the break-ing down of the doors or the destruction of the oily sheaths that protect the centers leading from the physical into the astral and psychic bodies. Once these sheaths are destroyed, the person is no longer able to close the doors and so becomes an easy prey to the denizens of the astral. Such an one becomes a helpless victim to *any* and *all* sorts of psychic imposition and deception.

There is no such thing as a "lost Soul," but it is possible for the personality to persistently refuse the guidance of the Higher Self and ultimately break away from it entirely and become a lost human-animal. The animal life-force of such a soulless entity may incarnate several times, each time growing more degenerate, until it has finally exhausted the force obtained during its contact with the Soul and

the aggregated atoms disintegrate and return to the elements from which they were gathered. The Soul in such
cases is not lost but is indrawn to await a new opportunity to gather up the materials necessary to clothe itself
in a personality.

There are several abnormal ways in which the oily
protecting sheaths can be broken down and the doors
thrown open, chief among which are the use of alcohol
and narcotic drugs. Chemically speaking, ordinary alcohol is ethyl-hydroxide. The ethyl (the spirit) vibrates
to the highest rate reached by mere physical matter, the
point where matter transcends the physical and enters
the astral, the ethyl actually functioning on both planes.
Narcotic drugs also contain an ethyl element. The ethyl
when taken into the body immediately seeks to escape
into the astral, and it naturally follows the usual avenues
of communication between the two planes. But in escap-
ing it passes through the centers in a reverse direction to
the normal current and gradually burns off the insulating
sheaths until in time they are utterly destroyed, just as an
electrical insulation might be burned off by interference
with the normal flow of the current.

This breakdown may be very rapid, as in the case of a
habitual drunkard or drug fiend, or it may be insidious and
not show markedly for several incarnations, but the result
is certain and every indulgence in the substances mentioned is a step toward the end. Ultimately this leaves the
doors unguarded and open for all the horrors of the lowest
astral-plane to rush in and take possession of the "Temple
of the Living God" thus desecrated. Bulwer-Lytton
gives a realistic description of some of these horrors
in his occult novel. "Zanoni." In that story the student

opened the doors abnormally by the use of drugs and being unable to close them through fright at the sights that met his gaze, was haunted until his death. Tobacco although classed as a narcotic does not contain the elements so destructive to the psychic centers, in fact when not used to excess is rather soothing. It does however, injuriously affect the heart and nervous system. From an occult standpoint one of the greatest objections to its use is its tendency to form a habit. It goes without saying that the aspirant for the spiritual life must be master of all conditions and functions and a slave to none. Hence while tobacco is not rigidly prohibited in the earlier stages of growth, its use is strongly advised against.

Tea and coffee are stimulants but not narcotics in the sense we use the term, as they do not contain the injurious elements. Their excessive use does affect the nervous system injuriously, although many sensitive persons find that their moderate use has a beneficial and tonic effect, but their use should not be abused.

The drunkard and the drug habitué open the doors while in a state of debauchery, and in such a condition, being particularly unable to defend themselves, they practically invite all the fiends of the underworld to enter and take possession.

It is our duty to give our sympathy and help to this class of sorely afflicted ones, for since it took many lives to break down the protective sheaths, it will require a long hard fight to rebuild them. Hence do not let such unfortunate ones become discouraged. No matter how many times they may fall back into the old habits, every effort to conquer aids in the rebuilding. And the very fierceness of the struggle will ultimately strengthen the Soul. But no matter how sincerely they repent, or what spiritual advance they make as a result of the sufferings they undergo, when the aura is tainted with narcotics or filled with fumes of alcohol, and until the protective sheaths of these centers are rebuilt, it is utterly impossible for a Master or Messenger from *The Great White Lodge to contact* (or come anywhere near), such an one, *no matter how great the student's psychic or spiritual development.* On the contrary they will have a bitter fight to keep out of their auras entities from the astral plane, and it will require many incarnations of such fighting ere the sheaths can be rebuilt. These sheaths are not broken down in one incarnation, but since in each incarnation there is a tendency to repeat the same old mistakes until they are conquered, so in each incarnation there is a tendency to increase the weakness brought over from the past until the final breakdown comes. The rebuilding must necessarily follow the same law, *i.e.*, be brought about by gradual accomplishment through determined and persistent constructive effort.

We read in the *Bible* that no drunkard can inherit the Kingdom of Heaven.[1] In this sense the Kingdom of Heaven means the highest spiritual-plane, which can be reached only by the perfect control of the doors or centers through which alone communion is possible. The *Bible* does not say that no drunkard can be saved, but that he cannot reach into the higher spiritual realms and come into conscious touch with his Father-in-heaven until he has conquered. He has destroyed the means of communication, and it is only after earnest and persistent effort, through many lives, that such an one can gradually rebuild the sheaths,

---

1   I *Corinthians* VI, 10.

purify the centers, and again make the body a fit Temple for the coming of The Christ. Many drunkards desire to stop drinking but, being open to the astral-plane, they are unable to resist the urge of those disembodied ones who have passed out of physical life while addicted to drink and have no means of gratifying their desires in the astral world. In order to gratify them they must come into touch with the physical-plane by entering into or obsessing someone on the physical-plane ere they can again experience the effects of the drug. On the other hand there are drinkers who simply say "I am done with drink" and never touch it thereafter. In such cases they are unconsciously rebuilding the centers until finally a point is reached where the doors can be closed at will, and it only requires some strong emotion to put the will into effect. This will is often aroused in a dramatic manner at the sudden "conversions" which so frequently result from various forms of religious excitement.

It is only in a normal, purified, strong and healthy body, with every function at its highest degree of development and every center under perfect control that The Christ can fully manifest on earth. You can live The Christ-life and attain to a high degree of spirituality and take many advanced steps without meeting all these requirements, but you cannot reach Mastery without fulfilling all the Law.

One of the most noticeable karmic results of the use of narcotics and alcohol in past incarnations can be seen in the numerous non-spiritual, subjective mediums, *of the irresponsible type*, who are to be found on every hand. Their doors, destroyed in past lives, now stand wide open leaving them at the mercy of *any* and *every* entity who desires to gratify its animal

senses upon the physical-plane. Truly, their lot is a piti-
able one; the more so because they know not the terrible
dangers they run.

Another karmic result of the action of alcohol and
drugs is to be found in a certain class of congenital
imbeciles whose psychic centers cannot even connect
with the ordinary centers of the physical body; in fact
many of them are the reincarnations of the soulless entities mentioned above. They have almost no voluntary
control of any but the lowest animal functions, and must
finish out their incarnation in a sort of vegetative animal
existence.

Still another way in which the doors are frequently broken open is by placing yourself in a passive, non-resisting
state and making the demand for psychic experiences, or
"sitting for development" as it is called. In this practice
you are placing yourself in a negative state in which *any
entity* dwelling on the lower astral plane can help you
break open the doors. This either destroys the doors or
abnormally forces the development of the psychic centers
instead of unfolding them as a natural accompaniment of
spiritual growth. When results have been thus obtained,
since the doors are not under the control of your will,
they are open to any entity who desires to obsess you.
Even if the obsessing entity is a disembodied friend of
good moral character your condition is not altered, for
he must he near you constantly to protect you from the
fiends.[1] This is what takes place in ordinary subjective
mediumship. As we said in *Letters From The Teacher*[2]
"The difference between spiritual communication and
subjective mediumship is a difference both of vibration and method. The right way to contact the higher
planes is to raise the vibrations of your physical and

1   See *The Shadow Land*, by Hamlin Garlin.
2   Page 44.

psychic bodies and their centers until they vibrate in harmony with the key-note of the Soul-plane, at which pitch "no evil thing can come nigh thy dwelling." As we can only become aware of a thing when some part of our organism responds to its vibrations, the psychic must have the proper development to come into harmony with the spiritual-plane ere he can contact the Masters or respond to things which touch upon or vibrate within the octave of their key-note.

"On the one hand—spiritual communication—the psychic, through spiritual living, loving thoughts and helpful actions in many lives, must build into his or her character enough of the divine principle of Compassion for all humanity to raise the vibrations of all the bodies, either temporarily or continuously, to the note of spiritual love to which the Masters of Compassion naturally vibrate. On the other hand—subjective mediumship— the psychic, through various means, either mentally by stilling the thoughts, or physically by various Yogi practices such as gazing at a crystal, a black spot, or sitting in a constrained position, through breathing exercises and many other still more objectionable practices—has gained the power of stilling the physical vibrations and becoming negative; or when through the oily sheaths having become weakened or destroyed the psychic is naturally negative. In such a state the physical atoms, not being held together by the vibratory rhythm to which they naturally respond, slow down and fly off to such an extent that any discarnate entity clothed in atoms of, and vibrating to the note of, the astral-plane—which is next to and in its lower degrees overlaps the earth-plane—can gather up and clothe himself in sufficient of the physical atoms thus thrown off to temporarily vibrate to the key-note of the physical-plane and become temporarily recognizable on that plane.

"In the first instance the whole desire of the psychic is to uplift humanity; he is filled with compassion for the Race and desires to give himself as a willing sacrifice to bring enlightenment to the world. This is true spiritual development. The Teachers and Masters whom he contacts do not see the little individual difficulties, or if They do, They understand the Law and know that all is working out for the best, that only Wisdom can really help. Given Wisdom, Love and sustaining help, the disciples can, and indeed must, work out their own personal problems. As Paul says: "Work out your own salvation with fear and trembling." All spiritual communication is uplifting, and the *spiritual* atoms which the psychic has contacted and drawn into his body will rejuvenate and strengthen the physical, uplift the mental and advance him on the Path of Spiritual Attainment.

"In the second instance, by giving up the command over the life-forces and throwing open or breaking down the doors of the sacred centers, the vitality is drawn upon and the atoms thrown off are used to bring to the physical-plane the denizens of the astral. These may be pure or vile, and are attracted to the medium in exact ratio to the state of the atoms which he or she gives off during the negative "sitting." If you understand this, and the fact that most of the entities contacted upon the astral plane *are not Spiritual Beings*, but merely men and women with their most dense and outer garment (the physical body) removed, you will understand the danger of giving yourself up to their use. Since they are using astral senses they can see farther ahead than those of the earth-plane, but such advice as they have to give should be taken just as you would take the advice of any earthly friend—subject to your own good judgment and common-sense. Usually such entities are interested in the daily life of the sitters rather than their true spiritual advance, but, if evilly disposed or lacking Wisdom and a knowledge of the Law, they can and often do deceive. They can only come to earth as they left it, *i.e.*, clothed in physical atoms; the fact that to manifest on the physical-plane they must steal physical atoms from the medium and sitters is proof positive of this. Often their desire is to help alleviate earthly conditions, but their advice, while valuable in many cases, is still in accord with worldly standards. In fact their activity is much like that of a well-meaning but over-meddlesome friend on the earth-plane. They desire to help their friends out of difficulties, over hard places, and often give advice which helps to make money out of the credulity of their fellow-men. This, as you can see, but helps to sink the Race deeper into the mire of earthly affairs. The first is the *Constructive*, the second the *Destructive* method of communication. In no case — unless they are Masters, in which case they will manifest quite differently, as we will explain later — are they different from the people on earth, except that they are functioning in a body composed of finer matter.

"You cannot always tell which of the above mentioned methods have been used by the teachings received, for even in subjective mediumship the teaching may be of a higher moral character, just as some friend might give you a highly moral address. But no matter who the entity *claims* to be, he will *not* be a Master of Wisdom if the subjective method is used, for no Master of the Right Hand Path ever uses that method. In this case it is not a question of *what* teachings are given, but how they are given.

"One absolute test as to which method a psychic is

using and from whence the messages come is the effect on the physical body. In spiritual communication the psychic is clothed upon by spiritual atoms which self-effacement and compassion have drawn to him, and he grows more spiritual. If after the experience his vitality is augmented and a peaceful, happy and vigorous feeling remains, even for days afterward; if life seems fuller, trials easier to bear and love more abundant, you can rest assured that he has risen above earthly things and has been clothed upon by the Spirit, and has brought back lessons for the benefit of humanity. This is the form of communion with the higher planes that should be desired. But do not strive for it; let it come as a natural growth resulting from a life filled with loving, unselfish thoughts and deeds.

"In subjective mediumship, however, owing to the loss of physical atoms and vitality, the psychic is depleted and weakened, and soon shows it, not only in bodily health, but also in mental power. His nervous system is enervated, his mentality is dulled and a great stumbling-block has been placed in his path. If, after communicating, the psychic is exhausted, tired, nervous, cross, fretful and uneasy, even for days, you can rest assured that he has allowed some astral entity to absorb his vitality and contact him by the second and *destructive* method. It must be remembered, however, that even the psychic who uses the constructive or correct method of communication is far more highly sensitive than the average and hence is easily affected by any lack of harmony in surrounding conditions, either physical or mental, and often suffers from such conditions, although later is able to conquer or rise above them. This is one reason why in all ancient religions the Sibyl or inspired Priestess was always surrounded by love, beauty and harmony and sacredly protected against all forms of inharmony."

We are now nearing the end of the Fifth Root-Race[1] of the Fourth Round (having just entered its sixth sub-race) and are reaching a point where, if we have been diligent, we should begin to lift up our eyes and see our Father afar off and say: "I will arise and go to my Father." Many are beginning to unfold their inner faculties and realize the presence or perhaps hear the voice of their Divine Guide and Teacher, and receive messages and teachings from Him. While the teachings of the Masters are always true—for there can be no confusion, since they are all One, and give out identical teachings—yet psychics who have never studied the philosophy of evolution and re-birth, or the laws of communication with such Beings, cannot always grasp, hence cannot correctly interpret, the lessons given, and much confusion results owing to the intellectual limitations of the instrument they must use *i.e.*, the physical brain. The physical brain cannot grasp or respond to ideas of which the pictures, or at least some conception—the seed, so to speak—has not been acquired through the outer sense organs, *i.e.*, through study, obser-vation, etc. At this point there are many, many avenues of deception, hence the great necessity for the pupil to come under proper instruction, and above all to learn that strict obedience to the laws which ages of occult training have proved to be the only safeguards, is a necessity, which laws he cannot find out for himself in one incarna-tion. Nor can he find them out through the guidance of astral teachers, for no matter how well-intentioned such teachers may be, they are still limited to the stage of their own evolution. Hence only those who have passed through *all* stages of evolution and have *mastered* the Law can give such training. Such great Teachers do not

---

1 For an account of the Rounds and Races, see Chapters XV and XVII, also the Theosophical text books, such as "Ancient Wisdom, " "The Ocean of Theosophy, " etc.

impart this training through astral means, for they have left well-authenticated records and text-books of their philosophy. Hence like any other scientific study, only when the student has familiarized himself with the fundamentals of the science will the advanced Teacher attempt to communicate with him, for those great Teachers know only too well the temptations and deceptions of the astral-plane and their great desire is to protect humanity from these dangers rather than to lead into them. Much better for a teacher to throw a pupil into the water ere he had been told how to swim.

Just as a college contains the accumulated wisdom and experience of all who have made discoveries in any line of study, while an individual experimenting alone has only his own experience to guide him and must make many blundering mistakes which a college training would have prevented, so it is in occultism.

The *Bible* is full of references to these psychic centers. Whenever doors or gates are mentioned in the Scriptures the reference is to these sacred centers. The following are a few of the many references: "Lift up your heads, O ye gates; and be ye lifted up, ye everlasting doors; and the King of glory shall come in. "[1]

The Children of Israel were told to take the blood of the sacrificial lamb (symbolizing The Christ-force sacrificed in humanity) and "strike the lintel and the two side posts with the blood that is in the bason; and none of you shall go out at the door of his house until the morning"[2] as a sign that "the Lord will pass over the door, and will not suffer the destroyer to come into your houses to smite you."

---

1 Psalms, XXIV, 7.
2 Exodus, XII, 22-23.

The whole story of Job is but a history of an initiation. In it Job laments as his chief sin that he opened his door to the "traveler"[1]; and again he asks, "have the gates of death been opened unto thee? or hast thou seen the doors of the shadow of death ?"[2] Both of these statements are incomprehensible from any literal point of view, but are plain in the light of the above. Wisdom is spoken of as "she crieth at the gates, at the entry of the city, at the coming in at the doors."[3] In *Isaiah* we have the invitation: "Come, my people, enter thou into thy chambers, and shut thy doors about thee."[4] This is a condition necessary to entering into communion with the spiritual-plane, for the doors must be shut to the lower ere they can be opened to the higher. In the *New Testament* we have these directions as to prayer (spiritual communion), "But thou, when thou prayest, enter into thy closet, and when thou has shut thy door (*i.e.*, shut out all worldly and astral conditions), pray to thy Father which is in secret; and thy Father which seeeth in secret shall reward thee openly."[5]

A most significant allusion to the necessity for mastery over the doors is given in *St. Luke*.[6] "Strive to enter in at the straight gate: for many, I say unto you, will seek to enter in, and shall not be able. When once the master of the house is risen up, and hath shut to the door. . . . But he shall say, I tell you, I know not whence ye are; depart from me, all ye workers of iniquity." To whom can this dismissal apply but to those without the gates? This plainly alludes to that state of development in which we have gained such mastery over the doors that we can shut them to all undesirable influences, even though they

1   Job, XXXI, 32.
2   Job, XXXVIII, 17.
3   Proverbs, VIII, 3.
4   Isaiah, XXVI, 20.
5   St. Matthew, VI, 6.
6   St. Luke, XIII, 24-27.

have supped with us, and say, "Depart all ye workers of iniquity," and make them depart. For you must be the master of your house.

Again, in *St. John* X, 1-3, we read, "Verily, verily, I say unto you, He that entereth not by the door into the sheepfold, but climbeth up some other way, the same is a thief and a robber. But he that entereth in by the door is the shepherd of the sheep. To him the porter openeth: and the sheep hear his voice: and he calleth his own sheep by name, and leadeth them out."

Note carefully the promise given to the angel of the Church of Philadelphia, in *Revelation* III, 7-13: "Behold I have set before thee an open door, and no man can shut it: for thou hast a little strength, and hast kept my word, and hast not denied my name." This promise is now being literally fulfilled as these are the last days of the cycle, and this Movement is the "open door" referred to. The cry of The Christ rings in the ears of every student who reads this lesson: "Behold, I (The Christ-force) stand at the door, (the heart center) and knock: if any man hear my voice, and open the door, I will come in unto him, and will sup with him, and he with me."

Just as there is danger in opening the doors of the individual, so it is with all spiritual movements. Every movement really sent out by the Great White Lodge is a vital center or door in the great body of humanity, and as such doors are opened it becomes the duty of every student who enters therein to sacredly guard his door, and see to it that only The Christ-force shall enter, else, just as with individual doors, evil psychic forces will pour in.

The door which this Movement symbolizes is a door for all humanity. It is the door of the *heart center* through which the love-force is poured out to all the centers. If a movement be established through mere psychism, emotionalism, or the desire of some personality to shine as a teacher, then the evil forces of the lower astral-planes are poured out upon its followers instead of The Christ-force, even if some of the teachings given out are seemingly helpful. It will be noticeable, however, in such movements that the spirit of loving fellowship is absent and in its place is a tendency for their leaders to demand personal aggrandizement.

Therefore, all students of the higher life, when confronted with a spiritual movement should seek in the Silence the guidance, not of any mortal, but of their own Higher Self in regard to it. The question is not merely whether they find in the movement certain things which they can accept while rejecting others, but that they must determine what force is being poured out through that door (movement). *For every person belonging to a spiritual movement (as well as its leaders), is absolutely responsible for the force that enters the body of humanity through them, as well as for the force they bring into the movement.*

If any movement is brought to your attention, and it be a true spiritual movement, *it is the open door for you, and comes to you in response to your prayers for more light and help.* If it be not a true spiritual movement then it comes to you as a test of your ability to use your intuition and judgment. *Therefore do not accept the teachings of this or any other spiritual or occult movement until through prayerful consideration and meditation you receive the confirmation of your own Divine Guidance that it is the open door for your next step.*

CHAPTER VIII

A STUDY OF KARMA

Be not deceived; God is not mocked: for whatsoever a man soweth, that shall he also reap."
Galatians VI, 7.

The word Karma is of Eastern origin and has no exact equivalent in the English language. It signifies the working of a great fundamental law. "This law — whether conscious or unconscious — predestines nothing and no one. It exists from and in Eternity truly for it is Eternity itself; and as such, since no act can be coequal with Eternity, it cannot be said to act, for it is Action itself. It is not the *wave* which drowns a man, but the *personal* action of the wretch who goes deliberately and places himself under the *impersonal* action of the laws that govern the *ocean's* motion. Karma creates nothing, nor does it design. It is man who plans and creates causes, and Karmic Law adjusts the effects, which adjustment is not an act, but universal harmony, tending ever to resume its original position, like a bough, which, bent down too forcibly, rebounds with corresponding vigor. If it happens to dislocate the arm that tried to bend it out of its natural position, shall we say that it is the bough which broke our arm, or that our own folly has brought us to grief? . . . It has not involved its decrees in darkness purposely to perplex man; nor shall it punish him who dares to scrutinize its mysteries. On the contrary, he who through study and meditation unveils its intricate paths, and throws light on those dark ways, in the windings of which so many men perish owing to their ignorance of the labyrinth of life—is making for the good of his fellowmen. Karma is an Absolute and Eternal Law in the World of Manifestation; and as there can only be one Absolute, as One eternal ever-present Cause, believers in Karma cannot be regarded as Atheists or Materialists—still less as Fatalists, for Karma is one with the Unknowable, of which it is an aspect, in its effects in the phenomenal world."[1]

While Karma is the implacable Law of Cause and Effect, bringing to you in exact justice the net results of your past thoughts, desires and acts, it does not do so in detail and hence is not the avenging Nemesis it is so frequently represented to be. "For the only decree of Karma—an eternal and immutable decree—is absolute Harmony in the world of Matter as it is in the world of Spirit. It is not, therefore, Karma that rewards or punishes, but it is we who reward or punish ourselves, according as we work with, through and along with Nature, abiding by the laws on which that harmony depends, or—breaking them."[2] It is not your acts that are the cause of your Karma, but the possession or lack of certain Soul-qualities which is the cause both of your thoughts, desires and acts, whose effects are brought to you by the great Law of Harmony for readjustment. The "Lords of Karma,"[3] spoken of so frequently in the Oriental teachings would mean, in European parlance, the conscious forces which bring about the natural sequence of events. These forces, however, are not blind, unintelligent streams of force against which you must hopelessly battle, but are the conscious, intelligent Executors of the Law of Divine Harmony (Love). Their sole object is to spiritualize and perfect both the planet

---

1   *The Secret Doctrine*, Blavatsky, Vol. II, p. 319.
2   *Ibid*, Vol. I, 704-5.
3   Referred to in *Ezekiel* I, 5. as the "Four living creatures. And this was their appearance; they had the likeness of a man."

and its inhabitants. Hence disobedience to the Law *is not punished but is adjusted*, even though the adjustment brings about sorrow and suffering.

The decrees of Karma are not something to be endured as a punishment, but if in ages past you have made mistakes and failed to gain certain Soul-qualities which are necessary for your further progress, these great entitized Powers place before the Soul the conditions—which are made necessary by your past disobedience or inaction—which the Soul itself chooses as the best means of learning the needed lessons and acquiring the needed qualities. The personality may suffer during the experiences it undergoes in the conditions selected by the Soul; but just as a tornado brings destruction yet is beneficial in purifying the atmosphere and sweeping away old accumulated conditions which were detrimental, so with the karmic storms which sweep over the personality; for their purpose is to sweep away old false ways of thinking that new Soul-qualities may put forth and bear fruit. Although the tornado is a result of the inharmony and impurity created by man, still it is used as an agent of Karma to dissipate the accumulated forces of evil and to readjust the atmosphere and permit new conditions more advantageous for the evolution of the planet and its inhabitants to manifest. Thus the tornado was not the cause of the destruction of life and property in its path, it was merely the agent for adjusting the causes set up by man.

So with the storms of sorrow, disaster, and poverty in your life. Everything that comes to you as trouble or sorrow is simply the result of your own shortcomings, your failure to learn the lessons which less painful experiences should have taught you. The fundamental idea of Karma is Harmony. It is not a punishment; not even an inevitable law of suffering which you must endure. But in the course of your evolution your Higher Self chooses to incarnate in certain families and under certain conditions which will bring out the Soul-quality which is lacking. The conditions chosen may be the result of causes set up by you in past lives, owing to a lacking quality, or if all those previous causes have been worked out, they may be chosen by the Soul *de novo* to develop a new Soul-quality, without having had any previous connection with them. The main idea of Karma then is not one of punishment for past failures, but that you may learn your lessons and gain as quickly as possible the Soul-qualities needed, that you may fulfill your destiny, your special place and work in the Grand Plan. When the lessons have been learned and the quality gained the Law is fulfilled and there is neither Karma nor anything else to hold you to the old conditions, except your own free-will. And if you hold to them after you have learned the lesson you are but setting up fresh Karma.

Therefore, instead of sitting down dejectedly and saying that you will bear everything as your Karma, much as a child might stoically bear a whipping, rather be like the child who recognizes the justice of the whipping and sees behind it the loving desire of its parents to inculcate a needed lesson and whose heart is filled with sorrow that it has made the whipping necessary.

It is foolish to invoke your past Karma with the idea of working it out more quickly, for the Law will bring it to you as fast as you are able to conquer and learn the lessons from it. To thus demand that your Karma be precipitated is to be overwhelmed by terrible sufferings in order to learn the lessons which a little later you would be strong enough to learn with little or no suffering. To thus demand your Karma would be to set up your judgment as superior to that of the Lords of Karma, thus showing a lack both of discretion and humility. Hence special trials might have to come to you to teach you the lessons which otherwise you might have learned happily while working out the Law normally as life brought it to you.

While you must learn poise and calm under all conditions, at the same time you must seek earnestly within yourself for the Soul-quality which your trials are most fitted to bring to the surface. And when you have recognized it strive earnestly to cultivate that quality and manifest it in your life. Then the old conditions will quickly begin to fall away from you, although you will pass through a period of severe testing to prove whether or not you have really learned the lesson and built the desired quality into your Soul. Learning the lesson, however, does not mean merely recognizing it or gaining an intellectual conception of what is lacking, but gaining *the power to manifest* that quality, for the change must be within, not merely on the surface. Recognition of what is lacking is a necessary step in attaining it, but when recognized then comes the testing to see if you have really gained the quality or merely recognized the lack. For instance, if you know that your great lack is impatience or lack of control of your temper, as long as only its outward manifestation is controlled you will still suffer from the effects of anger, for your friends will say, "He managed to control his temper, but I could see he was boiling inside."

If your lacking quality is generosity and you recognize the necessity of being generous but give merely because you believe it your duty or because you expect gratitude in return, those who receive your gifts will instinctively feel the grudging attitude of Soul back of the gift and will not send out the feeling of gratitude you are seeking. You will thus suffer from ingratitude until you can give with true generosity of Soul. It is not your Karma to suffer from specific acts of anger or ingratitude, but it is your Karma to learn control of your temper and generosity of Soul. If you are driving an automobile and notice something wrong with the engine and stop and adjust it, no harm results. But if you are careless and do not correct the trouble and the machine is wrecked and you are injured, it was not your Karma to be injured by an automobile, but it was your Karma to be taught carefulness and common-sense. Hence it is not your specific acts that bring your Karma to you but the lacking of Soul-quality; and any available events, conditions or circumstances are used to teach you the necessary lessons. Your acts are like leaves on a tree, the result of the amount and character of the sap. If the sap is lacking in life-force or is diseased, the leaves will wither and fall; but if the following season the sap is enriched and regains its lacking quality the tree will put forth perfect green leaves. It was not the fault of the leaves that they dropped, but a lacking quality in the trees. As you realize that it is yourself who is responsible for all the disturbing influences which surround you and that it rests with you to overcome them by eliminating their causes, you have begun in the right way to work with the Law and gain Self-knowledge and Self-poise. Make yourself one with the Law and all its manifestations will work in harmony.

The above is but one phase of the Law. In addition to personal Karma there is the Karma of the family, the community, the nation, the country, the Race and the world, all of which modify and are modified by the personal Karma. For instance, we all suffer from the storms and rigors of climatic conditions yet some have ample shelter while others have none. We all endure the economic conditions of society, its inequalities, its injustices, etc., yet some suffer more acutely than others according to their personal Karma. All members of a family are subject to the same environment, but individual members modify or rise above it.

Thus the individual, the family, the nation, and the planet are, both individually and collectively, learning their lessons. The lesson for the individual is to recognize his responsibility in bringing about such conditions; also the necessity for doing all in his power to bring about better conditions, not only for himself alone but for all. For he cannot gain the Soul-qualities he is here to learn without advancing the evolution of the entire planet to a certain extent.

Many students of life feel that a great injustice has been done them in that the Masters whom they are trying to serve do not remove their physical burdens and push them into positions of ease where they will be able to devote their time and thought to the Master's work. The Masters are just as subject to the Law of Karma as is the lowliest of earth's children—They can work with it but not control it. A farmer does the best he can to cultivate his fields, but he cannot make a grain of wheat grow where a grain of rye has been planted. He can enrich the soil and cultivate it so it can bring forth a perfect crop of rye, but the environment (the field) and the climate will still be the same, and the grain will still be rye, not wheat. This law is a benign and beneficent one, for it is only by reaping what we have sown, and eating of the fruits thereof, that we can ever learn to plant wheat instead of tares.

Karma is looked upon by many as merely the result of their actions in past lives which determine their present condition and environment. It is this and much more. With the separation of humanity into the sexes at the close of the Third Race, or as the church puts it, "The fall of Man,"[1] the Lords of Karma took charge of the evolution of the personalized infant humanity and personal Karma became operative: the so-called "fall" of man being in reality not a fall but a necessary descent into physical embodiment.

Considering humanity as one, as the great body of the Heavenly Man reflected upon the lowest earth plane and broken up into myriad expressions, each Soul or cell of this Great Body starts out with but one primal controlling desire, namely, to gain the necessary experience to fit it to take its proper place and perfectly fulfill its function in the Grand Plan and become one with its Father-in-heaven. With this end in view the Soul marks out a path that influences it in all its future incarnations, the local Karma of each incarnation being but eddies along the main stream. While the Soul, in its higher aspect, always realizes its destiny, it must gain its experience in and work through various personalities and is responsible for the actions of those personalities. It must build them up from life to life and is responsible for their creation, even to the matter of which they are composed. Thus the Soul[2] becomes the Higher Self or personal God and Saviour of the various personalities. The personality may not heed the "still small voice" of the

---

1 *Genesis* I, 27; "In the image of God created he (the Elohim) him; male and female, created he them. "

2 Do not confuse the term "Soul" with the astral body. It is used herein as synonymous with the Higher Self.

Soul and may fail and fall and sin, but each failure must
be corrected and redeemed and the personality brought
back to its real work.

The number of incarnations depends upon how
swiftly the Soul gains its experience and learns its lessons, or in how many by-paths the personality is allowed
to wander, only to retrace its steps to the main path. It
is the retracing of these wandering steps that is ordinarily referred to as Karma—cause and effect—the cause
being the going astray, violating the Law, the effect the
retracing of the steps, the return to harmony. This is
beautifully condensed in the *Bible* story of the Prodigal
Son.[1] Often incarnation after incarnation is spent in a
sort of lethargy, experiencing again and again the same
things without learning the lesson they are intended to
teach. Sorrow and suffering and loss are often the only
weapons that can awaken the personality from its lethargy to ultimately accomplish the main work.

No two Souls have or need precisely the same experience. If we take the circulation of the blood, from the time
it is propelled outward from the heart to perform its work,
to the time it returns again to the center, we will have
a fair illustration of the working of the Law of Karma.
Humanity as a whole is the blood stream composed of
myriads of personalized corpuscles, all propelled by the
one living force and vitalized by the one Breath to accomplish its great work in the Heavenly Man. Man is
possessed of freewill in that his Higher Self has the will
to accomplish its great work, but the will of the personality is only free in a limited sense. It is free to stray
from the path, and the Higher Self cannot compel obedience but can only take advantage of every experience to

---

1   *St. Luke* XV, 11-32.

mould the personality and ultimately bring it into the main channel.

The Soul, being complex in its nature, must seek for experience upon the plane of differentiation (physical plane) through masculine and feminine personalities. Just as the blood corpuscles start out from the heart to accomplish their work in the tissues, and after having been purified by the breath return to the heart, so these separated expressions of the Soul start out from the center upon their great journey (called in the Eastern teachings, "the cycle of necessity"), and having been purified by the Spirit, return to their Father-in-heaven. The blood may have a long tedious journey and be met by apparently insurmountable obstacles ere it can accomplish its work and enter the stream that is returning to the heart, just so the Soul may have to overcome great obstacles before it can return to the heart center. This point of return is the awakening of the personality to its Higher Self. It may be called "conversion" or what you will, but it is a recognition of its immortal destiny and a determination to walk consciously in the chosen path, its will one with that of its Higher Self. This, however, does not mean that the old Karma has been wiped out, for as the Master Jesus plainly stated, "For verily I say unto you, Till heaven and earth pass, one jot or one tittle shall in no wise pass from the law, till all be fulfilled." [1]

Many ask how the doctrine of Karma can be reconciled with the doctrine of forgiveness of sins, but a simple illustration will explain. If a beloved child through disobedience should pull down upon itself some heavy object and break a limb, its parents would forgive the disobedience, soothe its suffering and lav-

---

1   *St. Matthew* V, 18.

ish love upon it, but the forgiveness could not prevent the
child from reaping the results of its acts, *i.e.*, could not
restore the broken limb, for that could be brought about
only by slow and painful readjustment — the knitting of
the bones — perhaps with some deformity remaining, no
matter how great the forgiveness and love.

All the obstacles encountered are not necessarily the
result of the Soul's minor Karma, but may be a necessary training to fit it for its chosen work. For instance,
if you wished to train a horse to be a hunter, you would
take it into the fields, put obstacles in its path and teach
it to jump, but if you desired it to be a staid family horse
you would teach it not to jump, but to jog quietly along
the smooth, beaten roadway.

You can see this Law exemplified everywhere in
Nature. The seed contains the future tree, and if it ger-
minates beneath a rock, or if its growth is impeded by
any untoward condition, it will struggle to overcome
that condition, and no matter how distorted the growth
of its form, it will finally develop into the exact species
of a tree pictured within the seed, even though its outward form is imperfect.

Therefore, going back to our first simile, if the stream
of your Karma carries you to the feet or the hands, to
the brain or heart of the Heavenly Man, *do the duty
that lies nearest you cheerfully* and to the best of your
ability, and diligently learn the lessons that its perfect
accomplishment will teach. It is the duty of the feet to
support and carry; the hands to execute; the brain to plan
and direct; the heart to furnish the life-force to all parts;
but unless each performs its duty *in its* own *place*, and
performs it well, the whole man must suffer.

Let go then, the things that are holding you back. Throw yourself into the stream. Push out into the current where you will not get stranded in the eddies. Cease to cling so desperately to the rocks and snags against which you are tossed, for they are a sign of shallow water. Have faith to believe that your brothers and sisters are also in the stream *in their proper place*, and are learning the lessons they have incarnated to learn. Have faith that your Father-in-heaven knows their needs as well as your own, and is watching over *them* as well as *you*, and has promised that "no good thing will He withhold from them that love Him."

CHAPTER IX

THE SELF

"1 AM, the resurrection, and the life: he that believeth in me, though he were dead, yet shall he live: And whosoever liveth and believeth in me shall never die." *St. John*, XI, 25-26.

"Saith the Great Law: 'In order to become the *knower* of ALL SELF, thou hast first of SELF to be the knower.' To reach the knowledge of that SELF, thou hast to give up Self to Non-Self, Being to Non-Being, and then thou canst repose between the wings of the GREAT BIRD. . . . Bestride the Bird of Life, if thou would'st know."
The Voice of the Silence, Blavatsky, Fragment 1.

The I AM which is the resurrection and the life is the True Self.

We are "dead" when our consciousness is identified with the lower personal self and bounded by the mortal body and its functions.

The personal self, however, can be made a good and faithful servant, hence it is not to be despised, killed out and swallowed up in the way so frequently interpreted, for without it the Real Self could not gain the experiences of physical existence. It is a garment worn to protect the Real Self from the coarse and harsh vibrations of physical life, just as a diver dons a diving suit to protect him from the pressure of the water when he wishes to explore the ocean's depths. But if it loses touch with the Higher Self it is doomed, just as is the diver when he loses touch with the upper world and his supply of air is cut off.

If you are wedded to the idea of the lower personal self and consider it all-important or all there is, you must reach a stage of growth in which your ideals, your enthusiasm and zest in life, which at one time gushed forth like a mountain freshet, must die or lose themselves in the sands of earth conditions or be dried up by the hot scorching sun of criticism and worldly disapproval. But if you bestride the Bird of Life or hold for your central idea the thought of the I AM—not the mere personality but the Higher, Divine Self or The Christos—even those former ideals though dead, shall rise again, be spiritualized and never die. Just as the diver, if he holds fast to his source of supply, will be enabled to do his work and when it is accomplished, will rise into the upper air and take off his clumsy accoutrements. Should he think, however, that the diving suit was himself, or should he lose his memory of the higher world, he could never rise from the depths and return to his real home.

If in the face of all obstacles you go on trusting and centering your ideals on the True Self which is immortal, your faith can never die, for you will know that the Real Self can never be affected by the changing conditions of earth life. This is bestriding the Bird of Life. As long as you hold firmly to this idea you hold the reins which shall guide the Bird of Life throughout eternity.

The I is the only symbol in the alphabet that stands both for Deity—the straight vertical line symbolizing Spirit descending into matter—and for personality. As you advance along the Path and reach up through and above the personality and follow the straight line upward into Divinity, the personality blends into and becomes the Individuality,[1] the son becomes one with the Father. The small letter i symbolizes the personality before its spiritual awakening, the self (perpendicular line) overshadowed by the Higher Self (the

---

1 *Individuality*, that which is indivisible. *Personality*, literally to sound through: a vehicle; a mask.

dot) who as yet cannot manifest on earth except as the germ of that which the lower self can reach up and merge into. The perpendicular line must reach up and merge into the dot before it can become the I.

Even the materially minded recognize that the only path to worldly success is implicit faith and belief in yourself. This is but the lowest octave of the true success which results when you raise your belief from the personal self to the Real Self. The relative value of the Real Self and the personal self may be represented by a capital I painted in gold upon a dark shadowy background designed to make the golden letter more conspicuous. The personality must always be the shadow on earth of the Real I, its office being to emphasize and give perfect expression to the Real Self and make its golden light stand out the more brilliantly because of the shadow.

Manifested life is compared to the Great Bird (*Paramhansa*), for just as a bird grows to maturity and lays an egg out of which hatches another bird, so the cycles of manifestation emerge from the World-Egg, mature and deposit their eggs (*laya centers*) out of which new manifestations (*manvantaras*) of activity emerge. The winged globe and the winged wheel have the same symbology, namely, that Time is fleeting but is forever progressing. This symbol is often called the Winged Eternity, eternity only in its eternal renewal of manifestation. The Bird of Life called Kalahamsa or Black Swan—black because unmanifested—symbolizes the Higher or Divine Self, the "I AM THAT I AM." Hence, to "bestride the Bird of Life" means to be master of all the manifesting expressions through which this great bird or winged wheel is passing, just as a rider must control and master his fiery steed. Our text therefore points out the possibility of such mastery and the only way by which it can be attained, *i.e.*, by an understanding of the Self, merging the personality into the Individuality over the straight line of your awakened spiritual consciousness.

To accomplish this think of yourself as one with the Silent Thinker, the Great Over-Soul, the Self, the Bringer-Forth of all things, and swallow up the little personal self in this greater conception of Selfhood. Always think of the Real Self as an emanation from or an expression of the Divine, of which you, the personal self, are but the shadow. While you should make the personal self a perfect shadow or reflection of the Divine, still even after that is accomplished it must take its proper place as the humble servant of the Self. If you make a sincere effort to do this, how much of misery, of unhappiness, of trouble will fall away from your life! As we have said in another work, "O ye seekers for the Way! . . . To you comes a message from all the spheres through which the Spirit of Life Eternal presses onward pulsating, rising, falling, beating the outward form into nothingness, that the immortal Spirit of all things may be revealed to you, the Soundless Sound."[1] What does this mean, this "beating into nothingness?" What is this "outer form?" It is the personality, your life in the outer world. But must all these things, my business, my pleasures, my friendships be beaten into nothingness? Yes, if they so completely occupy your attention that they prevent the Real Self from manifesting. For once you have set out upon the Path to Mastery, once having chosen to live the Higher Life, you have registered your desire and your willingness to let that Self manifest and all the forces of the universe work together to fulfill your vow. Therefore,

---

1   *The Soundless Sound*, Curtiss, p.9.

be not amazed at anything that happens to the little self, but instead ask Why? Why?

That which holds you back is the personal self. Almost every trouble that confronts you is centered in this little self and what others think of that self. Perhaps you are so humble that you think constantly of how little you are and dwell upon it so that it is impossible for the Silent Thinker to inspire you, perhaps to do a great work. Perhaps you magnify every little deviation from that conduct which you have decided makes for spiritual growth. Perhaps, instead of keeping your mind on your Higher Self, you are watching to see what others think of your beliefs, striving to shape your life to meet their approval or trying to live up to what others consider a spiritual life instead of listening to the Silent Speaker and following your own divine guidance. Perhaps you are following some great ambition, trying to accomplish some great thing for humanity. Perhaps some slight to the little self occupies your whole attention, perhaps some grief. There may be many seemingly laudable excuses given for allowing the little self to occupy the center of the stage in your life, but whatever they are, if you are honest with yourself, true and serious in your desire to be united to the mind of the Silent Thinker, you must admit that it is self that is occupying your attention and bringing about your troubles. This is comparable to the ignorance of the illiterate person who uses a small letter i where a capital I is indicated, for the little i is always subordinate and should never stand alone. You would not long fret or worry if, instead of focusing your attention upon the little self, its needs, its joys, its sorrows, its slights or perhaps its honors, you permitted it to be swallowed up in an effort to realize your Divine Self, to think of the personal self only as a vehicle or expression or shadowy background on the physical plane, of the Great Self, the Higher Self.

Many dream of a grand work for humanity, but the little self sets boundaries upon it or decides what the work is to be thus allowing many opportunities to go by while waiting for what they have decided is to mark the beginning of their great work. While the great work which each Soul has to accomplish is born from the Higher Self it must be accomplished through the little self or personality. Hence the events which mark its beginning will be just those which the little self can accomplish and by such accomplishments grow into greater things. To sit with folded hands for a miraculous beginning is just as disastrous as to try to use a capital I where the small i is needed. Again it must borne in mind that the work of each self will be brought to that personality by the Great Law, and that it will never be another's work.

Each personality is in very truth a ray from its Higher Self but in passing through earth conditions it has become clouded, obscured, distorted, just as a ray of light becomes distorted by passing through a dense medium. Therefore no person should try to pattern his life after that of another or after another's ideals, but after the ideal life of the Soul as set forth in the allegorical life of the Christ-man, Jesus.

He should take account of his own disposition and idiosyncrasies and seek to find the original intent of each characteristic or the germ of good within every fault. For this reason "know thyself" is the watchword rather than to pattern after another, be that other ever so godlike. For in the Grand Plan, while all are one in the unity of the godhead, still each atom or personality has its own part to play and is endowed with tendencies and characteristics which when corrected and sublimed will fit it to take its own place, a place no other can ever fill. Since your personality is the distorted image of your Higher Self it should be your first duty to straighten it out and discard the awryness due to the illusiveness of the medium through which it is functioning and permit it truly to express the Real Self. The important point to remember therefore is not to copy the actions of others or try to square your life with the ideals of others, but bravely seek deep within your own being for the germs of action implanted in the personality by the Higher Self and make the personality measure up to the ideal given you by your own Higher Self. In other words find yourself, do your own thinking and live true to your own divine guidance.

We are wont to consider selfish those who desire only happiness for the self or who refuse to let others have what they desire. We think ourselves very unselfish if, perchance, we strive to appear meek, seem humble, eager to talk about our littleness and the greatness of others and to prefer others to ourselves. But the truth is—and would we could speak it in tones that would vibrate from pole to pole—that it is just as selfish to permit your humility to occupy the foreground in your thoughts and continually impose it upon the thoughts of others as to continually seek your own pleasure. For even though you are dwelling upon your own unworthiness, nevertheless it is the little self that is occupying your attention. The little self is your servant and must be set to work in the vineyard of your life and not stand all day idle waiting for The Christ to come and give it work in the great vineyard of humanity.

On the other hand, many teachers gain a considerable following by reiterating their own greatness, sanctity and claims to holiness. They talk much of their wonderful experiences, their illumination and their Christ-like character, and followers like sheep flock to them. But if each Soul will do his or her own thinking such claims to sanctity will at once arouse suspicion, for all scriptures and occult authorities proclaim in no uncertain way that "whosoever shall exalt himself shall be abased." The true teacher must have evolved beyond the little personal self and to some extent merged his consciousness into the Divine, hence neither seeks nor permits adulation or worship for himself, but lets the Divine in him speak through his teachings.

Let your deep, abiding aims, your aspirations, be ever upward. In fact, bestride the Bird of Life and soar into heavenly realms. Forget to look down to earth. If you stumble, do not waste a moment's thought over it, but remember the lesson from it and say: "I must be up and doing. That is past and gone and it shall not hold me back." Truly nothing can hold you back unless you hold to it. If the Bird of Life is chained to a perch it cannot fly. "It warbles not, nor can it stir a feather; but the songster mute and torpid sits, and of exhaustion dies." If you were running a race and tripped and fell, would you waste time carefully inspecting the spot where you fell and wondering how it happened? No! you would be up and on, intent only on reaching the goal, not even conscious of the bruises you have received. Thus must you run this race which ends in Mastery. Be so intent on climbing the mountain that you have no time to think of your hurt feelings, no time to sit and cry, no time to enumerate either your personal grievances and slights, or your honors and exaltations, no time to grieve over lack of appreciation of your efforts by those around you.

While you are not to go over and over in your mind the things belonging to the little personal self, still you must not waste your opportunities. Do your full duty in life, be kind, loving, just and true, yet always have your gaze fixed on high, and on the realization of your oneness with the Real Self like a thread of fire forever penetrating your being and filling your consciousness. The little self continually seeks to sit upon the throne of the Higher Self, and when you think you have made it the servant in regard to earthly things, it begins to assert itself on the higher planes as spiritual selfishness and spiritual pride.

Determine that you will not remain identified with the servant (the personality) but will identify yourself with the Master (the Higher Self).

This life is but one day in the school of the Soul. Your real life is not at school but at home in your Father's house. If things in school do not go just as you would have them, nevertheless realize that everything that belongs to you or is a part of your Soul is yours upon the Soul-plane. There are many expressions of the Soul and these expressions may manifest in absolutely different ways upon the different planes. That which belongs to you is yours upon the Soul-plane, therefore accept it upon the Soul-plane, but do not insist upon its physical expression also until the Great Law brings it to you, for its physical expression may not be for the personal self during this day at school. And if it does not belong to the personal self, why pin the Self down to the little self which, while learning its lessons in school must have many of its beautiful possessions kept from it until study hours are over? You only prolong the deprivation by refusing to pay attention to your lessons. For you thereby attract earthly atoms which do not belong to the Real Self and which must be taken from you, making the little self bleed and suffer. You are like a ship which, while in the ocean, even if blown temporarily from its course, is still victor over currents, winds, tides and storms. But if this same ship anchors for a time in ever so beautiful a harbor it will become covered with barnacles, things that do not belong to it. And the longer it lies there the greater the encrustation. The only way it can be set free is to have the barnacles scraped off — a painful process. Try to understand and realize that anything you cling to for the mere gratification of the personal self, no matter how desirable it may seem, is but a barnacle holding back your spiritual advance. Your Higher Self has now everything necessary for its perfection and will and must scrape off the barnacles ere it can indraw the little self into its own Divine Consciousness and perfection. Dwell then in the Higher Self which does not need the physical expressions you desire but has the Reality in the oneness of the immortal Soul of All, forever in the Godhead.

One of the greatest temptations of those who are progressing and beginning to develop the higher consciousness is to think that they have reached the point where the divine illumination of conscious oneness with the Higher Self is soon to take place. So instead of merging their consciousness into the Divine they develop a great spiritual ambition for the little self to have an experience which shall lift them above their fellows and give them prestige. This is one of the most subtle temptations of the little self which must be carefully guarded against.

You can carry the burdens of the little self only along the first steps on the Path. Long ere you enter the Fourth Gate[1] you must have left them behind.

---

1 See Chapter XXII.

Like Christian in *Pilgrim's Progress*, you must find them falling from your shoulders into the abyss and be able to let them go without a murmur. The abyss is the only place for that of the lower self which cannot be swallowed up, digested, transmuted and permitted to manifest under and within the great Divine Self. Tear from your eyes the bandages of darkness and ignorance! why will you suffer so long? why put between you and all the loving Great Souls who are anxious to help you such a barrier, such a tremendous barrier as this lower self and its petty concerns? The Spirit within you is immortal, Divine. The Soul of you is part of the Soul of the Heavenly Man, and you owe it to your own Soul to work with all your powers for humanity. This you cannot do while your horizon is filled with the little self, while you remember that you are a separate entity or anything but an expression of your true Higher Self who is one with Divinity. The Real Self, being one with all, is concerned only that the personal self learn the lessons necessary to bring it into conscious at-one-ment with the Divine, hence refuses to be turned aside from its purpose by the little trials and tests the personal self has to pass through. It sees only the great end, only the Divine Power working through the little selves and leading humanity up to the Divine. The self must become the True Self, the Higher Self.

CHAPTER X

"And, behold, I come quickly; and my reward
is with me, to give every man according as
his work shall be. I am Alpha and Omega, the
beginning and the end, the first and the last."
Revelation XXII, 12-13.

The Order of the 15 was put forth by the Great White
Lodge for a definite work in helping to prepare the way
and make a place for the coming of the great World
Teacher, the Avatar. For ere such a Divine Being can
appear on earth there must be a nucleus formed of
awakened Souls who not only ardently long for His
advent, but who are sufficiently instructed in the Law
and developed through love, to recognize Him when
He comes. The time has now come to give to our pupils
such further information concerning this great event as
the times permit.

"What is an Avatar? for the term being used ought
to be well understood. It is a descent of the manifested
Deity, . . . into an illusive form of individuality, an appearance which to men on this illusive plane is objective,
but it is not so in sober fact. That illusive form having
neither past nor future, because it had neither previous
incarnation nor will have subsequent rebirths, has naught
to do with Karma, which has therefore no hold on it."[1] In
other words a true Avatar is a focusing of the universal
cosmic Christ-principle into and through the individuality of a Great Soul who has reached divinity—hence has
no Karma. Such a Great Soul must be an Initiate into the
Mysteries, one who has overcome and reached nirvanic

---

1 *The Secret Doctrine*, Blavatsky, Vol III, 364.

bliss, but who voluntarily incarnates in the flesh for the purpose of becoming a vehicle for an individualization of The Christos, that it may accomplish a special definite mission in humanity. Such an one sacrifices His life in the spiritual realms and offers Himself as a vehicle because of His great love for suffering humanity and in answer to its great need for a more direct manifestation of Divine Love and Wisdom.

The whole doctrine of Avatara is so hedged about with mysteries whose elucidation belongs to the higher initiations, that only a more or less imperfect outline can be given here. Generally speaking, however, an Avatar is not a mortal, but a Divine Being, who descends from the spiritual realms and suddenly appears on earth in a body composed of atoms which vibrate to the rhythm of the spiritual plane and hence are immortal. The Ophites and Nazarenes taught that, "Therefore, Christos, the perfect,[1] uniting himself with Sophia (divine wisdom) descended through the seven planetary regions, assuming in each an analogous form . . . (and) entered into the man Jesus at the moment of his baptism in the Jordan.[2] From this time forth Jesus began to work miracles; before that time he had been entirely ignorant of his own mission."[3] This is the true interpretation of the symbol in which Jesus is said to be born of a virgin, *i.e.*, he descended from the great Celestial Virgin, Sophia, as a direct Avatar. From the life of Jesus

1   The Western personification of that power, which the Hindus call the Vija, the 'one seed or Maha-Vishnu-a power not the God-or that mysterious Principle that contains in Itself the Seed of Avatarism,"

2   The Baptism in the Jordan is the Rite of Initiation, the final purification, whether in sacred pagoda, tank, river, or temple lake in Egypt or Mexico. The perfect Christos and Sophia . . . enter the Initiate at the moment of the mystic rite, by transference from Guru to Chela, and leave the physical body, at the moment of the death of the latter, to re-enter the Nirmanakaya or the astral Ego of Adept." Ibid, Vol. III, p. 159.

3   *Ibid*, Vol. III, p. 151.

as given in the *Bible* it may be inferred that he was not a direct Avatar, having been born of woman. Nevertheless He was a direct Avatar, for that story is not a history of His physical life, but an allegorical account of the Soul-life of every great Initiate.

As above indicated, The Christos becomes individualized upon all planes, beginning with the highest spiritual plane and gradually descending to earth. In the case of the coming Avatar this individualization has already reached the higher astral plane, the next above the earth plane.

When the mission of an Avatar requires an appearance upon the physical-plane His spiritual body responds to His will, lowers its rate of vibration to the key-note of the physical plane (somewhat similar to the way steam can be condensed into ice), and He appears among men in a body to all intents physical, "an appearance which to men, on this illusive plane, is objective, but is not so in sober fact," in that it is not a mortal body confined to the physical plane and subject to death and decay. Such a divine Being is not born of woman, but simply appears in a body far more glorious, sensitive and powerful than any mortal body could be. Such a body can manifest upon any plane of consciousness in response to the will of its possessor. Since such a Great Soul is one with His Father-in-heaven He has all knowledge and all wisdom, hence would require no earthly instruction or schooling, for His consciousness would be one with The Christ-consciousness, hence all-knowing.

His manifested personality would transcend all racial characteristics and limitations; would be the type of perfected man. Hence He could not be pointed out as belonging to a particular Race, but would embody the perfections of all Races and therefore would not arouse the race-prejudice of even the most advanced.

The appearance of an Avatar is determined by the needs of humanity and the manifestation is as great as the highest ideals of the most advanced of mankind demand. He comes in answer to the cry of many, many hearts for more love and light, for higher ideals and for a clearer understanding of the universal spiritual truths contained in the one Wisdom Religion. As more and more hearts send up their cries the demand creates a vacuum or a negative vortex into which the positive complementary force of The Christ-principle must flow and find an embodied manifestation in humanity. In *The Bhagavad Gita*[1] Krishna—the Christ—says: "I produce myself among creatures, O son of Bharata, whenever there is a decline of virtue and an insurrection of vice and injustice in the world; and thus I incarnate from age to age for the preservation of the just, the destruction of the wicked, and the establishment of righteousness." This law is illustrated by the popular saying, "The darkest hour is just before the dawn." Therefore, when we find that humanity has reached a point of great spiritual, mental and social unrest, during which the established and recognized spiritual teachers have gotten so far away from their true spiritual guidance that the great mass of humanity are like sheep without a shepherd, and are sending out their heart-cries without ceasing, What is Truth? Who shall show us the Way? "How long, O Lord, how long?" this cry must bring forth its answer. In other words, when the enlightened thought of the day recognizes—as it does today—that its spiritual teachers are no longer in personal touch with the higher realms and are no longer divinely

---

1　Chapter IV.

called, guided and appointed to their offices, a new
regime is demanded. When the ceremonies employed
and the sacraments administered by priests and ministers no longer carry divine potency, it is time for a
true priesthood to be established. When the covenant
of marriage is no longer a sacred sacrament, but has
degenerated into the mere recital of a few words before
one who has no spiritual power to discern whether or
not the man and woman belong to each other spiritually—as all divinely ordained priests have—and when
through such ignorance the resulting mistaken marriages degrade the Divine Creative Power into mere
sex gratification, impurity and lust, then there must
come a fresh outpouring of Divine Love, Purity and
Wisdom. For there is never a sincere prayer uttered by
the children of men that does not, by the very law of
the universe, create its answer. Neither social, political nor economic injustice and inharmony can ever be
truly adjusted and regulated and graft abolished until the
divinely appointed priesthood, who are under personal
conscious direction of the Progenitors and Guides of
the Race, is re-established. The question of the marriage sacrament alone demands a divinely appointed
and trained body of spiritual teachers—a true priesthood—who have the power to know who should partake
of that sacrament together and who should not. If there
were no other need in humanity for an Avatar this alone
would be sufficient to call one into manifestation, that
a new order of true priests of the Lord or the Divine
Law might be established. But there are many other
crying needs expressed in present-day social, economic
and political conditions, as well as the awakening of
many, many hearts to the need of more direct spiritual
teachings. Hence all the signs of the times point to the

necessity for a fresh outpouring of Divine Love and Wisdom in this present age.

As the Avatar descends through the higher worlds and draws near the earth-plane, all hearts who are open to His influence or respond to the key-note of His message come into more or less conscious touch with Him interiorly through the illuminating power of His Divine consciousness and feel an unquenchable desire and an irresistible urge to purify, uplift and make more harmonious that phase of work for humanity in which they are interested. And today all classes, types and conditions of mind are feeling the influence of a great spiritual awakening which is giving them a greater vision, a greater realization of the needs of humanity and the possibility of their filling a wider range of usefulness and accomplishing greater results. And this no matter whether they are more or less blindly following the urge to do good along philanthropic, humanitarian, sociological or political lines of endeavor, or whether they are occultists who understand the Law and are working more or less consciously under the inspiration and direction of those Great Souls, the Masters of Wisdom, whose Love, Wisdom and Power is back of and working through every effort for the betterment of the Race in direct proportion to the ability of the various channels to assimilate and make use of Their help.

An Avatar then is the focusing and embodiment of the same Christ-principle that has manifested in all ages in all Avatars, each of whom thus became The Christ for the age in which He appeared. Each direct descent of Deity into physical embodiment, however, is preceded by many lesser and incomplete manifestations called Avesha Avatars. In these cases an advanced Soul who has not yet reached full Mastery, but who is sufficiently pure, loving and compassionate, is chosen and overshadowed by The Christ-principle for a certain time and for a certain purpose. In every organization, society, order or movement working along truly spiritual, occult or mystic lines, there will be certain advanced members who will be able to reach up into the spiritual realm and come into conscious communion with the Avatar. From these advanced Souls one who is especially pure, gifted, well trained and worthy, will be chosen as the mouthpiece through whom the message of the Avatar will be given out to his particular society or movement. It is necessary, however, that this vehicle be capable of receiving and transmitting as much of the Divine Wisdom, in its purity, as the stage of evolution and degree of spiritualization of his bodies is capable of expressing. Hence such a vehicle must be carefully trained, disciplined and prepared that his faculties and powers may reach their greatest perfection. In each case the chosen one is a Christ only during the period of the overshadowing, at all other times being but the human and mortal personage. Not that there is any limit to possible revelation, for the overshadowing is always The Christos which is not a being, but that Essence of Divinity which is Everlasting Law, Everlasting Wisdom, the Essence of Truth from the beginning, from everlasting to everlasting. Jesus speaks of this overshadowing Power as "the Comforter" and tells His disciples that it is expedient for Him to go away that the Comforter might come. This simply means that, being the Avatar, He condensed or focused The Christos in Himself which at His departure would be perceived by mankind apart from its manifestations through His personality and shine in every heart prepared to correlate with it. "But the Comforter, which is the Holy Ghost, whom the Father will send in my name, he shall teach you all things, and bring all things to your remembrance, whatsoever I have said unto you."

In other words each truly spiritual, pure and sincere society and movement will have some illumined Soul who will be an Avesha Avatar to that society or movement to prepare his followers for the coming of the Avatar, as John the Baptist prepared the Hebrews for the coming of Jesus. No doubt in many instances such an Avesha Avatar will be considered by his followers to be the Avatar in person. But this is easily determined if you remember that an Avatar is not a mortal. When such a claim is made for any human being, however great or wise, you may know that he could not be more than an Avesha Avatar and be mortal. Nevertheless the essence of his message would be that of the Avatar, for water is still water whether measured by a thimbleful or by an ocean. Furthermore, if he be a pure and enlightened Avesha, he will not only refuse the title of Avatar, but will exclaim with John the Baptist: "One mightier than I cometh, the latchet of whose shoes I am not worthy to unloose." He will also discountenance all adulation and personal worship. The characteristics of his teachings will include not only the much abused "universal brotherhood" but also the true tolerance that arises from a recognition of the divine guidance of other teachers and Aveshas. For one evidence of a true Avesha must be a recognition of the divine mission of others.

Necessarily the messages of the various Avesha Avataras will differ in details, methods of presentation, etc., for the ability of such a channel to give out the teaching depends upon such factors as the line of endeavor he is interested in, his race-thought, his mental and spiritual capacity, his habits of life, his knowledge of the laws and philosophy of the higher life and the intellectual training his mind—through which all the teachings must pass—has received. In this way the members of every Society and movement shall hear the divine truths spoken in their own language wherein they were born, *i.e.*, couched in the terminology, symbols and characteristic methods of expression peculiar to their own avenue of truth. Thus all classes of humanity will be given the opportunity to do their part in preparing for the coming of the Great One by forming an universal Center in which He can manifest. This does not necessarily mean a Center in the sense of a segregated community, but an universal Center in the thought-world from which the currents of force will radiate that shall affect the minds and hearts of the whole world. Each Avesha Avatara will no doubt found a community for his own followers and out of each community there must ultimately be chosen those advanced disciples who have been able to recognize The Christ "in the air" or on the higher planes and hence are able to recognize Him when He manifests in the flesh. These will be gathered together to be His immediate disciples and body-guard. The Avatar will not come to any one society, movement, order or sect, but will come to humanity. His truths will be so divine and perfect, yet so simple, unbiased and unprejudiced by the characteristics of any cult, that they will be equally applicable to all, no matter what their Race, creed or special trend of thought may be.

We have in the Gospel of *St. John*, in language so simple as to be a complete and incomprehensible blind to all but the initiated, the whole doctrine of the Avatara. We read: "In the beginning was the Word (The Christos) and the Word was with God, and the Word was God," God in that it was and is the totality of Spiritual Wisdom, the creative Word, the manifested Christ. "The same was in the beginning with God. All things were made by him; . . . In him was life; and the life was the light of men." The Christ-principle is the essence of Divine Life without which there can be no life, and being Divine this life is "the light of men" and is distinct from mere animal life which is but the outward and densest covering of Divine Essence. "And the light shineth in the darkness; and the darkness comprehended it not," *i.e.*, it is hidden in a human body. These verses also bear testimony that this Light of the Christos is once more to be manifested in humanity as it has been manifested periodically "from the beginning." This is but another and more compact statement of a deep esoteric truth, and a most sacred mystery, which has filled volume after volume in more ancient scriptures.

In all religions now on earth there is an exoteric or public and an inner or secret teaching. Something analogous is true of the manifested Christos; it has its exoteric manifestations and its inner Essence. Heretofore, in every manifestation of an Avatar, it has been the outer covering, as it were, of this Power that has manifested through the vehicle; and even this has been more than humanity could grasp or understand. In the coming Avatar will be manifested more of the inner Essence of The Christ than has ever before been possible, because thousands in the world today are shaking off the garments of their dense materialized conceptions of life and are responding to the higher siritual ideals.

Every Great Teacher, such as Zoroaster, Gautama, Jesus, etc., has founded a new religion or at most, a new expression of the One Religion. They have all taught the Wisdom Religion, but in ways which appealed to the different peoples to which they came. While each of those Great Teachers has taken the world a step onward and emphasized some one phase of Divine Truth, still they have founded but larger sects, rather than brought the world into one Universal Brotherhood. The Christian religion is universally acknowledged to be the greatest factor in modern civilization, and the time has now come for it to take an advanced step through the awakening of a sense of the deep, underlying, vital truths common to all religions in the hearts of all earnest seekers among Christian people; thus taking the first step on the return journey to the one Wisdom Religion.

There are many prophecies in the *Bible*, and elsewhere, relating to the Avatar who closes this cycle, which have never been fulfilled *in any sense*. The Book of *Revelation* is distinctly a history of the preparation for the coming of such an Avatar. In it is allegorically set forth all that must occur in the world during an avataric cycle. A careful study of this book will prove that it contains teachings identical with the above, as well as with those of all ancient revelations pertaining to the Mysteries. This will easily be understood if the student will remember that the *Bible* covers the whole period of an avataric cycle, *i.e.*, from the first coming to the reappearance of the Avatar at the close of the cycle. Jesus, speaking of The Christ-principle within Him, said "I am Alpha and Omega, the beginning and the ending, . . . which is, and which was, and which is to come, the Almighty,"[1] a

---

1   *Revelations*, I, 8.

most blasphemous assertion if referring to His human personality. This emphasizes the fact that it was not the *man* Jesus, but The Christos that manifested, and that it was the same Power in all ages and in all manifestations, and that the same Divine Power which manifested through the personality called Jesus will be the Power to manifest through the Avatar who closes this Messianic cycle and plants the seed for the new. But instead of this return being merely the founding of new religion or sect,—humanity, having passed the lowest point of the downward arc of the cycle and begun laboriously to climb the upward arc—the coming Avatar must fulfill the prophecies already given, bring to earth as much of the Divine Wisdom as humanity can attain to by the end of the sixth and seventh sub-races, and plant the seed for the future Sixth Great Race, whose manifestation will usher in the Golden Age.

The time of His coming cannot be given out; but it will be in exact accord with the astronomical and numerical cycles hinted at elsewhere. Moreover, all who will be drawn into the coming Brotherhood will find that they are in some mysterious way connected with the secret cycles of the Messiah. The Avatar cannot come until the cycle is fulfilled; until the stars are in their proper positions. As we said in a former lesson:

"It is a fact that the creative force flows in cyclic waves, and in a cycle corresponding closely to a century of earth life. The ebb and flow of this great force is first downward. The first quarter of the century it passes from the spiritual world into the mental and psychic; the second quarter down into the physical, and then, in the last half of the century, back again into the spiritual-plane, following the reverse order. But the deductions that have been drawn from these facts by some, are arbitrary and misleading.

"As the force descends from the spiritual plane into the psychic in the first quarter of the century (1 to 25), it causes great creative activity in the psychic and mental worlds, and the Masters take advantage of this fact to work with the tide. Consequently all those who have developed their faculties so they can reach the higher psychic plane can meet the Masters upon that plane (not upon the astral) and can benefit correspondingly by the great activity of that period.

"Later, during the second quarter of the century (25 to 50), the force descends into the physical world and touches the lowest point of its arc; but it is still spiritual creative force. The natural deduction from this is, therefore, that the first quarter of the century (1 to 25) is, most emphatically, the planting and growing time, corresponding to the springtime of the year. It would be during this quarter of the century that an Avatar would first manifest Himself to His more advanced disciples and plant in their hearts the seed of His teachings.

"The second quarter of the century (25 to 50) corresponds to summer; the time when this spiritual creative force, having penetrated to the earth-plane, must bring forth its fruit upon that plane. Whatever has been planted must bring forth its fruit, provided it has been a fruitful season; that is, providing the work has been faithfully done and the spring growth carefully nurtured. Should this part of the cycle of the century coincide with certain greater cycles, it would be possible at this period for the Avatar to manifest openly among men, He being the fruit of the culminating cycles. The Master Jesus was spoken of as 'The first fruits of them that slept,' the word 'slept' indicating not in manifestation. Should the Avatar come, the result of His teachings, and His contact with the earth would mature during this period. At the end of this quarter of the century the force, having reached its lowest point, would turn upward, and His teachings would raise humanity with it.

"The third quarter (50 to 75) corresponds to the autumn when the fruit is harvested; when 'we which are alive and remain shall be caught up together with them in the clouds, to meet the Lord in the air; and so shall we be ever with the Lord.'"

"The last quarter (75 to 100) corresponds to the winter time, when the ground is frozen. At that time, after the harvest has been gathered and the spiritual forces indrawn and the world has again fallen away from the true teachings, it becomes necessary for The Lodge of Masters again to send out an agent, or agents, on the physical-plane, to break the ground and prepare for the new springtime. At such a time much of the activity of The Lodge is directed to the physical plane through physical embodiments.

. . . . "Consequently these early years of the century are pregnant with power. As the years go on this Great Creative Force of Love must be brought down to earth by those who can receive it; for only as we are able to reach up into the higher psychic realm, and there meet and correlate with the Great Teachers, is it possible to prepare for the coming to earth of the Fruit, or the embodied power of The Christ-force, in the person of the Avatar whose coming the culminating of many cycles now makes possible. 'And then shall appear the sign of the Son of Man in heaven.[1] Already the Watchers have seen The Christ-star—the star that has announced to all

---

1   *St. Matthew* XXIV, 20.

wise men, in all ages, the appearance of an Avatar. Consequently we believe that the Avatar will soon come, not in a physical body born of woman, but in a more ethereal or spiritual body, capable, nevertheless, of appearing objectively as a physical body as occasion demands.

"Instead of this being a time to sit down and con old lessons, it is time to be up and doing; but on lines altogether different from those suitable to the period of the breaking of the ground and the sowing of the seed. This is why *The Order of the 15* is now put forth; to enable all who are ready, to grow to the point where they can, through special instruction, come into personal touch with the Masters and the Avatar."

"It is asserted by many advanced thinkers that the present wave of psychic unrest is a sign of the near advent of the Avatar, and that a widespread development of psychic faculties will usher in His coming. This is, indeed, a sign of the coming; but it is not strictly correct to say that it will be the characteristic; for, although there will be a period of great psychic activity (not, however, due to new senses, but to the use of the present faculties upon the inner planes) it will but serve to prove that mere psychic development is not the end to be desired. 'Behold, the days come, saith the Lord God, that I will send a famine in the land, not a famine of bread, nor a thirst for water, but of hearing the words of the Lord: And they shall wander from sea to sea, and from north even to the east, they shall run to and fro to seek the word of the Lord, and shall not find it. "[1] The spiritual understanding of the people shall be darkened and they shall wander from sea to sea seeking the word of the Lord. Today many are running

---

1 *Concerning Various Misconceptions*. Now out of print.

to and fro after self-advertised teachers, seeking to develop their psychic faculties. And many who have begun to use these faculties on even the lowest stratum of the astral-plane set themselves up as teachers or write books giving the world minute directions covering the whole field of thought and action, from the feeding of their animal bodies to the attainment of Adeptship. With the fragments of knowledge thus obtained such teachers claim that every other psychic who has gleaned a few different fragments is wrong. This psychic awakening, conflict and confusion will come as the first step in a wonderful wave of activity in all walks of life, tending to extreme selfishness and unbrotherliness; for each will claim the Truth and start sect after sect, and, like a pack of wolves tearing a carcass in pieces, each one will be ready to fight to the death to maintain and guard his bone against the whole pack. Then shall begin 'wars and rumours of wars' and the struggle for supremacy. 'Now the brother shall betray the brother to death, and the father the son; and children shall rise up against their parents, and shall cause them to be put to death.'[1] This will be but the beginning of the end; and the prospect would be hopeless, indeed, did we not know that out of those who 'run to and fro,' one by one there will come the few who will open their *spiritual* faculties, sweep away the mists of prejudice, and see the Light of The Christos shining in their brother's heart. These few will band together to help spread the Light rather than to increase the confusion; and they will be the remnant who will survive the physical catastrophes and usher in the golden period of the present *Kali Yuga* age. These will not seek the Kingdom through psychic development, but, through the

---

1   *St. Mark* XIII, 12.

awakening of their love and compassion, they will find The Christ-light illumining their hearts and opening all the psychic doors normally and without effort. These will be the 144,000 who will 'meet the Lord in the air,' *i.e.*, in the higher spiritual plane to which they can penetrate because of the love and compassion developed. Only when the Christ-love has manifested and has thus awakened the hearts of a considerable number of disciples can a center be formed in which this power can be focused and individualized in the person of the coming Avatar."[1]

When the birth of Jesus was announced, it was only after a particular Angel had announced The Christ that the angelic hosts of heaven joined in the chorus. So today all who are faithfully guarding their flocks upon the mountain top will first hear the announcement and then the response.

The Order of the 15 is put forth in an effort to awaken The Christ-love in the hearts of men, rather than to cater to the intellect or the desire for psychic development. For only those who can correlate with this Christ-power can be gathered together as His disciples. The aim of this Movement is especially to help all Christian people to find the deep, underlying vital truths common to all religions in their own, and thus truly, and in the only way possible, prepare for an Universal Brotherhood on earth in which each Soul shall find the same vital truths spoken in his own language, *i.e.*, couched and taught in terms of the religion in which he was born.[2] This is the only real way of bringing about Brotherhood. For to dream of a Brotherhood in which all classes of hu-

---

1 Since the above was written (1908) many of the prophecies have been fulfilled, as even a superficial study of the signs of the times will show.

2 See Acts II, 6.

manity and all varieties of race-thought are forced to flow in one direction and accept as final Truth couched in one set form—no matter how lofty the form or how beautiful its trend—is but a fantastic chimera born of the human mind, and whose attempted practical establishment has always ended, and always will end, in confusion, antagonism, and unbrotherliness far more intense than before the attempt was made. It is only by touching the deep, underlying springs of Universal Love that Universal Brotherhood can be attained. Therefore, we ask one and all to seek to develop The Christ-love in their hearts, remembering that only when it shows in their lives and makes them more Christ-like, can it be said to have germinated. A seed may lie dormant for ages, but the instant it opens its heart to the life of the sun it begins to grow. So it is with The Christ-seed. The Christ-light is in every man, but we can say the Christ-star has arisen only when it shines forth and illumines our daily life. The Christ-love is a consuming fire, and all fire spreads. If the life remains cold and dark and selfish the Fire is not yet lit. This is the first step toward Universal Brotherhood, for when we find The Christ in our own hearts we seek for it in every other heart.

CHAPTER XI

A STUDY OF REINCARNATION OR REBIRTH

"He asked his disciples, saying, Whom do men say that I, the Son of man am? And they said, Some say that thou art John the Baptist: some, Elias; and others, Jeremias, or one of the prophets." *St. Matthew*, XVI, 13-14.

When the old teaching of reincarnation was revived in the Western world, it was necessary to bring to bear all the powers of logic to prove its reasonability, and its ancient and world-wide acceptance. Today this truth has permeated all classes of society, filling the world's literature and furnishing the *motif* for many successful stage productions—thus proving that the public is eager for the subject. This itself is an evidence of rebirth, for what else can this widely renewed interest in the subject be but a reincarnation of an ancient world-wide belief? For detailed proofs of its reasonability we refer the student to other authorities.[1]

Like many other things that are true and generally accepted, proof that would convince all is out of the question, for what is proof to one is not to another. For instance, a spiritualist might say that, if he had lived before, something might be given him by discarnate entities about a former life that could be verified by historical records. This would be no proof at all, for it would be an easy matter for any discarnate entity capable of communicating, to secure the information from any records accessible to the investigator. As far as absolute proof goes each one

---

1 *Reincarnation*, Walker. *Reincarnation and the Law of Karma*, Atkinson. *Reincarnation*, Anderson.

must take this law as he takes many other laws—upon its reasonability. If it fails in this or in its ability to afford a rational explanation for the many discrepancies of life which are otherwise unexplainable, he is at liberty to reject it. But for those who do accept it we will make an effort to remove some of the misconceptions and clear up some of the vagaries which, like barnacles, have attached themselves to this truth.

"Intimately, or rather indissolubly, connected with Karma, is the law of Re-birth, or of the reincarnation of the same spiritual Individuality in a long, almost interminable, series of Personalities. The latter are like the various characters played by the same actor, with each of which the actor identifies himself and is identified by the public, for the space of a few hours. The *inner*, or Real Man, who personates those characters, knows the whole time that he is Hamlet only for the brief space of a few acts, which, however, on the plane of human illusion, represent the whole life of Hamlet. He knows also that he was, the night before, King Lear, the transformation in his turn of the Othello of a still earlier preceding night. And though the outer, visible character is supposed to be ignorant of the fact, and in actual life that ignorance is, unfortunately, but too real, nevertheless, the *permanent* Individuality is fully aware of it, and it is through the atrophy of the 'spiritual' Eye in the physical body, that that knowledge is unable to impress itself on the consciousness of the Personality."[1]

When the physical body is left in the tomb the Soul is clothed in an astral[2] body and lives for a time upon

---

1   *The Secret Doctrine*, Blavatsky, Vol. II, p. 320.

2   *Astral*: A finer state of matter than the physical, the etheric; the next kingdom above the physical; the state between the intensest physical activity and the slowest mental activity; the region of the play of all feeling and desire of the human Soul, whether incarnate or excarnate; the state in which it becomes conscious on leaving the physical.

the astral-plane, in the exact environment for which its development fits it. A period of time is passed in digesting and assimilating the lessons of the past life, in the reverse order of their acquirement, and in realizing the inevitable trend of all its desires and actions while on earth. The progress made is in the growth and development of the seeds of good and evil sown during earth life. For this reason, unless reincarnation had been brought to one's attention upon earth, he would be very unlikely to know anything about it or come in contact with those who did, for there is nothing in his astral environment to suggest it any more than there was in his physical environment. After having passed through the various subdivisions of the astral world and passed on to higher states of consciousness, there comes a time in his evolution when, after a long period of rest—during which he has exhausted or experienced the spiritual bliss resulting from the realization of all his earthly ideals—he realizes his limitations and chooses once more to clothe himself in flesh. He does this firstly, from a comprehension of the great work of the redemption of humanity and the globe which he has gained upon the higher planes and of the necessity of fitting himself, through further earthly experience, for his necessary part in that work; and secondly, because of a strong desire to help on the evolution of the Race, which evolution can only be accomplished by the purified Soul clothing itself in fleshly atoms that it may train and purify them. The Soul realizes that its lack of experience limits its usefulness, and a deliberate choice is made once more to function through a physical body.

Being one with God the Soul has the power of choosing its path and its environments, subject to the

Law of Karma, the one desire being to quickly fulfill
the "cycle of necessity" and return to the Father's heart.
Therefore it chooses an environment, not as a personality would choose—for wealth, ease or happiness, for it
realizes that spiritual happiness must be born of earthly
experience; must be the giving up of self for the upliftment of all—but an environment which will give it the
best opportunity to gain the experience it lacks—the
best environment that its Karma will permit. It naturally
incarnates among its old associates unless, as sometimes
happens, there is some Karma or needed lesson that
takes it temporarily into a new set of associations (a side
issue). This clothing itself in flesh involves the training of a new instrument (brain and body) which is not
correlated with the memory of the Real Self, and thus
the "why" is forgotten, for otherwise the lessons would
be no lessons at all. This experience of the Soul might
roughly be compared to a person away on a pleasure trip
in a foreign country where he suddenly realizes there is
some task he has failed to perform ere leaving or that
there is some loved one who needs his help, and he returns to take up the duty, even though the task be sordid
and repulsive, and the loved one unappreciative. There is
no person, therefore, who can say that at the present time
he is having his last incarnation; for only when the Soul
reaches the stage where it weighs itself in the balance
and realizes that there still lacks something of earth's
experience to fit it to take its destined place in the Grand
Plan; only then can it be known whether or not the earth
urge will draw it back into incarnation. This urge is not
always from karmic necessity, except during the earlier
stages of evolution, for many Souls return through pure
love and compassion to help the world, even after they,

as separated individuals, have gained all the necessary experience and wisdom. Therefore it is foolish for pupils or disciples to talk about this being their last incarnation; for were they advanced in wisdom they would know that their attitude proclaimed aloud that they were lacking in even ordinary discretion and common-sense.

We must also bear in mind that there are many more Souls excarnate than incarnate. Many of them are waiting for the wave of civilization to rise to the special point that will permit them to fulfill their destiny in accord with karmic law. If the student will refer to what was said about the color Rays in the chapter on *Evolution*, it will be found to apply here. Since all Souls belong to one of the seven Great Rays they must wait for incarnation until the Ray and subray to which they belong is in manifestation. Thus, if a Soul started its special work during the manifestation of a certain sub-ray of the Red Ray, while under special conditions hinted at elsewhere, it might incarnate and work out side-issues in other sub-rays, yet the main work could not be continued until the same sub-ray was again manifesting.

There is no regular set time during which Souls remain excarnate. It depends upon many conditions, and ranges all the way from almost immediate rebirth to five hundred years, and in some cases far more. There is almost as great a diversity in times and seasons for rebirth as is found in the affairs of men.

When it is taught that a Soul incarnates sometimes in one sex and sometimes in another, or in each sex for seven incarnations alternately, only a very small fragment of a great truth was hinted at. This partial truth as time passed has developed some ridiculous and irrelevant conceptions. Again it is asserted by

many that sex does not inhere in the Soul, but the fact
is that sex inheres in every manifestation of consciousness, although on the higher planes sex manifests in
quite a different way from that which we know as sex
in the physical body. While the great mystery of sex,
in its fullness, is as sacredly guarded today as it has
ever been, still, as this is the beginning of a new cycle
or the reincarnation of a period of the manifestation of
this great mystery, it becomes the duty of those Masters
and Teachers connected with this special line of work to
again give to the world a suggestion of the inner truths
connected with sex. But alas, the time is not yet ripe to
entirely tear aside the veil and reveal the mysteries of
this subject although an effort is being made from the
higher side of life to open the understanding of the few
who can realize the divine possibilities of sex, that they
may penetrate behind the veil.

It is not the rule for a Soul to change its sex when
incarnating, but is rather the exception. Since the separation of the sexes during the Third Race the positive
and negative rays always retain their characteristics
and tend to incarnate in a body corresponding to their
polarity. The exception occurs principally for two reasons. The first one, which alas, at this period, is only
too common, is that if a Soul gaining experience either
through a male or a female body fails to appreciate the
lessons of the opposite sex; if it despises the other and
either cruelly treats it, or holds itself superior to it, such
a Soul at its next incarnation may find itself in a physical body of the despised sex; for this would be the only
way that such a Soul could learn the lessons of that sex
and reap the Karma it had created. However, the sex
of the incarnating Soul would not be changed. It would

always be a male Soul in a female body or vice versa. The world has no trouble in recognizing this, for such misfitted Souls are frequent in every community, and there is no difficulty in noting the discrepancy between the sex of the incarnating entity and its body.

Every male contains the potentiality of the female, and every female that of the male, and while we would not speak of this duality as sex upon the spiritual plane, as we use the term sex on the physical plane. Still, if the student will remember what was said in the chapter on Karma in regard to each Soul being a part of the Great or Heavenly Man and having a special work to do and a special place in which to fulfill its destiny, comparing it to the body as we have done, it will be seen that some organs (Souls) must fulfill the function of the positive expression (masculinity) while others express the negative (femininity). Any other condition would be unthinkable, for while we know that all expressions of life, from molecule to God, are perfect epitomes of the Cosmos and contain the two opposite poles (positive and negative) within each, yet in the aggregation of either atoms, organs or Souls, each must function with either the positive or negative expression predominating. It is just as though you took a horseshoe magnet and cut it up into pieces. Each piece would be a perfect magnet with positive and negative poles, and if you could separate it into atoms each atom would have its positive and negative poles. But when you put the atoms together to form a Grand Magnet, each would take its place on either the positive or negative side and express either attraction or repulsion. To carry this simile further, by reversing the current through the magnet it would be easy to make that which was the positive pole become the negative, and vice versa. This is what takes place when a masculine entity clothes itself with a feminine body.

As to man evolving into an androgynous being in which both sexes manifest coequally, as long as mankind is manifesting in separated sexes it is a waste of time and energy to try to imagine such an existence; for until you have learned all the lessons possible in separated bodies you can have no realization of what such a manifestation would be like. And you will never learn those lessons as long as you despise any function and refuse to master it. The two sexes can never blend into one until each has reached a perfect expression of his or her sex and they have learned to work together in perfect harmony while separated. The lesson is not for one sex to avoid or ignore the other, but to learn how the twain may become one in all things, in heart, mind and body, thus fulfilling the great Law of Sex.

The second and rare cause for a change of sex is that a Soul may have reached a degree of Mastery, yet, owing to the World-Karma, and to the restrictions of conventionality, such a Soul may never have fully grasped or understood the opposite sex. For instance, a Soul expressing the masculine principle might be deeply desirous of entering into the experience of the inmost depths of the opposite Soul-expression so as to see its temptations, feel its oppression and learn its limitations, and thus be ready to take up a special work in the coming age, whose keynote is the equalization of the sexes and the liberation and the restoration of woman to her proper place. Therefore, a Great Teacher in preparing to take the place of Leader in such an age might naturally desire to be clothed for one life period with a female outer covering. But even in this case it would be evident to all thinkers that the sex of the entity differed from that of the body. Such a Great Teacher, moreover, might use that period (which would be her last earth experience), in entering into all phases of life. She might use the power possessed by all such Teachers to merge the apparent personality into various other personalities. Thus, for a time, she might have to become one with and apparently manifest the qualities of a depraved sister, a swearing, roistering, swashbuckler, a pirate, a learned scholar or any other phase of humanity. She would thus, in a measure, be gaining the experience of humanity in the only way that would make the experience her very own, knowing all the temptations and also the inner germ of love and hope that even the most degraded hide somewhere within. Such a Great Teacher might be compared to an author who, in gathering data for a coming work, lives for a time in each class of society. But in the case of the Great Teacher the power would be hers to absolutely become, for a time, the personality she desired to study. Thus when her Great Work began she would know just how to deal with all types of brothers and sisters, and from the higher planes be ready to direct the reaping of the golden grain sprung from the seeds of Divine Truth planted during her last earthly incarnation. Such a complex personality was she who planted the seed of the Wisdom Religion in the Western world. And she is still directing its garnering from the higher planes.

CHAPTER XII

"Alas, alas, that all men should possess Alaya (Divine Essence), be one with the Great Soul, and that, possessing it, Alaya should so little avail them." *The Voice of the Silence*, Blavatsky, Fragment II

For God hath not given us the spirit of fear; but of power, and of love, and of a sound mind." *II Timothy*, I, 7.

Man is made in the image of God. This image, however, is not the corporeal likeness of a personal God, for God has no personality which can be imitated. But if we take God to mean that Supreme Power which is sent forth from the Absolute, and through whose many manifestations all things are brought forth, then we must recognize that this God must have all power. It is in the image of this All-power that man is made. Jesus, who stands as a symbol of perfected man, said: "All power is given unto me in heaven and in earth."[1] If this be true of the highest type of man, it is potentially true of all men, for all power is given unto man because he is created in the image of God, although in most men this power is latent because man in the aggregate has not yet come into his birthright, at-one-ment with his Father-in-heaven or Higher Self. The omnipotent powers of God operate through intelligent centers of power in the manifested universe. And to make it possible for perfected man to have "all power in heaven and in earth" and to fulfill the prophecy that he shall "become as one of us" (the gods), these centers of power must

---

[1] *St. Matthew* XXVIII, 18.

have their more or less active reflections in man, for
man is truly the microcosm of the macrocosm. All the
lower kingdoms have certain powers but only man has
the powers of the Godhead, with which, when he manifests them as his own, he can create the new heaven
and the new earth of the Apocalypse, wherein dwelleth
righteousness. When man awakes to a realization that
all powers in heaven and in earth are latent within himself—in heaven the powers of the Godhead, in earth the
powers of all creatures and all Nature—he will begin
to reclaim his lost heritage, lost only in the sense of his
having deserted it.

In most Eastern teachings we find hints of these wondrous powers and are told that they represent steps up
which every candidate for Mastery must laboriously
climb. The Western world is awakening to the use of
some of these powers, especially the powers to control disease and dominate environment. The powers of
man are six in number, synthesized in a seventh—the
Astral Light of Eliphas Levi—and correspond to the
seven principles of man.[1] Each power has its seat in a
certain sacred center in the body. These seven centers,
each with its seven subsidiary centers, are sometimes
called the "forty-nine crucified saviors," signifying that
the vital power of these centers is at present misused and
crucified, and ere they can become man's Saviors they
must be resurrected from the tomb of matter and made
to function in a higher state. They are called the forty-
nine fires because their light guides man to super-man.

These powers are (1) the Supreme Power (*Para-
shakti*); (2) the power of Intellect (*Jnana-Shakti*);
(3) the power of Will (*Ichchha-shakti*); (4) the power
of Thought (*Kriya-shakti*); (5)the power of the Life-

---

1   See *The Seven Principles of Man*, Besant.

principle (*Kundalini-shakti*) and (6) the power of Speech
(*Mantrika-shakti*). Each power is an emanation from
one of the Elohim, hence must be reflected in man to
make him the image of God, for God, like the white
light, in passing through the prism of matter, manifests
in a seven-fold manner. Each power has its positive
and negative aspects, and until we can correlate with
the positive ray of its Progenitor we are buffeted by its
negative aspect.

It is impossible to consider these powers separately,
for without the cultivation of all none can be truly operative. The Supreme Power is the power which man has
of correlating with Divinity through the breath. All creatures breathe, and we are accustomed to say that "breath
is life," and ordinarily when man ceases to breathe he
ceases to live objectively, but man alone, because he
can bring his other powers to bear upon it, can make
the breath more than the mere drawing in of physical
life. Within the auric zone of the earth there are many
subtle forces unknown to science and barely mentioned
by even the deeper students of mysticism because so
sacred, so potent and so powerful that their very names
must scarce be whispered. Breath, combined with Will
and Thought, is the power by which man reaches up to
the higher worlds and opens an avenue through which
these potent forces may reach his Inner Self and lift him
above mundane things, and at the same time regener-
ate his physical body. There are those who, holding the
thought of health, breathe for physical health and obtain
it, but it is possible to use the breath to obtain far more
than mere physical health. Its misuse or negative aspect
can also bring disasters undreamed of by the pseudo-oc-
cultist. Realize that you are responsible for every breath
that you breathe, for through the breath you are spreading

either God-love or disease. It is commonly thought that the outgoing breath contains a virulent poison, and so it does if you permit it, for it carries off certain effluvia from the decaying atoms within you. Are you willing to be a source of infection? If this is your will and your thought then it is what you become. When the breath is foul you are abusing your body, it is sick and out of order. It is within your power to be healthy, to be a source of inspiration and life to all. For health and life and love are as infectious as their opposites. Therefore, every time you become conscious of it, use your power of the breath to breathe in Divine Love, to breath in Spiritual Life that it shall so cleanse and transmute your physical atoms that your breath shall become as that of a little child.

Mind or intellect should not be confused with the power of thought. The human mind is the reflection in man of the great Universal Mind, the Divine Ideation or what some call Cosmic Consciousness. It is the vehicle through which thought operates. In man mind manifests in a threefold manner, the subconscious or animal mind, the conscious or human mind and the super-conscious or Divine Mind. The subconscious mind is composed of the consciousness of every cell, organ and nerve ganglia synthesized and overshadowed by the animal soul. A reflection or shadow of this power can be traced in all the kingdoms, even those in which it is still latent and which have no power of thought. Being the mind of the animal soul it is below the consciousness of the human reincarnating Ego. To its control are relegated all those functions which operate without man's conscious control, *i.e.*, respiration, circulation, secretion, excretion, etc. But when these functions are deranged beyond the power of the subconscious to restore it appeals to the human con-

sciousness for aid through pain or discomfort and man
becomes aware that something is wrong. The subconscious mind is the vehicle of the passions and desires
normal to the animal soul and which it seeks to gratify, but which must be controlled and directed to their
highest uses by the will of the human Ego. This lower
or animal mind functions through centers in the me-
dulla oblongata, the cerebellum and also in the solar
plexus and other nerve ganglia containing gray matter.
When these centers are upset by inharmony or the baser
emotions—fear, hate, envy, jealousy, sorrow, etc.—the
functions controlled by them are inhibited or perverted,
and the physical, mental and moral health suffers, while
if they are stimulated by peace, tranquility and harmony
or exalted by joy and love their normal functions are
activated or increased with corresponding welfare of the
whole organism. Habits are the result of training the
subconscious mind to act in a certain way. Most vague
and illogical dreams are the result of the subconscious
mind wandering about in the astral world during the
absence of the human Ego from the body during sleep
and therefore without its guidance or supervision. Hence
it is comparatively easy to train the subconscious mind
not to wander so that only the spiritual lessons given
by the Higher Self through symbolic visions or logical,
well-remembered dreams will be brought back to the
waking consciousness. From the above we will see that
we should treat the subconscious mind—as well as the
body—as a good and faithful servant, but should not look
to it for a higher degree of intelligence than we could expect from the highest animal, and certainly should never
look to it for guidance in moral or spiritual problems.

   The conscious or human mind (manas) is the consciousness of the human reincarnating Ego inhabiting

the body and limited by its faculties. It functions through the cortex of the brain, through whose centers it controls the subconscious. It is the great battleground where the Ego is influenced from below by the animal mind and from above by the Divine Mind, yet having free-will to choose its own course of action. It is called lower or higher *manas* according as it identifies itself with the desires of the animal mind or the desires of its Father-in-heaven. Its characteristic is self-consciousness, the feeling of I AM I. "The following are *some* of its manifestations *when placed under the influence or control of material conditions.* (a) The power of the mind in interpreting our sensations. (b) Its power in recalling past ideas (memory) and raising future expectation. (c) Its power as exhibited in what are called by modern psychologists 'the laws of association,' which enables it to form *persisting* connections between various groups of sensations and possibilities of sensations, and thus generate the notion or idea of an external object. (d) Its power in connecting our ideas together by the mysterious links of memory, and thus generating the notion of self or individuality. The following are *some* of its manifestations *when liberated from the bonds of matter*: (a) Clairvoyance. (b) Psychometry."[1]

The super-conscious or Divine Mind is the mind of the Higher Self or Father-in-heaven, one with God. This Divine Consciousness overshadows the human mind much as the human overshadows the subconscious. It is from this source that the higher guidance called conscience and intuition comes, and its Voice is often mistaken for the voice of some Divine Being or Master. It functions through the pineal gland and pituitary body located in the middle of the brain.

---

1 *The Secret Doctrine*, Blavataky, Vol. I, p. 312. I & II

The power of Will is truly a godlike one, for it enables man to follow the will of God or, setting up his own will, to follow his own desires in opposition to the will of God, or the Great Law of Good. If God's will were merely reflected in or imposed upon man, he would of necessity have to follow that will, which would then be not a power given him to use as he would, but a leading-string which he must follow. Man alone has free-will. The animals are subject to the will of the Entity governing the Group-soul of their species. An animal acts because of instinct, not because of free-will. Man, through his power of Will can reach up into the world of Divine Mind and bring to himself all the power of Mind, or he can grovel with the beasts in the World of Desire and by his superior powers intensify its evils. Thus it is that in a world created by a God of Love man has the power to create evil. Will is a power bestowed upon man, for the use of which man alone is responsible—he is not a mere puppet, forced to follow the will of God.

Thought is the power by which man creates images or moulds within which Divine Ideation manifests, while imagination is the power by which he comprehends the subjective ideal, the outer semblance of which may come into objective manifestation through thought. For instance, a painter may in imagination comprehend ideal love, but he must use thought to mould the details in his effort to represent it on canvas. Psychology says that "every thought tends to express itself in terms of muscular activity unless counteracted by a more powerful thought of opposite character." Thus through the powers of Thought man creates his world, or, as the Bible expresses it, "As he thinketh in his heart, so is he." And because of this mould-making power, that which is repeatedly thought of will ultimately manifest. If we think continually of ourselves as poor or sick or unhappy we are making it more possible for poverty, sickness and unhappiness to manifest. In fact we are creating a mould into which they must flow. Conversely if we think of peace, plenty, health and happiness they are just as certain to manifest.

Thought manifests in a dual way. It is the middle principle and together with Mind and Breath, can be used to draw inspiration from the Divine or it can be dragged down and made to waste its force on trivialities, self-pity, etc. When you recognize its power to make images or moulds into which the life-forces naturally flow and shape themselves and become objective, it is not to be wondered at that if wasted on every ache and pain or poverty, troubles or petty worries they grow apace and become objective.

The power of the Life-principle is that magneto-dynamic force which correlates man with Nature and through which he either dominates it or is dominated by it. It works in Nature to readjust and harmonize Spirit and matter. It is the power of rhythm, the power of all forces which take a serpentine path. Frequently persons say they know a storm is coming by their aches and pains, and we know that all animals are warned by this same power to protect themselves from the approaching storm. In man this power is far more than a common consciousness with Nature, for by it, if he wills so to be, he is literally the ruler of Nature or the Lord of Creation. It is through this power that he impresses his state of development upon the

Cosmos. When storms, earthquakes, tidal waves, volcanoes or catastrophes of other kinds take place, many say, "Behold the work of God! How insignificant is man !" This is false. God never made a storm, an earthquake or a catastrophe of any kind, for God is the great Law of Love. They are all evidences of man's power. Had man never sent out evil thoughts, wicked words, blasphemies and curses, the earth's aura could never be so charged with destructive forces that a catastrophe was necessary to dissipate them and bring about equilibrium. Had man never exercised demoniacal cruelty to his brother man, neither the animate nor inanimate worlds would be at enmity with him. When a cataclysm takes place, instead of saying that man is but a helpless atom before the manifestations of Nature we should say, Behold how powerful is man! For it is by the misuse of this power of the Life-principle, exercised through freewill, that man has brought suffering and destruction into a world created by love. So is it with man's body. Unless it has been purified through love and spiritual aspiration this power of the Life-force—which in ordinary man is almost dormant—will bring about readjustments in his body comparable to earthquakes and cyclones. Therefore to meditate upon this force or its center in the body and strive to rouse it into activity is extremely dangerous, for such practices have been known to cause insanity and instant death. The disciples said of Jesus, "What manner of man is this, that even the winds and the sea obey him !" This indicates what perfected man can do when he uses his powers according to the Law of Love.

To overcome fear is the first step on the Path, for fear can be conquered only by love. If fear were conquered absolutely, ere man learned to correlate his

powers with God-love, conditions would be far worse
than today, for even fear is the servant of God. Fear
is a paralyzing and disintegrating force, and if it were
not that the catastrophes caused by man's disobedience
engendered fear, the mistakes of man would become a
solid wall of darkness shutting him away from God. Fear
is continually working as the Great Disintegrator, in reality helping the force of the evil created by man, which is
like a miasmic mist, to precipitate and exhaust its power
upon the earth in the form of storms and catastrophes,
and in the human body as sickness, disease and death,
instead of accumulating indefinitely. When mankind
learns the Law of Love, fear will have no more work to
do, and will cease to appall man at every step. God did
not give man fear. Man himself brought it into manifestation. From another aspect fear is love perverted. In one
sense fear is the Angel of the Flaming Sword guarding
the entrance to Eden, Eden being a perfected earth and
a perfected physical body, with its trees bearing every
manner of fruit good for man, *i.e.*, his powers. It was
the tree which grew in the midst of the Garden, or this
Kundalini or serpentine force which functions in the
spinal column, that proved man's undoing.[1] Only when
this force is mastered and fear vanquished can man re-
enter Eden, cultivate the trees and eat of the fruit thereof
as a faithful husbandman. To conquer fear you must
resolutely use all your powers to create Good, for as
long as you create evil you must have fear to help disintegrate and dissipate it. "Beware of fear that spreadeth,
like the black and soundless wings of midnight bat,
between the moonlight of the Soul and thy great goal
that loometh in the distance far away. Fear, O Disciple,
kills the will and stays all action. . . . The Path that

1 See Chapter XVIII.

leadeth on is lighted by one fire—the light of daring burning in the heart. The more one dares, the more he shall obtain. The more he fears, the more that light shall pale—and that alone can guide."[1] Dare, Do, Keep Silent. Become one with the Silence in which all forces are potent.

Speech is one of the greatest powers, for it includes the powers of sound, number, color and, when written, form. We are all more or less familiar with the power of sound, both in the spoken word and in the chanting of mantra, etc. One who masters this power has the world at his feet. This is illustrated to a slight degree by the ease with which an eloquent speaker can sway an audience. In this chapter but a hint can be given, for it would require a separate lesson to even outline this subject. The point of development each Soul has reached is revealed in the tones of the voice, just as nature-tones indicate Nature's stage of evolution. We may carefully control our words and manner of expression, but the tones of the voice will reveal the true feeling back of the words. This inner attitude is quickly recognized, especially by children and animals. In fact, tone is the key-note of man's power over the animal kingdom; for by the tone he either arouses enmity or love and obedience. The spoken word can never die, but will go on working out the potency and power, not only of its tone, but also of its color, number and form and the thought-pictures created by it in the minds of its hearers, together with the power of the Will which sent it forth. Every word and tone spoken by man is registered upon the etheric substance of the Akashic Records. This principle has been demonstrated and its truth verified in a physical way in the phonograph. Speech is the first power for man

---

1   *The Voice of the Silence*, Fragment III, Blavatsky.

to master as a medium through which all his powers may be made operative on earth.

It is said that, "Before the voice can speak in the presence of the Masters, it must have lost the power to wound." To speak in the presence of the Masters means speaking as a Master or that the spoken word will carry with it the mastery of conditions. To bring to your minds some of the practical effects of this power we would ask you for one day to note carefully the effect your words have on those about you. Many pupils ask for something *practical* to do to develop occult powers and manifest the higher life. Noting the effect of your words is *practical* and most important and a practice which can be indulged in without fear of dangerous consequences. And until at least some conception of the power of speaking kindly and lovingly but to some purpose and *some degree of mastery over it has been attained* the development of all other occult powers will be retarded if not actually prevented.

God spake the word and the world was created. Man speaks one little word and a new world of gladness is created in his brother's life, or man speaks a word and a brother is disheartened and gives up the fight, or a sister's good name is taken from her and she is pushed out into the darkness, is pushed down under the feet of the multitude. Think what one kind word can do! How it can bring sunshine and peace and courage into your own life and the lives of others! Waste no force in frivolous or negative chatter, speak only positive words, words of love, words of power. If your brother offend you, speak words of love that your heart may send back nothing but love. Never withhold a sincere word of love or endearment or a word of help, encouragement or

health. A kind word spoken even to a stray dog will
not return to you void. Know well that until you have
mastered this power and can speak words of health,
strength, cheer, courage and love you would better follow the injunction, "Let your communication be, Yea,
yea; Nay, nay." For remember well, "whatsoever is
more than these cometh of evil." The meaning of this
is that any unkind, boastful or untrue word is bound to
return for you to prove and adjust, probably just when
you think you have conquered. Be especially careful
in regard to written words. When the world begins to
understand this power there will be fewer misleading
statements sent out under the guise of occult teaching
which become snares and wiles to mislead those who
are seeking enlightenment. We cannot emphasize too
strongly this fact: "That every idle word (either spoken
or written) that men shall speak, they shall give account
thereof in the day of judgment."

As to how to attain and use these powers: They are
yours now. They are in constant activity and, unless consciously directed toward the unification of mankind in
God-love, they are adding their force to the misery of life,
both in your own body and in the whole Cosmos. Hence,
there is but one thing to do—realize that God is Love, and
that Love is the one great Law of all Life, manifesting
in you in this seven-fold Path of Power. If this realization seems difficult, set to work at it in earnest. Repeat
it to yourself again and again. Breathe it. Vitalize it with
the Life-principle. Think of it. Will it. Grasp it. Impress
it upon every atom of your manifested expressions
of being. And the ultimate result can only be Victory.
When you synthesize your six powers in the seventh,
the power of becoming one in consciousness with God-

love—which is the power proceeding from the heart and always spoken of as the power of the Diamond Heart or the Heart Doctrine—then you can have nothing to fear, for "perfect love casteth out fear." This is the power of becoming one with your Higher Self. Its seat is in the heart, for in the heart are centers corresponding to and connected with all the centers, as an electric switch-board may be connected with many sub-stations. Therefore by cultivating the heart qualities and dwelling in peace and love you can awaken and dominate all the centers and make their cultivation easier.

This is not some far-off possibility, for the instant you synthesize all your powers in the heart and seek to subserviate your life and action to the Law of Love you are one in aim with your Higher Self, and this Higher Self will manifest more and more through you. Then will there be no death, for death will be swallowed up in victory. You have nothing to fear for you are all-powerful. You have but to direct your powers in accord with the universal Law of God which is Love.

Look around you and see the evil man's powers have wrought when working contrary to the Law! Then think what they could accomplish if they had this Great Law working back of and through them! If but two or three are gathered together "in my name" (The Christ-love), ready to believe the spoken word of power as herein delivered to you, *i.e.*, that you are today as gods and that all power is given unto you in heaven and in earth if you really will to become one with the great Law of Love, then the regeneration of the world would quickly be accomplished. And if but seven Souls, or even three, can be gathered together and work con-

sciously in a perfect realization of this truth, making
a determined effort to work with the Law, soon there
will manifest on the earth-plane a practical Center of
Right Living of such force and social magnitude that
the whole earth will feel its influence, and the deplor-
able conditions under which the world now suffers will
begin to adjust themselves. There is no use reading a
lesson such as this and thinking it a mere theory, for it
is more than mere theory. It comes to *you* as the Word
of Power. It says to each Soul: What are *you* going to
do about it? On which side of the battle will *you* fight?
Into whose coffers will you pour your substance, God's
or Mammon's? Choose ye this day whom ye will serve.
"O fearless Aspirant, look deep within the well of thine
own heart, and answer. Knowest thou of Self the powers, O thou perceiver of external shadows? If thou dost
not then art thou lost."[1]

---

1   *The Voice of the Silence*, Fragment III, Blavatsky.

CHAPTER XIII

Just as the Law of Karma is indissolubly connected
with the Law of Reincarnation, so is reincarnation indissolubly connected with the Law of Evolution; for
without reincarnation, evolution could not be carried
on. Hence, a brief outline of the chief factors in evolution, on this planet, will first be considered. But in this
short chapter we do not attempt to cover all phases of
the subject. We merely view it from one angle, with a
full recognition that it may be viewed from many angles.

As correctly stated by the naturalist, Agassiz: "All
things had their origin in Spirit—evolution having originally begun from above and proceeding downwards,
instead of the reverse, as taught in the Darwinian theory."[1]
At the first rebirth of our earth—for the law of cyclic re-
birth applies to planets and systems as well as to men—it
was brought into manifestation, or "created"[2] by a ray of
pure white light from the Absolute penetrating into the
chaotic debris of previous world-periods. As a ray of light
in passing through a prism is separated into seven color-
rays, so this Ray of spiritual light in passing through
the prism of manifestation was separated into seven
great differentiations or color-rays called Hierarchies.
These are composed of spiritual Beings manifesting
the creative power of their color. For just as science has

---

1 *Principles of Zoology*, p. 154.
2 Not, however, out of nothing.

demonstrated that every color has its special and characteristic work in the world, so each of these spiritual color-rays has its own part to play in the evolution of both man and the lower kingdoms. Each Ray is presided over by one of the manifestations of Deity collectively spoken of in the *Bible* as the Elohim and in Eastern teaching as the Rishis, Sons of Wisdom, etc., who needed this manifestation to perfect their experience, and to prepare conditions to further the evolution of the lower beings—the humanity of this globe—under their charge.

The great Spiritual Masters, constituting the higher degrees of each Ray, gained their god-like perfection in previous world-periods[1] of almost immeasurable length, and gained mastery over the cosmic forces while upon the lunar chain of globes.[2] Hence, they are called our Lunar Ancestors or Fathers (Pitris). But they still needed the experience of guiding the evolution of this darkest, because lowest, of planets, the earth, to perfect them in wisdom. After they had enjoyed a rest, or period of withdrawal from activity in manifestation, for incalculable aeons, they took up the formation and evolution of this planet. By the power of concentrated Divine Will and Wisdom, they consciously formed and brought into manifestation our earth as an advanced field wherein to train and further the evolution of humanity. They did this

---

1 Great Life Cycles or Manvantaras. See Chapter XV.
2 "The Sun is the Giver of Life to the whole Planetary System; the Moon is the Giver of Life to our Globe; and the early races understood and knew it, even in their infancy." *The Secret Doctrine*, Blavatsky, Vol 1, p. 415. "It is, then, the Moon that plays the largest and most important part, as well in the formation of the Earth itself, as in the peopling thereof with human beings. The Lunar Monads, or Pitris, the ancestors of man, become in reality man himself." *Ibid*, Vol. I, p. 206.

by first projecting from themselves into the centers[1] where the inert matter for the new planet was sleeping in darkness, the thought-forms of that which was to be, and later projected their astral bodies This inert matter comprised all that material on all planes which they, in the course of their evolution toward Godhood, had thrown off and had not had the opportunity to spiritualize and redeem. Hence it was laid aside until they had gained the godlike power which would enable them consciously to redeem all their emanations and creations. If each Soul was required to redeem in one life all its mistakes and spiritualize every atom with which it had been connected in even one life, the Cycle of Necessity would be never ending. Instead of this all tasks that are beyond the strength of the Soul in any one incarnation are held back until it has grown strong enough little by little to work them out. However, the essence of all the mistakes remains with the evolving planet as a part of the World Karma, so that when the evolving Soul reaches the point where it can begin consciously to redeem its leftovers it will also help to redeem the same influences in the World Karma.

During the first two cyclic day-periods[2] of the earth the Elohim are said to have passed "through the whole triple cycle of the mineral, vegetable and animal kingdoms, in their most ethereal, filmy and rudimentary forms, in order to clothe themselves in, and assimilate, the nature of the newly formed Chain."[3] After ethereal human forms had been evolved by these Lunar Fathers, at the close of the third day-period, they gradually became so dense

---

1 Called laya-centers.
2 Periods of activity called Rounds. See Chapter XV.
3 *Ibid*, Vol I, p. 197.

that it may be said that they clothed themselves in flesh—"coats of skin," as the *Bible* puts it.[1] This was done consciously for the sake of evolution and experience, and not, as theology teaches, as a result of a "fall" through disobedience. It was a "fall" only in the sense of a descent into matter. These human forms, created and informed by the Lunar Fathers, had no self-conscious (only animal) mind (instinct), and could not continue their evolution until they had been endowed with human mind (self-consciousness).

Animal consciousness attains to its ultimate perfection in reason while human consciousness attains to its ultimate perfection in the direct knowledge gained through intuition. As the whole of a species is guided by one Group-soul, instinct is the power of the animal to respond directly to the consciousness of the Group-soul. The human-animal being guided by his own Father-in-heaven or his own individual Soul, in intuition consciously recognizes the direct guiding voice of his divine Higher Self. Hence intuition stands exactly over instinct on the spiral path of evolution. Both are the voices of their respective Souls, in the animal imparted collectively to the species, in man personally to the individual. The gift of mind was accomplished at the beginning of the Fourth Root Race, by the projection into man of the Divine Spark from a still higher class of Spiritual Beings, the Solar Fathers (Pitris). It was at this time that the history of man as a corporeal being began.

There are three streams of evolution going on in man at the same time, each advancing along its own path and each inextricably interwoven with and as-

---

1   *Genesis*, III, 21.

sisting the other.[1] It is this complexity that makes so
much confusion in the study of reincarnation. There is
the evolution of the animal body, evolved and informed
by the Lunar Fathers; the evolution of mind implanted
in the bodies by the Sons of Mind, the Solar Fathers;
and the evolution of character, which is the result of
the overshadowing Spirit—a Divine Emanation from
the Absolute—working through both the Solar and
Lunar Fathers and forming the Divine Indweller, the
God-within-us.

The history of humanity shows that each of these lines
of evolution has been made the object of worship. (a)
There are those who worship the perfection of the animal body, holding that their first duty is to bring it to
perfection, maintain its health and prolong its life upon
the physical-plane. Yet prolonged life in a physical body,
without spiritual perfection, would be a curse rather than
a blessing. This doctrine reached its greatest perfection
among the Greeks, many of whom are now reincarnating
and are putting forth the old ideas. (b) There are those
who worship the mind, considering it the supreme power.
The so-called age of reason in reality is the age of the
worship of mind. (c) There are those who give exclusive
worship to the studies which make for spiritual advance,
even at the expense of physical and intellectual life, her-
mits and *yogis* for example. Perfect evolution, however,
can be obtained only when the three go hand in hand,
for spiritual evolution can manifest perfectly only as a
result of the harmonious blending of all three, a perfect
mind in a perfect body, illumined by spiritual intuition.
The above accounts for the many discrepancies in life
and evolution, for it is impossible for any human being to

---

1   *The Secret Doctrine*, Vol 1, p. 213.

say that one is more advanced than another; one may be advanced along one line while another may be equally as advanced along another line.

Although we speak of the Lunar Fathers as our physical Progenitors, it must be borne in mind that they are Divine, having attained at-one-ment ere the evolution of this planet began. After the astral forms or models were produced by the Lunar Fathers, "The evolution of the *external* form, or body round the *astral*, is produced by the terrestrial forces, just as in the case of the lower kingdoms; but the evolution of the *internal*, or real, Man is purely spiritual. It is now no more a passage of the impersonal Monad through many and various forms of matter . . . but a journey of the 'Pilgrim-Soul' through various *states*, not only of matter, but of self-consciousness and self-perception."[1] Thus it was that, aided by the Emanations from their Progenitors, the Celestial Solar Fathers—who stand to the Lunar Fathers as our Higher Self stands to us—the Lunar Fathers became the Progenitors of humanity. These great classes of Spiritual Fathers, who are still living and guiding human evolution from the higher realms, are the Divine Men known to us as the Masters of Wisdom. There are many accounts of the presence of these Divine Men— the gods—on earth, founding nations, establishing laws, teaching and guiding humanity face to face, to be found in the sacred writings of all ancient peoples, many of whom still claim to have sprung from the "gods."

The seven great groups of these Spiritual Beings are classified in a manner similar to the groups of colors in our solar spectrum, each group being called a Ray, bearing the name of one of the seven

---

1   *Ibid*, Vol. I, p. 198.

DIAGRAM III[1]

THE SEVEN HIERARCHIES AND THEIR SUBDIVISIONS

Color-rays	Sub-rays	
VIOLET	VIOLET Indigo Blue Green Yellow Orange Red	Violet
INDIGO	Violet INDIGO Blue Green Yellow Orange Red	Indigo
BLUE	Violet Indigo BLUE Green Yellow Orange Red	Blue
GREEN	Violet Indigo Blue GREEN Yellow Orange Red	Green
YELLOW	Violet Indigo Blue Green YELLOW Orange Red	Yellow
ORANGE	Violet Indigo Blue Green Yellow ORANGE Red	Orange
RED	Violet Indigo Blue Green Yellow Orange RED	Red

1   *The Secret Doctrine*, Vol. III, 483.

colors, viz., the Red Ray, Yellow Ray, Violet Ray, etc.
Just as the colors of the spectrum are emanations from
the one White Light, so are these Spiritual Creators emanations from the Divine One—the Absolute.[1] These
Rays constitute seven great Hierarchies, which are presided over by seven still greater Celestial Beings,[2] each
of whom is called the Progenitor or Father of His Ray. It
must be borne in mind, however, that each Ray contains
representatives of all the other Rays. (See *Diagram* III.)
In looking at the sun we see a halo composed of the
seven colors in concentric rings. These rings represent
the Hierarchies and in reality conserve the forces of the
colors composing them. The same law is illustrated in
the rainbow although only one segment of the circle is
visible.

Each great Ray, or Hierarchy of Masters manifests in
turn, and, like the notes in the musical scale, in rhythmic cadence, its Progenitor or Father presiding during
its manifestation as Captain of the Host. All the Masters
belonging to a Ray are most active during the manifestation of their Ray, while those belonging to all the
other Rays, even the Progenitors, are, for that period,
subservient to the Ray that is manifesting in activity.
This does not mean that the other Rays are dormant, but,
like a grand symphony, when one note or Ray is dominant, all the others are complementary. Thus absolute
harmony results. While we say a certain Ray or color

---

1   While there can be but one *God*, the Absolute, there are many gods. *i.e.*,
    Spiritual, Creative, Emanations.
2   The Seven Creative Spirits, the Dhyan Chohans, who correspond to the He-
    brew Elohim. It is the same hierarchy of Archangels to which St. Michael,
    St. Gabriel, and others belong, in Christian Theogony." *Ibid*, Vol. 1, p. 73.
    "The Seven Spirits of God sent forth into all the earth." *Revelation* V, 6. "The
    seven spirits which are before his throne." *Ibid*, I, 4. "And I saw the seven
    angels which stood before God."*Ibid*, VIII, 2.

is presiding, in reality it is man's consciousness that is passing through that band of color or Ray of force and consciousness, learning its lessons and gaining its forces. For example, a Celestial Being * * * is the Progenitor or Father of the Red Ray or Hierarchy of Masters. Under Him are the masters of His sub-rays and lesser sub-rays, and so on down to those Souls who are achieving mastery and entering the ranks from the races now on earth. It is the aggregate of all these Masters that is known to us as the Great White Lodge. It is called the White Lodge because, like the white light, it is the harmonious blending of all the seven Rays.

The Great White Lodge is divided, just as is humanity, into seven great classes or Degrees, each of which is sub-divided into seven Orders. The seventh or lowest Order of The Lodge overlaps or blends into humanity, just as humanity overlaps or blends into the animal kingdom.[1] Not that the Masters of the lowest Order are not human, but more than human. The Masters of this lowest Order are still upon the physical plane, using physical bodies and working with and teaching humanity. There are also certain Orders of Masters who are guiding evolution below the human kingdom as Group-souls.

Each of the Masters composing the higher Degrees is the Progenitor or Father of many human beings; for, while gaining the perfected wisdom of former planets during their long periods of evolution, they were consciously creating, both by the power of Divine Will and by emanation. Every emanation of their life-substance, and every cell composing their various bodies, has now evolved into the human kingdom, and the Master of Wis-

---

1 See Chapter III.

dom who originally sent out the emanation or cell, is
called its spiritual Father, no matter what its present
stage of evolution. Hence, all mankind are the children
of one of these great Spiritual Creators. In the same
manner we are the Progenitors, and sometime must become the Guides and Saviors, of every cell that has
composed our various bodies in all our incarnations,
as well as all the creatures created by our thoughts and
desires, when, aeons hence, they have evolved to a point
analogous to present humanity; for they are the children
of our creation. They are not, however, redeemed as
individual atoms, but as more or less composite units.
Each separate cell does not evolve into a separate human
being, but according to its nature and stage of evolution
when cast off will it become a part of an organ in a human body. Man's body therefore is an aggregation of
many sentient lesser centers of consciousness, hence
the necessity for man's ruling his subconscious mind,
as it is the synthetic product of the consciousness of the
lesser centers.

In the early days of the Fourth Root Race, when humanity were but children, having newly received the
gift of self-consciousness (mind), they were guided and
taught face to face by the Fathers—the Elohim—just as
a father and mother (for these great Beings were both
Father and Mother—androgynous)[1] might guide and
teach a child. But when the child has grown to manhood it must leave its parents' guiding care and go out
alone to meet the trials and temptations of the world and
prove how much of the parents' teachings it has built
into character. This is what humanity has been doing

---

1   "In the days that God created man, in the likeness of God made he him; male
     and female created he *them*; and blessed them, and called their name Adam."
     Genesis V, 1-2. It was from the androgynous first Adam that Eve was taken
     i.e., the sexes were separated.

ever since that time; for by the end of the Fourth Root Race humanity had grown up and become disobedient. With the destruction of Atlantis began the individual working out of that disobedience, and an endeavor to put into practice the lessons learned. The Red Ray is now manifesting through humanity, and has been for an immense period of time (Fourth Round), the whole *Bible* being but a history of this Ray. Consequently the Great Being * * * who is the Progenitor of that Ray, is what might be called the Commander-in-chief of the forces of evolution operative throughout this cycle. Humanity has to evolve all the way through this Red Ray, from its lowest sub-ray to its highest. Having passed the middle point of its densest manifestation, humanity is now upon the upward arc toward more spiritual states of Being. As the occult maxim, "As above, so below," and vice versa, holds good for all planes and all laws—in reality there being but one Great Law—to form a conception of what lies before us we have but to consider what the lower aspects of red stand for. Red is the color of the blood which, in the body, carries the life-force. Hence, in its lower aspects, red is expressed by anger, passion, war, anarchy and bloodshed. It is through these expressions of the force of the Red Ray that humanity has been struggling until it has reached the point where the lessons of the lower octave must be registered in the higher. The lifeblood of humanity has reached the point where, laden with the vileness and the effluvia of animal man, it is being purified by the Breath of the Spirit, and henceforth must take on a new tint, just as the physical blood is purified and changes its color in the lungs. Anger purified becomes love-force and energy that will conquer all difficulties; passion must be turned to fervor and ardor for spiritual union; war turned to spiritual warfare, where good triumphs over evil, light over darkness; anarchy becomes the one Law of Brotherhood; bloodshed becomes the pouring out of the spiritual life-force, for as blood carries the physical life-force its correspondence on the higher planes is the vehicle for the spiritual life-force. The highest tint will be reached when the Spiritual Sun shines through this Red Ray, and permeates it and brings out the rose tint of Christ-love and Brotherhood.

The vision of St. John, as portrayed in the *Book of Revelation*, and commonly accepted as a description of the end of the world, is simply the winding up of the dominance of the Red Ray. Although the same symbolic teachings arc given in the *Book of Enoch*, it does not mean that St. John copied from Enoch, but that both were teaching the same universal truths received from the same divine Progenitor.

In the *Bible* much prominence is given to the word blood and "The blood of the Lamb which was slain from the foundation of the world." This refers to the force of the Red Ray, which is the life-blood of humanity, predominating as it does at the beginning of every sub-race, and thus running through and permeating the whole Root Race. Those "which came out of great tribulation, and have washed their robes and made them white in the blood of the Lamb"[1] are the ones who have learned the lessons of the Red Ray—the lessons of the vital life-force—and have thus washed their garments (body) white and pure in the stream of living spir-

---

1   Revelation VII, 13-14.

itual force. They are those who have fought the good fight and are crowned victors, ready to take up the lessons of the next dominant Ray. Only by evolution through all that pertains to the Red Ray (spiritual life-force of the Soul — its blood, so to speak) can humanity be washed in the blood of the Lamb and be redeemed.

Certain texts in the *Bible* regarding blood which are repulsive[1] and inhuman in their exoteric meaning, if looked at in the light of the above explanation, at once take on a new significance. Even that most abused and revolting hymn—

> "There is a fountain filled with blood
> Drawn from Emmanuel's veins,
> And sinners plunge beneath that flood
> Loose all their guilty stains"

becomes quite comprehensible when viewed from this standpoint. You have no real spiritual life in you until you have correlated with the higher aspect of the Red Ray which is, indeed, the Blood of The Christ.

---

1   "Except ye eat the flesh of the Son of man, and drink his blood, ye have no life in you. " *St. John*, VI, 53-55.

CHAPTER XIV

THE LAW

"Love is the fulfilling of the law." *Romans*, XIII, 10.

"Study the hearts of men, that you may know what is that world in which you live and of which you will be a part. Regard the constantly changing and moving life which surrounds you, for it is formed by the hearts of men; and as you learn to understand their constitution and meaning, you will by degrees be able to read the larger word of life (Law)." *Light on the Path*, Rule 12.

All life is law. There is but one law, Love. All life and all law is vibration. Hence the Law of Love must manifest through the whole gamut of vibration, becoming thus both the Law and the fulfilling of the Law.

When God (Love, Law) sent His only begotten Son (the Light) to earth, there shot forth a great shaft of living fire, vibrant with creative force, into the darkness (the germs of unmanifested life) where at once a cyclic motion was begun in every atom, and all things began their cyclic evolution—worlds, creatures, atoms, each with its own innate potency awakened to activity by the light,[1] the Spirit or Breath which moved on the face of the waters. Some faint conception of how this ray of force cleaves the darkness can be gathered by watching a skyrocket shooting up into the blackness of the night. For some distance it is apparently a solid shaft of fire, yet in reality every particle is in rapid cyclic vibration; every molecule is swirling at a high rate, and only because of this vibratory force is the rocket propelled onward. The

---

1   See Chapter XXIV.

law followed by the tiny atoms of fire in the path of the rocket is the same law that governs worlds, planets, suns and systems. Each turns around its own axis, yet all continue upon their own appointed paths upward and onward into new regions. While each turns upon its own axis and circles around its own sun, still the whole universe is being propelled onward through space, changing conditions through which it passes and by the very force of its cyclic vibration setting all it contacts into a motion of its own. It is this great Law, Divine Love, which creates all things and holds them to their appointed paths, that they may evolve their germs of good and transmute their germs of evil, for evil is but opposition to the Law.

The Light is the first-born and only begotten Son of God for it is the first expression of God-force or Love to manifest, just as terrestrial light is the primeval manifestations of our visible sun—and light includes within itself all vibrations. Just as the rays of the sun start the seed to growing in the earth and ultimately draw back again the force of the perfected tree, so the only begotten Son of God, through Love, both plants the seed of Immortality in earth conditions, matures it and brings it to perfection, that it may be indrawn into the Father.

The Law manifests in seven major aspects: (1) Order, (2) Compensation, (3) Cause and Effect or Karma, (4) Vibration, (5) Cycles or Periodicity, (6) Polarity, and (7) Balance or Poise. No one aspect manifests alone, but while each may predominate in turn all the others manifest at the same time as subordinate factors.

(1) Order. Not a grain of sand blown by the wind on the seashore but is following the Law as order, for the wind acts as the servant of the Law, there being no

such thing as chance. Everything in life comes in orderly sequence. Nothing can come into your life outside of this law. There is always a place and a time for everything and a reason why it comes. It is according to the Law as orderly sequence. Everything is brought to you at just the right time and place to bring to you the help or the lesson needed to take your next step. All comes to you through Divine Love.

(2) Compensation. The Law works as compensation in that in every experience, be it painful or otherwise, there is a compensating power to be gained or a reward which is well worth the suffering necessary to build it into Soul-growth. This is also Love. "A woman when she is in travail hath sorrow, because her hour is come: but as soon as she is delivered of the child, she remembereth no more the anguish, for joy that a man is born into the world."[1] In the lower forms of life when an eye, for instance, is needed, it is gradually developed by the extreme sensitiveness acquired by the repeated stimulations given to the nerves of a certain part by the continual bumping of the organism into objects which it cannot see to avoid. The compensation is an organ of sight.

(3) Cause and Effect or Karma. Inextricably blended with the Law as Compensation is that aspect known as Karma. That is, effects of causes set up in previous times or former lives are brought to you in orderly sequence to be worked out, and in turn to set up fresh causes. The great point to understand in this manifestation of the Law is that Karma is neither a reward nor a punishment for past deeds—and still less is it an avenging Nemesis remorselessly exacting "an eye for an eye and a tooth for a tooth"—but is

---

1 *St. John*, XVI, 21.

the effect of causes in the sense that it brings to the Soul *the* o*pportunity* to learn certain lessons which it has not learned in a past life, hence which the Law of Love brings to it through this manifestation that it may gain the Soul-quality needed for further progress.

(4) Vibration. All the events which are brought into your life in orderly sequence with the intention of compensating you are brought through the aspect of cause and effect by the Law as Vibration. This teaches you to correlate and attune yourself to the infinite vibrations of Divine Harmony so that through the Law as Vibration the evil or inharmonious aspects of life may be dissipated and the rhythm of all life be attuned to the Infinite.

(5) Cycles or Periodicity. There can be no concept of life outside of or apart from vibration, and all vibration is cyclic. Everything manifests in cycles from the sprouting of the tiniest blade of grass, its fruition and decay to the times and seasons of suns and systems (manvantaras and pralayas). Every event is governed by cycles, a period of activity, a period of rest, corresponding to the downward and upward sweep of manifestation and obscuration or the outbreathing and inbreathing of the Great Breath of Brahm. The life of each individual is also governed by cycles within cycles. All students notice periods of great spiritual uplift followed by periods of depression and deadness. These extremes can only be overcome by a knowledge of the Law as Periodicity or Cycles. When the period of depression comes, balance it with the force received during the exaltation. Recognize that it is the period of inbreathing, the time to indraw and digest the lessons of the active period. Only thus can Balance or Poise be attained.

(6) Polarity. Until all the aspects of the Law have been brought into perfect polarity and attuned to the divine rhythm of the great Law of Love, Polarity is broken up into many lesser polarities which manifest under the Law of Opposites, good and evil, light and darkness, male and female, etc. If we break a magnet into a thousand pieces each piece will have its positive and negative pole, but its power will be but a faint reflection of the power manifested in the one. When true Polarity is attained all will be in perfect harmony with the positive pole of Divine Love, the negative pole of human love reaching up unwaveringly and merging itself into that Love, and all the forces interacting in perfect rhythm from pole to pole. The polarity of the Law has literally been broken and separated into its various aspects instead of manifesting in its entirety. Man through his disobedience has broken the Law, yet he must become one with the Law, or the Hammer of Thor will break him in pieces. Just as a ray of white light in passing through a prism is broken up into its seven aspects or colors, each manifesting an individual force, so the Law of Love in passing through the dense darkness of physical life is broken up and deflected so that its seven aspects work individually, bringing about chaotic conditions. If we isolate the red ray, at one extreme of the solar spectrum, its effect would be heat and over-excitement tending toward feverish and inflammatory conditions, with little illuminating power. At the other extreme of the spectrum the action of the violet ray would be to kill low forms of life—both bacterial and organized cell life—and in higher forms to cause disorganization and insanity. And each of the other color rays has been found to have its own special action which when separated from the others is inimical to man;

but each when used with wisdom or synthesized into white light contains a quality of helpfulness. In fact, these various aspects are the forces, each with its own individual work to do, alluded to as the "seven Sons of Fohat" or the seven differing manifestations of Force, all of them contained within the one white light of Divinity. Only when these seven Sons are united in their parent ray can there be light, for while separated they manifest color rather than light. So it is with the Law of Divine Love. When the Law is broken and its differing aspects strive to work individually, as they do in this world of effects, there is confusion, darkness and a turning away from God or a manifesting of the opposite pole of Good, evil. But in reality this is only a lack of positive polarization.

(7) Balance or Poise. The heart of these various activities of the Law is Balance or Poise. For only when Poise is attained or that center where vibration is so rapid as to be peace can all the aspects of the Law be synthesized and perfected.

All temptations met with on the Path come through the various aspects of Love, even Jesus in the wilderness, being obliged to face and conquer the love of power, dominion and ambition.[1] On earth we see Love manifesting as love of gold, love of power, love of self, love of pleasure, love of animal gratification and so forth, all perverted or negative polarizations of Divine Love. Divine Love and human love are often thought of as quite separate while in reality they are but opposite poles of the One Force. There is no manifestation of the Law on earth capable of touching the depths, or reaching the heights in its cyclic sweep as Polarity or human love when not wedded to Wisdom. Through Love perverted has man touched the

---

1   *St. Matthew* IV, 1-11.

depths of degradation, yet because Love is the Divine
Law, One from the beginning, it must forever sweep
upward and onward, and like a mighty whirlwind gather
up all it touches. In its journey back to its source Love
gathers up and synthesises its seven manifestations and
thus fulfills the whole Law of Being. "God is Love" and
God so loved the world that He sent His only begotten
Son (Light or Love made manifest) to descend into the
darkness of the unmanifested mass of substance (matter) that out of it Love might work the fulfillment of
the Law. From the earliest dawn of creative thought to
the present moment has Love thus worked its way up
through matter.

Many say that before Jesus came there was but the
thundering of the inexorable Law of the Old Testament
or what the Hindus call Karma, but that Jesus came to
substitute for the Law the glad tidings of redemption
through Love. But Jesus Himself says: "I came not to
destroy the Law but to fulfill it." The Law which we
are wont to call inexorable justice in reality could be
neither just nor inexorable were Love left out, for Love
is the one and only reality which endures from eternity
to eternity. Hence Jesus the perfected man did not come
to do away with the Law but to straighten out man's
misconceptions of it; to emphasize the fact that justice
becomes injustice and cruelty when Love is left out; that
Law is Love, and that which we look upon as an awful inexorable punishment is in reality but the force of
Love striving to counteract man's disobedience to the
Law and lead him back into the path where Love alone
can redeem. Hence the glad tidings of Jesus were simply
to point out to the world that Love is the fulfillment of
the Law; is the recognition that the Law is Love, and that
only through Love can it be fulfilled. There can be no

punishment, injustice or fear for those who recognize and live at one with the Law of Love.

A careful analysis will show that every test, trial or temptation is brought about through the negative polarization of Love, by a breaking up of the Law, a refusing to find balance and a consequent revolving around an individual center, a getting out of harmony with that which keeps all things in their appointed paths. This negative polarization is the cause of so many unhappy marriages. Man feels the stirring of the Divine Love-force within, pushing his whole nature onward toward God-consciousness, and instead of at once polarizing himself to this Divine Love he often seeks to polarize himself to some human love which the Law does not bring to him and thereby forces both himself and that other out of harmony with the Law. And sooner or later the Divine Fire in both atoms must die out and like burned out cinders they fall back to earth filled with disappointment, sorrow and coldness. He fails to realize that just as he focuses his consciousness upon the positive pole, all that belongs to him — his own, the little swirling love atom that is his earthly complement — must come to him as he becomes one with the Law, for its lawful place is by his side and without its help he could not fulfill the Law of Love.

Heretofore man has been misapplying the Law and placing himself under its negative aspect — evil — and through the ensuing suffering has been learning to lift up his eyes afar off and long for his Father's home. But the time will come when man must balance the effect of the negative aspect — suffering — by manifesting under the positive aspect — Love — and reap his reward. The suffering may be the means of turning man God-ward, but the ultimate knowing of God can only come through Love. The negative aspect of Divine Love has evolved up through humanity until the turning point was reached, and now the positive aspect must come into manifestation. Jesus outlined to the world a grander conception of the Divine Law in what is known as the New Dispensation, but it takes very little thought to realize that this New Dispensation has never yet manifested in humanity as a whole; it has never been more than a grand ideal to which only a few isolated examples have attained. This New Dispensation can never be realized until man begins to polarize his whole life to Divine Love and manifest its positive or good aspect as he has its negative or evil, thus gaining perfect equilibrium.

This is the esoteric meaning of the injunction, "Seek ye first the kingdom of God, and his righteousness; and all these things shall be added unto you." In other words when you have polarized all your life and love to Divine Love and when you are living thus harmonized to your proper place in the stream all that is yours must be swept onward with you. As long as you refuse to understand the Law and think of yourself as an atom separated from the mass or pick out for yourself another atom to revolve around you are destined to remain in the negative polarization and fall to earth again and again, as do the sparks in the sky-rocket which have lost their oneness with its fiery heart.

"Men loved darkness rather than light, because their deeds were evil." Their deeds may not be absolutely wicked but they tend away from the positive pole of Light (Divine Love) and hence must manifest darkness rather than light. The lesson to be learned is that you do not have to seek for something afar off or foreign to your nature, for you are living in a world of love, created by a Love which embraces every atom in the universe in its fiery Heart; that you will suffer until you learn to desire the Light; that Light (Love) is turned into darkness as long as it is broken up into lesser loves. There is but one way, the way of The Christ, the only begotten Son (the Light) which is the way, the truth and the life. You must deliberately turn your heart toward Divine Love and realize that the instant you thus turn you are vibrating with the stream and must of necessity be swept onward and upward and must draw with you every other atom that is in any way harmonized to you. Then help, strength, power, comradeship and love must come to you because you are harmonized to the stream of Divine Love which is ever working toward perfection. You suffer only as you get out of harmony with the Law by passing it through the prism of your lower personality and hence producing various colors rather than light.

The world is struggling in the stream. The rocket has been shot from its mortar and cleaves the darkness in one swirling stream of fiery particles. Many in the stream know not whither they are bound, but they are in the fiery current. They whirl round and round, each little Soul a vortex of fire, each cycle of each spark seeming to be a complete universe shutting out all else, apparently vibrating to some force whose center is within the atom, yet in reality all are being drawn onward and upward in Love in a straight line back to the source whence they came, as the fire and force of the rocket are drawn to their source, the sun—the storehouse of both light and force—while that which belongs to earth—the stick and the ashes—falls back to earth. Love fulfills the Law for each atom, for each Soul. The lessons of each are brought

by Love. Only the hearts that are cold and dead to Divine
Love and persistently seek some human polarization fall
back to earth as cinders, those that are alive and glowing
sweep ever on.

As you go out into the world you must dwell in this
current of Divine Love, and as you feel its force thrill-
ing through you know well that its center is not in the
little puny life round which you revolve, but in the Heart
of the One Life; that the main lesson is not that you
find satisfaction in being in the stream, but that you
lend the fire in your heart toward propelling the rocket
ever higher, and that fire within must be the indwelling
Christ-force. The positive pole cannot manifest without
the negative pole; the Divine cannot manifest without
stirring up earth conditions. Your temptations will come
through Love; that which is purest will seem to stir up
the most impurity; that which is Divine will bring sorrow and discouragement. How then shall you become
one with the Law? By polarizing your love to Divine
Love, by merging your spark into the heart of the vortex
where all is rest and harmony and peace.

This is the work of this Order, and this is your work.
You cannot expect the world to attain peace and love
unless you manifest peace and love, not merely to one
atom, but to all. You must demonstrate your ability to
stand still amid the swirling currents of life and hold
on to the center of the whirlwind, the Heart of Love.
Recognize that the turbulence and disasters and sufferings are but the results of the outpourings of Divine Love;
that they come not as karmic retribution but that through
the vibrations of Love the Law may be fulfilled. You
must lend your love to make this Order a great fiery
stream of Divine Love that shall draw to it and make

glowing all the little fiery hearts that are following crooked paths and growing cold and falling back into the darkness. Your mission is to point out how that which is apparently evil can be polarized to good, how discouragement can be turned into ardor, how suffering can be turned to joy.

Study the lessons in the Book of Life. On every page will you find the word Love. Many pages may be clouded and obscured, many may be almost obliterated with tears, many may be besmirched with mire, but because you have been drawn into this fiery stream of Divine Love you will have the power to decipher the pages, to trace the story of the Love that has been guiding you through all the darkened, sorrowful pages. You can show the stricken ones and the heart-hungry that they are still in the stream; that it is Love that is leading and guiding them; that the Law is whirling them round and round only to bring them and theirs back to God; that there are other pages in the book, pure and unsullied, whereon they may learn to write their names.

CHAPTER XV

"Thus the heavens and the earth were finished,
and all the host of them. And on the seventh day
God ended his work which he had made." *Genesis*,
II, 1-2.

"Whirling, glowing ether, fluidic but cohesive, throwing off sparks. Encountering moist air it sends up clouds of vapor in its rapid motion. The Great Mother sends out her breath to blow cool and moist upon the fiery offshoots of the Father. Little by little it gathers density until the children suited to its condition begin to move in its fiery heart like tiny flames, yet flames that have life and independent motion. All life is now 'gaseous light.' The spirits of the gases hover over the glowing vapory mass. They fan it with their wings that it may cool and harden. Within the womb of the World Mother an infant globe slowly takes form. At last upon this whirling sphere there descends, in one great rush, the spirits of the Great Ones destined to prepare this ethereal dwelling place for humanity. These are men indeed, MEN, Divine Men, Manus, who reached their godlike state on former chains of worlds. They begin their work on the first and earliest globe of this chain in its most ethereal condition. Their work is to inform and prepare this life-essence for future use.

"They blow their cool breath upon the glowing vapory globe and lo! it solidifies into the prototypes of that which becomes rock and mineral, imprisoning the Spirit of Life. Their life blood becomes currents of living force. They hover over the face of the

Great Deep. Into the waters they breathe their life breath and the waters are filled with innumerable living forms. From the waters and the cooling rocks a great mist arises.[1] It is the Spirit or life-element of the coming humanity. It separates into masses. They take form and become ethereal beings floating like clouds over the still ethereal planet. Through all this first Round the Creators are engaged in preparing the earth, informing the prototypes of that which is to be. It is the breath of their nostrils, the blood-stream of their life forces that is both transforming and reappearing in the life of the elements.

"Ere the earliest types are ready to take on denser ethereal forms they pass into a sleep, which in this early stage is but a slight cooling down of the globe. Then a new day dawns, the Second Round. A new form of life appears, the vegetable. Once more must the Parents of the Race guide the pure but as yet incorporeal beings, the Second Race, and teach them how to inform the planet. The Manus must enter, through the breath of their nostrils, into the formation of the new globe. They must permeate the mineral to give it consciousness and penetrate the vegetable, very like the water of the ocean flowing through coral or some spongy substance, leaving behind its informing principle. As yet humanity is globular and ethereal, but must become acquainted with the globe on which it dwells. It becomes the mineral, the stone, the water, the air. The oceans are of carbonic acid, and the air is saturated with its evaporation. Gigantic trees form from the carboniferous exhalations of the early Races. The immense coal beds were thus created by the informing Beings, the Progenitors of the coming humanity.

---

1   See *Genesis* II, 6.

"After a pralayic night of short duration they are ready for a new globe; they awaken to a new condition, the Third Round. Different strata have been formed. The earth's crust has formed over the minerals and the giant trees. Now gigantic reptiles and beasts roam the earth, with bodies and functions adapted to the existing conditions. Humanity is not yet ready to take solid form.

"In the Fourth Round humanity falls into generation; is endowed with mind by the Sons of Mind. God breathes into man's nostrils the breath of life and he becomes a living Soul. As humanity reaches the lowest point of this Fourth Round, the human body solidifies. The spiritual powers and psychic faculties are now limited and all but lost in the dense physical envelope; mind begins to develop. From this point onward man must work out his own redemption, together with that of the earth. Up to this time his evolution and that of the earth had been guided and directed by the Manus or the Rishis, the Progenitors of all that lives and breathes on Earth."

The above is an extract from a cryptic lesson given by the Master to the Order explaining the formation of a 'World Chain, but which the limits of this lesson are far too short to fully explain. However, although there has been much speculation and much confusion in the minds of students concerning these World Chains, we will endeavor to explain herein only certain of their most practical phases, for a complete understanding of the subject belongs to the Mysteries of the higher Initiation.

Just as man's body is the lowest expression of his seven-fold constitution, so is each visible planet but the lowest, densest aspect of a seven-fold Chain, called by occultists a "World Chain." A World chain is composed of seven globes of differing states of matter and consciousness, all existing at the same time and all interpenetrating. The globes of any one Chain must not be identified with the visible planets, for only one globe of each Chain is visible, each physically visible planet being the physical globe of its own Chain, just as the Earth is the physical globe of the Earth Chain. The other six globes of each Chain arc composed of finer and more ethereal states of matter to which our physical senses do not respond. They are invisible and hence to us apparently do not exist.

In its descent (involution) into physical manifestation life appears successively on each of the seven globes during one day-period called a Round, seven of such day-periods or Rounds being required to complete the cycle of manifestation (involution—turning point—evolution). "Our Earth, as the (now) visible representative of its superior fellow-globes, ... has to live, as have the others, through seven Rounds. During the first three, it forms and consolidates; during the fourth (our present Round), it settles and hardens; during the last three, it gradually returns to its first ethereal form; it is spiritualized, so to say."[1]

It may appear as though the evolving lives stepped from globe to globe of the Chain, but in reality they merely evolve into new states of matter and consciousness. A new globe or plane of consciousness manifests when the consciousness evolved in the preceding Round can no longer express itself on the old globe. In passing from globe to globe a new principle is developed on each. Man can penetrate into the consciousness of the states through which he has passed, but can not penetrate into the realms that embody principles which he has not yet evolved. As man

1 *The Secret Doctrine*, Blavatsky, Vol. I, 133.

evolves, his consciousness is born into a new globe or state of consciousness, literally born into a new world which did not exist for him before, where all the familiar things of his daily life and of Nature appear in a new and hitherto unsuspected light. This is due to an expansion of consciousness which enables him to respond to the vibrations of a higher globe, enabling him to grasp deeper meanings and understand teachings which he formerly regarded as mere vagaries of unbalanced minds or mystical word pictures of no practical value. "Cycles and epochs depend upon consciousness: we are not here for the first time; the cycles return because we come back into conscious existence. Cycles are measured by the consciousness of humanity and not by Nature. It is because we are the same people as in past epochs that these events occur to us."[1]

Undeveloped man responds chiefly to the vibrations of the physical globe, those things which he can see, hear, taste, handle, etc., and can not comprehend or function in the globes belonging to the psychic and spiritual planes. Many so live in and for the gratification of their animal appetites, desires and passions that although they are living on earth they are dwelling in the World of Desire or the globe embodying the desire-principle, where desire reigns supreme. For such, every thought, act and experience of life is interpreted from the standpoint of animal desire. Others dwell so completely in the mental world that the desire world, and even the physical world, has little power over them. Many function in a dream world, the astral envelope of the physical earth, in which the physical, desire and mental worlds are all reflected. Some are able to reach up into the

---

1   *Ibid*, Vol III, 563.

Soul World and receive their mystic Soul birth, while a few receive their birth into the Spiritual World where their consciousness becomes one with their Father-in-heaven. The phenomenon of true "conversion" is but the birth of the consciousness into the Soul globe or plane. The majority of humanity, however, function in the three lower worlds (physical, mental, desire) at the same time or vibrate from one to the other. The mental world, however, has two aspects, a high and a low, and since man is endowed with free-will, he can chain mind to the lower worlds and make of this great gift but a servant to gratify desire and intensify physical life, or he can use his gift of mind to reach up into the higher worlds of Soul and Spirit. Man must ultimately function and gain experience on all seven globes at the same time, checking up, balancing and perfecting the experience of one by that gained on the others, thus rounding out his seven-fold nature into the Real Man. Only thus can he gain Mastery over the portion of goods given him by his Father-in-heaven.

What is referred to in the above quotation as taking place in each Round is the ultimate characteristic evolved while the life-wave was passing around the Chain of seven globes during that Round, and what is referred to as "humanity" or "man" is, of course, not man as we know him today, but stages in the involution or descent into matter of that which became man at the middle point of the Third Race of the present Fourth Round. During the First Round the center of the stage of action was occupied by the mineral kingdom; the mineral dominated the entire Chain, reaching its greatest density on the fourth globe. In the rocks formed during that period science finds no traces of either vegetable or animal forms.

During the Second Round the vegetable kingdom occupied the center of the stage and dominated the Earth
Chain, the mineral kingdom being subservient. It was
upon the fourth globe of that Round that giant vegetation flourished in an atmosphere of carbonic acid gas.
The remains of that vegetation are still preserved to us
in the form of coal. The rocks formed during and after
that period record the characteristics of the vegetation
but no trace of animal life, for the animals had not yet
taken on or descended into solid physical form. During
the Third Round animal life dominated the globe in the
form of giant reptiles and monstrous animals whose
remains science has found preserved in many places.
During this period both mineral and vegetable kingdoms
were subservient to the animal. The rocks of that time
contain traces of both vegetable and animal life but not
of man, for he was still astral or super-physical. During
this present Fourth Round it is man who descends to
the physical-plane and dominates the globe through the
power of mind, all the lower kingdoms being subservient to him.

Since man is the microcosm of the macrocosm, in his
spiritual evolution he must pass through stages analogous
both to his own physical evolution and that of the planet,
just as during his inter-uterine life he passes through the
evolutionary stages of the early Races—vegetative, animal, human. The first three Rounds would be represented
in man's spiritual evolution by the innocence of ignorance. During this period he goes on his way actively
doing neither good nor evil, vegetating, indifferent to the
higher ideals yet not groveling in the lowest. Persons in
this stage take life as they find it, with little thought as to
its significance or its deeper problems. They are happy

and carefree, neither very good nor very bad—average good natured persons with whom the world goes well and who experience little sorrow or suffering. There must come a time, however, when, like the planet, the evolutionary urge involves them in still deeper, denser conditions. Their carefree condition changes. Since they pay little attention to the higher ideals of life and concentrate all their efforts on physical gratification, they come to live more and more in their animal natures. They become carried away with animal desires, with the love of money for the gratification of creature comforts, with ambition, with great selfishness resulting in extreme cruelty to their brother men. All these conditions gradually plunge them into the denser animal realm where, like the immense animals that roamed the earth during the Third Round, they prey upon one another, living only to enhance and gratify their animal natures and prolong their animal pleasures.

In this period of spiritual growth the animal passions dominate. Man now seeks to escape sorrow and suffering through indulgence in animal desire. In obeying the inner urge toward harmony (happiness) he madly plunges into all manner of animal excesses and self-indulgences with little regard for the rights of others; but freedom from suffering still eludes him. Ultimately he reaches a point where the Real Man begins to control, corresponding to the period when man began to dominate the earth. As with the planet so with the Race and the individual. The vegetative and animal stages lead steadily toward a condensation of conditions. Just as the passing of the gigantic vegetation of the Second Round added to the density of the globe in the form of coal and the enormous animals of the Third Round by their deposits of bone, so during the corresponding periods of his evolution has man helped to create for himself denser physical conditions, karmic conditions of suffering and sorrow which he must experience and redeem.

Little by little, through sorrow and suffering, he awakes to the realities of life. Sorrow and suffering are to man what matter is to Spirit, the sinking into the densest and most limiting conditions of expression. And the object is the same, i.e., for Spirit, to gain experience in physical conditions and thereby redeem matter; for man, to gain his Soul experience and thereby redeem the causes in the world which produce sorrow and suffering, namely sin and disobedience, as well as to redeem the matter in which he clothes himself. Hence, while the Law as Karma will bring to all the suffering they have earned, at the same time as they conquer they become redeemers for the Race, for they can not conquer for themselves alone. They have been born from the world of thoughtless action into the realm corresponding to the period when man was endowed with mind. They have begun to respond to their Higher Mind. Once having reached this point they can go no more back. Life no longer flows smoothly. They can no longer be thoughtless and carefree, for they must henceforth take in their own hands the working out of the great problems of their spiritual lives, just as man at the corresponding stage took over the guidance of his physical life. They must seek for themselves the solution of life's problems.

When you have reached this stage you have entered the Fourth Degree[1] of humanity where you consciously take up the work of spiritual regeneration.

---

1   See Chapter III.

In this Degree you consciously start out upon the Path and must conquer all the kingdoms below you, both in yourself and in the world. All who are interested in these teachings, for example, have reached this point. And to you we will say that you are not mere creatures of impulse, driven hither and thither by a relentless fate, but are children of your Father-in-heaven. You have reached your majority and are being tested. You are encouraged to take up the great work of your own redemption. Your guidance is now no longer that given a schoolboy, but rather the supervision of a loving parent over one who must of his own free-will follow the principles taught by that parent. It is comforting, however, to realize that you have this power to walk alone or you would not be where you are today. If you were still a child in spiritual leading-strings the great problems of life would not confront you, for the Law of Divine Love brings to the Soul only such problems as it has the strength to meet and conquer. Your Heavenly Father would not that any perish. Yea, not one sparrow falleth to the ground but the Father knoweth.

Seek then to reach up in consciousness to the Soul World, to the globe of Divine Love, a new world in which you can dwell if you will. Your Heavenly Father has prepared a mansion for you in that world which you do not have to pass through the change men call death to enter. But you do have to let go and cease clinging to the things of the lower worlds, for that to which you cling and in which you permit your mind to dwell is the world in which you must function. You may do your duty in the lower worlds and still dwell with your Father in His world of love and glory. Realize that He is watching over you and that His world envelopes you and will manifest to you if you will but open your heart to let it in. Like a human parent, but in a degree far transcending the human, your Father suffers with you, yet understands the necessity for you to conquer alone. The greatest gift to man is free-will. It must be your will to reach out for the guiding hand that is always within reach, even in the darkest night, ere you can find it.

All is Law, and all Law is Love. It is the life-essence of this Law—The Christ-force—which has overcome the world or which has brought about the physical evolution of the planet. Hence it must also bring about your spiritual evolution and bring to perfection all who choose to work in harmony with The Christ. Nothing can overwhelm you if you make this great truth the foundation on which you build your life.

CHAPTER XVI

PURITY

> "What? know ye not that your body is the temple of the Holy Ghost which is in you, which ye have of God, and ye are not your own? For ye are bought with a price: therefore glorify God in your body, and in your spirit, which are God's."
>
> I *Corinthians*, VI, 19, 20.

Your body is the Temple of the Living God. It is your duty to see that in every way it is kept a fit dwelling place for the God within. The chief requisite for this is absolute purity of body, mind and heart. When we speak of a Temple it naturally suggests the idea of sacredness, hence you should not only look upon your body as something to be kept clean and wholesome and in perfect health and strength that it may be a fit instrument, but you should also sanctify it and keep it holy and undefiled. Nothing must be allowed to enter it, either as food or drink, that will injure it, make it unhealthy or lessen your control over it.

This animal body of yours has certain desires and tendencies which are perfectly natural to it, just as they are to any animal, but since you, the Immortal Self, are dwelling in it, you, the Immortal Self must control the animal with its desires and tendencies, and make it subservient to the Law of Being. The lower animals—having no individualized spark of the Divine dwelling in them—receive their touch with the Divine through a Group-soul which guides the evolution of each particular species collectively, through instinct. Hence the animals follow their natural tendencies

when not perverted by contact with man, and these tendencies, not being perverted, are necessarily right and
proper, but man having a higher guidance than instinct
must control the animal tendencies instead of being controlled by them.

No natural function of the body but is pure and wholesome when used for its proper purpose. No natural act
is, of itself, impure. It becomes impure *only through
impure thoughts concerning it*. The animal can follow
only its normal instincts but you, by debasing your God-
given intelligence, have the power to sink lower than
the beasts, or by claiming your birthright and asserting
your manhood, to rise far above them.

Love in its highest expression is the one power which
you possess in common with the gods. It is a divine force
of attraction which seeks equilibrium in the union of
the masculine and feminine expressions of the Divine.
It is a natural force expressing itself in perfect purity
on all planes, spiritual, mental and physical. When it is
confined to the physical-plane you are apt to lose control
of it, and the animal body, through which it is expressed
physically, is left to follow its own devices. Thus the
animal perverts this divine force, and by the aid of intellect devises abnormal ways of gratifying its appetites
instead of expressing the pure love of a spiritual being
for its mate. What was Divine Love becomes debased
and impure, the body is defiled and the Temple of the
Living God desecrated.

Not alone impure acts but also *impure thoughts*,
even if only subconsciously held, are a source of defilement. Science has demonstrated that thoughts are
things, forces which create ethereal forms that attach
themselves to their creators seeking expression through

their bodies. The science of psychology (the science of the mind) teaches that every thought tends to express itself in a bodily act, and does so express itself unless counteracted by a stronger thought of opposite character. Therefore your impure or evil acts are not committed because some devil stands at your elbow urging you to do the impure or evil deed, but you yourself are responsible, for you have created the impure thought-forms that are but striving to express themselves through their creators. Or you have so attuned your mind to impurity that the impure thought-forms created by others are drawn to you. The normal animal passions when excited and inflamed by impure thoughts find abnormal, and necessarily impure, expressions. The whole problem rests upon your ability to purify your thoughts concerning all the forces and functions of your bodies. Learn that there is no natural function of your body that is not normal and right if put to its proper use and governed by pure thoughts.

"Thou shall not let thy senses make a playground of thy mind." [1]

To keep the thoughts pure you must fight every impure thought the instant it appears. Learn to take an interest in pure things and fill your mind with thoughts concerning them. Determinately *conquer the tendency to investigate impurity*. Do not be always hovering on the borderland of suggestion, seeing in every word and look some hidden suggestion of impurity. Expend as much energy and take as much interest looking for Pearls of Purity as is generally spent in seeking for the impure; for what ye seek ye shall surely find. Determine not to entertain an impure thought any more than an impure visitor

---

1   *The Voice of the Silence*, Blavatsky, Fragment III.

would be entertained in the bosom of your family. By
interesting yourself in purity and filling your mind with
pure thoughts you cut off the supply of life and energy
from the impure thought-forms and, if you persistently
create their opposites, after a fierce struggle for life,
they will soon cease to trouble you, for you have created thought-forms of purity which will transmute the
impure, and *will and must* express themselves in pure
thoughts and actions. These pure creations will become
the Warrior who fights for you. Often it is a great sur-
prise to find that the thing you looked upon as such a
dire temptation a short time ago will now scarce attract
a passing glance. You have conquered it.

This divine creative force of Love, which is the link
that unites you with God, finds its greatest earthly expression in the sex-forces. It also has a corresponding
expression on all planes, spiritual, mental and physical. The *sex-forces are always creative* and cannot be
brought into operation without a definite creation on
all planes, their higher aspects creating upon the higher
planes, their lower upon the physical-plane. The spiritual essence will create upon the spiritual-plane; the
mental will create upon the mental-plane, following out
the patterns set by the thought-forms which are fashioned by the desires, thus making them conscious living
entities which attach themselves to man, their creator,
express through him, and demand that he sustain them.
Thus if only gross animal thoughts are held at the time
the forces are used you create gross animal thought-
forms which drag you down, so that you grow more and
more animal. But if pure love and high aspirations as
for a holy sacrament are held at the time, you will be
able to express more and more clearly the ideal held.

The physical essence will create upon the physical plane, but if denied its natural expression on that plane, *i.e.*, the creation of a body in which a divine Soul can incarnate, it will still create upon the physical plane. Being perverted from its normal and thrown into abnormal channels, it will send its quota of creative energy toward the creation of disease, death and pestiferous plagues, for its natural function is completely perverted and that which should have been put to the highest use and which should bring the greatest blessing to mankind has now become its curse. When the creative life-force is brought into activity in purity and love, as it finds embodiment in the lower kingdoms it will clothe itself in forms helpful to man, but since the opposite conditions are too often the rule the creative force adds its power to those forms which are antagonistic to and prey upon man.

These evil things, however, are not a direct creation, but are the result of the impure thoughts and perverted creative force of man permeating the atmosphere of the earth and filling its aura with life-force expressing itself through living entities working in a reverse way, seeking avenues through which to bring forth evil instead of good in all parts of the earth, even where man has never trod. The entities thus created, being man's perverted physical creations, must draw their sustenance from mankind. Just as a child draws its life and nourishment from its mother's breast so these unnatural creations must also flourish and in some way draw their life from man's blood (blood sucking parasites, cancers and all pathological bacteria, for example). Do not blame God for sickness and disease. They are man's creations.

Humanity as a whole has created these conditions for ages, until the aura of the earth is saturated with what is known to science as disease breeding germs, bacteria, parasites, etc. Scarcely anything you eat or come in contact with is free from these enemies to human life, making every one born under the flesh in bondage to the flesh, as the *Bible* puts it or, in occult parlance, subject to the world's Karma to a greater or lesser degree. Nevertheless, although the microscope shows that the germs of disease are constantly entering your body through air, water and food, to the pure in heart and mind and body these abnormal creations will prove harmless. Thus is literally fulfilled the promise "Behold, I give unto you power to tread on serpents and scorpions, and over all the power of the enemy: and nothing shall by any means hurt you."[1] Know well there are no evils created to tempt or diseases to harm you but those of man's own creation. Since man has thus proved himself a creator of evil it is time for him to realize this fact, recognize his power and determine to create good instead of evil.

Cohabitation must never take place except between persons legally married to each other. *There can be no possible exception to this rule.* Legally married means that the law of the land in which they dwell must legalize in the eyes of the world any sexual union. But unless the union has already been made in heaven through pure love, the physical union cannot bring about peace and happiness, for like all true sacraments it must be entered into and registered upon all planes. Nothing can be gained by breaking the laws of the land; if they are crude or inadequate your effort should be to uplift them. Every principle which evolution has proved to be for the benefit of mankind must ultimately be used for its highest purpose. Cohabitation outside the legal married state is but breaking the law and

1   *St. Luke* X, 19.

adding complications to be worked out later in sorrow and suffering. Even though the marriage law is but a man-made law and is far from perfect, it is nevertheless a shadow on earth of the Divine Law, the divine Marriage of the Soul. Man's marriage laws have many objectionable features, but the lesson for humanity to learn is that marriage is a holy sacrament, not to be lightly entered into or lightly set aside. Hence if through ignorance and perversion man degrades this sacrament he will never learn its sacredness, especially by ignoring it or refusing to bear the consequences of his acts.

The fundamental teaching of this Order is that in every Soul there is a Divine Guidance which, if the human personality will listen, will clearly indicate what is right and what is wrong. Hence no one is forced into an unhappy marriage without going against this inner urge; he either enters it because he is blinded by passion, because of a desire for worldly position or for some reason other than the one great reason, namely, because the Soul speaks to its mate in Divine Love. The Law of Divine Love will bring to each Soul its true marriage, a union in perfect purity on all planes. This according to the one life-theory is of course impossible for all; but since reincarnation is a fact, the Soul, through repeated experiences, learns to follow its Divine Guidance, hence will ultimately find its true mate. But they can be spiritually as well as physically married to their mates only when the old accounts of both have been balanced and the old complications set up through the mistakes of the past have been worked out. To ignore the lessons necessary to be learned is but to prolong the period of separation between the two, for they can never come together in perfect purity until each has learned the

lessons which keep them apart and have found out how
to fulfill the Law on all planes; that is, have reached a
point where nothing but the spiritual attraction or true
love leads them into a physical marriage. To break the
Law on any plane by refusing to bear the results of your
acts simply results in your having to come back and
take up the same old lessons where you left them and
continue in them until they are learned.

The marriage state is the highest and holiest relation
between man and woman. Anything that detracts from
its holiness should not be tolerated. The idea that it is
inherently wrong is an insult to an institution which
was placed before man as the earthly expression of
his highest attainment, the union of the Soul with the
Divine. Until you have grasped at least something of the
holy reflection on earth of this Divine Marriage, your
consciousness can never enter into it upon the higher
planes. Hence if you are not ready to enter into this holy
sacrament with a realization of its sacredness, its purity
and the possibility of overcoming the vile ideas which
the world has cast upon it, you would better not swear
falsely before God and man by taking upon yourself its
vows. If mere companionship or a so-called "spiritual
mate" is all that is desired that can be attained without
physical contact. But mark well that mere companionship or "spiritual union" does not include the privilege
of personal contact or physical union.

It is not the words pronounced by minister, priest,
or magistrate which bind you, no written documents,
but the spiritual potencies of the Law which you invoke by your vows and the intent of your Soul in
making the vows. And it is these forces which will
demand the fulfillment of the vows, no matter what
verbal or written contracts to the contrary you may

make or what mental reservations you may hold. If you
refuse to fulfill them in one way you must pay the price
in another, for you will be free only when the debt is
fully paid. It makes no difference whether the ceremony
be Catholic, Protestant, Mohammedan, Mormon or
civil. Whatever land you are in and whatever law you
invoke to bind your Soul is the one with which you
should comply, for it is the power of one Divine Law
you invoke no matter what the ceremony employed.
Whatever law you accept at the time of the marriage as
a representative of the Divine Law, and make your vows
accordingly, that is the law that holds you.

There are three parties to the marriage vow, the man,
the woman and the law of the land. This vow can be
annulled and withdrawn with the consent of all three
parties. Also if one of the parties has violated the vow,
he or she cannot hold the others to it unless they choose
to overlook the violation and thus in effect renew the
vow. If, however, one overlooks the violation and ac-
cepts the resulting conditions let him not complain and
seek sympathy for his hard lot, for he has deliberately
chosen that lot and must abide by his choice, work out
its Karma and learn its resulting lessons.

If man and wife cannot fulfill the vow by living
in love and harmony, it is far better for their Soul-
growth to ask the third party—the law of the land—to
release them from it. For there is nothing more detrimental to spiritual advance than nuptial inharmony,
because of the perpetuation of the inharmony through
the creative power and because of the inharmonious
and impure creations brought forth. It is also far better for the children of such a union to pass through
the experience a legal separation of the parents might

entail than to be brought up in an atmosphere where love, trust and understanding were lacking and inharmony reigned.

When the Laws of God and man have been complied with, the consummation of the union in pure and holy love is a sacrament.[1] Under such conditions, if at the time the thoughts are exalted and pure, and the creative energy is permitted to function through its normal and natural channel, there will be upon the spiritual-plane a creation which will correlate with the Divine Creative Force and draw to the participants a wonderful blessing and help, while upon the mental plane thought-forms of purity will gather as a protecting band around the unborn child to ward off all inimical and evil influences, and a perfect body should result. Also, through the spiritual force drawn upon, an advanced Soul may be attracted to the body. If the desire is to create the body of a child it should be looked upon as a sacred and religious rite; for there is nothing more important to the Race than the perfecting of the vehicles for its continuance and its upliftment. This is far more important than building churches, preaching sermons or sending missionaries to the "heathen." The thoughts of both parents should be concentrated upon an exact mental picture of the body they desire and the creative act should be carried out with this ideal in mind, and in the greatest purity of thought. Thus there can be created a beautiful love-child which will be a blessing and a joy throughout life. If a physical body is created when it is not wanted it is created by the mere husks of the creative force, while the real power of creation is expended on other planes in following out whatever

---

1   "A sacrament is an outward and visible sign of an inward and spiritual grace."

pattern is set by the desires. Since the thoughts were not concentrated on the physical plane to produce a perfect body, such a child is robbed, and will naturally lack a part of its birthright, the whole Race being proportionately defrauded.

All life comes from the One Life of the Absolute and normally should evolve back to God in perfect purity and harmony, but instead everything that grows, be it herb or animal, has to contend with the malign influence of the perverted currents of life-force, the result of man's misuse of the creative power. This is a literal fulfillment of the curse recorded in *Genesis*,[1] "Cursed is the ground[2] for thy sake." The curse was not pronounced because of the act of one man and woman, nor was it because the Third Race (symbolized by Adam and Eve) fell into generation, for the power to create was the great gift given to the humanity of this globe by the Elohim. With the gift the Divine Guidance to use it aright was also given, but as early as the latter part of that Race in direct disobedience to that Guidance mankind began to abuse and pervert it. And humanity has perpetuated that mistake ever since. The curse was not pronounced as a punishment, but was merely a statement of the natural consequences which would follow the use of the creative power in a perverted way. "Thorns also and thistles shall it bring forth to thee," and also "in sorrow shalt thou eat of it all the days of thy life." Even in eating our choicest fruits, when partaken of ere they have gained the victory (ripened) over the adverse conditions resulting from currents of perverted life-force, we suffer.

If the Race is to be propagated in vileness, every child that is born must bear the burden of a thought

---

1 III, 17.
2 Meaning the entire planet, mistranslated "ground."

of something vile and impure connected with its birth. It is no wonder that children so conceived have little love or respect for their unwilling parents. Children born in love and purity, while subject to this world Karma or "in bondage to the flesh," will still be overshadowed by a mantle of purity which will ward off many temptations to impurity and vileness, and will find their environment such as to lead them in paths of purity rather than in byways of evil. For this reason the salvation of the Race depends upon the pure in heart conceiving children in love and purity, for if the perpetuation of the Race is left to the impure and ignorant, conditions must grow worse.

Without this thing which we are wont to look upon as vile and impure the Race would very soon become extinct. And if mankind continues to debase and degrade this great gift the Race will still become extinct, for, as we have said above, nearly all diseases can be traced to the perverted activity of the creative force.

In reality sexual desire is but the effort of the Soul to express Divine Love through the physical vehicle and should be looked upon as the lower or negative pole of that Love, and God is Love. When we debase, degrade and befoul sexual desire we are debasing the highest physical expression of the God within us. Just so long as parents fail to fill their children's minds with thoughts of the purity and the holiness of the sex relations, the thought that it is evil or vile will be perpetuated in the Race. Just so long as it is thought of as something unclean and vile, just so long will it be so; for the creative power of thought will clothe itself in the vile garments of the impure ideas, and the sins of the fathers will be visited upon the children unto the third and fourth generation.

Purify, then, not only your acts, *but your thoughts*. Persistently refuse to entertain impure ideas. Combat them with ideas of Purity and Divine Love. This does not mean, however, that you should deliberately close your eyes and refuse to admit or recognize that there is evil in the world. For a wise physician must recognize the first symptoms of a disease that he may combat it ere it gains a foothold. Remember, always, that knowledge is power. Learn to look things in the face with a full consciousness of *your power to create good* where evil now exists. For, "As a man thinketh in his heart so is he."

NOTE: For the methods of transmuting the sex-forces in those who are not married, see the chapter on "The Sex Problem" in *Letters from The Teacher,* Curtiss.

CHAPTER XVII

THE ORIGIN OF MAN

"In the day that God created man, in the likeness
of God made he him; male and female created he
them; and blessed them, and called their name
Adam, in the day when they were created."
Genesis, V, 1-2.

"Man is a little world—a microcosm inside the
great universe." *Isis Unveiled*, Blavatsky, Vol I, 212.

There is much speculation among students of all
schools in regard to the origin of man. Some hold to the
orthodox idea that God literally fashioned a man out of
clay and in some mysterious manner animated him with
breath. Others hold to the Darwinian theory that man and
the ape descended from a common ancestor, both being
the result of a wholly physical and more or less mechani-
cal evolution. Between these extremes the great mass of
thinking people are seeking something more satisfying to
a rational mind than the former and more elevating than
the latter. To this great class there comes from out the ages
the arcane teachings of those Great Souls who reached
their godlike state before this world was born and who
have been the manipulators of the evolutionary law under
which this planet and its inhabitants have reached their
present state. These Great Souls have always been and
still are the Guides and Teachers of mankind, hence those
whose reason postulates or whose intuition recognizes
such godlike Beings can safely accept Their teachings,
for They are in a position to know. This ancient wis-

dom has never been lost, but because of man's gradual refusal to accept and follow it during his ages of darkness and ignorance it has been temporarily withdrawn from the public teachings and carefully preserved, although always accessible to every Soul who seeks it by the right method and in the right spirit.

There are reasonable grounds for both the above mentioned theories. Man has both a spiritual evolution which comes from above and a material evolution which belongs to the earth. His physical body is the highest attainment of a physical evolution through all the lower kingdoms where it has passed through stages analogous to the mineral, vegetable and animal, in an ethereal form corresponding to the stages through which the planet passed in previous Rounds.[1] His spiritual evolution is the result of the voluntary descent of Immortal Egos into more or less perfected human-animal bodies, and Their subsequent effort to control and spiritualize those animal organisms. These arcane teachings, preserved in their purity upon imperishable records through all the ages, tell us that during each Day-period or Round seven Great Races follow each other successively, each being made up of seven sub-races which in turn are composed of many tribes, kingdoms and nations. These Races and sub-races do not begin suddenly or end abruptly to make way for the next, but overlap for untold ages ere the old gives way to the new. For example: "The majority of mankind belongs to the seventh sub-race of the Fourth Root-Race. The . . . Chinaman and their off-shoots and branchlets (Malayans, Mongolians, Tibetans, Hungarians, Finns and even the Esquimaux)

1　See Chapter XV.

are all remnants of this last off-shoot,"[1] although humanity is already entering the sixth sub-race of the Fifth
Great Race of the Fourth Round. And some few children
are even now being born who will become the teachers
and prophets who will prepare for the coming of the
Sixth Great Race.

Following the cyclic Law, each of the tribes, nations, sub-races and Great Races has its humble birth,
its youth, its maturity (during which it reaches the zenith
of its power) then its gradual decline, decay, and final
disappearance, as the recorded history of nations known
today clearly shows. All that a Race acquires, however,
is stored up to reappear in its purity in the next Race.
The reason for the decay is that the Race has acquired all
that its physical evolution enables it to express. Further
accumulation of knowledge must be postponed until a
finer and more responsive organism has been evolved.
Therefore while an entirely new Race seems to appear,
in reality it is but the reincarnation of those Souls who
composed the former Races. In this Round the majority
of persons in the western nations have evolved through
the Fourth Great Race and through the sub-races of the
Fifth (Aryan) to the point where they are now just entering its sixth sub-race, although among all nations there
are laggards belonging to less evolved sub-races.

During the first Great or Root- (Polar) Race, the
germs of that which was to become man were sleeping as it were through the chaotic conditions of the
then ethereal world, a sleep of oblivion in the waters
of the uncreate. Hence man today can have little comprehension of this First Race. As the Spirit of God
moved upon the face of the waters misty or cloud-
like forms composed of but two elements — air and

---

1   *The Secret Doctrine*, Blavatsky, Vol II, 188.

water—arose, having a sentient life yet not human intelligence. These cloud-like forms "composed of the most ethereal matter compatible with objectivity" took the shape of "gigantic semi-human monsters, the first attempt of material nature at building human bodies."[1] This was the Second or Hyperborean Race. This Race was sexless, their mode of reproduction being by fission or division, just as a cloud might separate into two parts. These misty forms became more and more dense by the gradual absorption of a new element, earth, until "The Second Race being also sexless, evolved out of itself, at its beginning, the Third, Androgyne Race by an analogous, but already more complicated process. . . The emanations that came from their bodies during the seasons of procreation were ovulary; . . developing into a large soft, egg-like vehicle, which gradually hardened, when, after a period of gestation, it broke and the young human animal issued from it unaided, as the fowls do in our Race."[2] Not a strange procedure when we remember that even today a child is born in a membranous sack or "a large soft egg-like vehicle." At the middle point of this Second Race "He is still gigantic and ethereal, but growing firmer and more condensed in body; a more physical man yet still less intelligent than spiritual, for mind is a slower and more difficult evolution than is the physical frame."[3] These primitive beings were still composed of astral matter and today would not be visible, hence they left no physical traces by which science might discover them. "The evolution of the *physiological* man out of the astral races of the *early* Lemu-

---

1   *Ibid*, Vol. II, 146.
2   *Ibid*, Vol II, 175.
3   *Ibid*, Vol I, 211.

nan age—the Jurassic age of Geology—is exactly par-
alleled by the 'materialization' of 'spirits' (?) in the
seance room."[1] Only toward the middle of the Third
Race (Lemurian) did solid bones develop, the sexes separate, the body become "clothed with coats of skin" and
take on the human form as we know it today, although
at that time it was of gigantic proportions.[2] It was from
this point onward that truly human evolution began, as
symbolized in the *Bible* by Adam and Eve. Previous to
this time the Races were cold-blooded like the present
day amphibians, reptiles, fishes and the invertebrates,
taking on the temperature of their surroundings, but
from this point on humanity gradually became warm-
blooded and maintained a constant body temperature.
Thus it will be seen that man is truly the microcosm of
the macrocosm. For in his physical development and in
his modes of procreation he has passed through all the
stages Nature has used and still uses in the lower kingdoms. The mineral reproduces by exuding its essence;
the vegetable by budding or by seeds, each part of the
plant as a slip being capable of reproducing the entire
plant just as a part of Adam's body (his rib) reproduced
Eve; and the animal by the sexual process.

The above refers merely to the evolution of the animal body of man, and in some respects may resemble
the Darwinian hypothesis, the great difference being
that according to these teachings the beginnings of
man were not upon the physical-plane and all stages
were not passed through in physical matter. This is
why science has ever failed in its search for the "missing link" or the "common ancestor" of man and the

---

1   Ibid, Vol. II, 778.
2   "There were giants in the earth in those days; and also after that." *Genesis*,
    VI, 4.

ape. Man did not descend from the ape or from a common ancestor, but the ape descended from man, being the perverted and degenerate offspring resulting from the sins of the latest Third and early Fourth Races.[1]

After the middle of the Third Race a dual evolution begins. Spiritual Beings (called Solar Fathers or Pitris) who had reached their high estate on previous World Chains, consciously descended to earth and breathed into the human-animal forms "the breath of life," as recorded in *Genesis*. That which is called the breath was something with which animal man was then endowed, a power and capacity added to the mere animal consciousness he possessed before; for it was the breath of Divine Life, a human Soul, a spiritual overshadowing. This same teaching is represented in *Genesis* by the Adam of the first chapter being created but a sexless animal, the culmination and last of animal creation; the Adam of the second chapter first being created a bi-sexual animal, then being endowed with a human Soul. This Adam (the early Third Race) was created before the animals and each animal was brought to him to be named. Later on this Adam evolved out of his bi-sexual state into that of the separated sexes, Adam and Eve. Then "the Sons of God (semi-divine Beings) saw the daughters of men (the evolved human-animal forms) that they were fair; and they took them wives of all which they chose,"[2] and begat the future sub-races. The union of the Sons of God with the daughters of men added to the elements in humanity (air, water, earth) a new element, fire, or intellect. Fire is a sacred and higher element which only comes to earth as the gift of the gods to man and man alone of all creation

---

1   See Chapter III.
2   *Genesis*, VI, 2.

can control it and use it unafraid. But only the highest of
the human forms were ready, hence comparatively few
received the divine incarnation, while many received
the spark of self-consciousness and still more received
but an overshadowing of the semi-divine Beings who
in future stages of evolution were ultimately to become
their Fathers-in-heaven. "Some projected a Spark. Some
deferred till the Fourth. . . Those who entered became
Ahrats. Those who received but a Spark, remained des-
titute of (higher) knowledge. . . . The Third remained
mindless.' This stanza contains, in itself, the whole key
to the mysteries of evil, the so-called Fall of the Angels,
and the many problems that have puzzled the brains of
the Philosophers from the time that the memory of man
began. It solves the secret of the subsequent inequalities of intellectual capacity, of birth and social position,
and gives a logical explanation of the incomprehensible
Karmic course throughout the eons which followed."[1]
These differences were not the result of injustice, but
were due to the inequalities of the animal organisms,
just as we find today in a field of wheat—all of which
was planted at the same time, with the same seed, and
in the same soil—varying degrees of perfection, some
ripe for the harvest, others unripe, others not yet begun
to head out. The great Law shows no partiality. All will
reach their perfection in due season.

As involution progressed the response of matter to the molding and guiding power of Spirit
became less and less, proportionate to the increasing density of the forms through which it had to act.
And only when the human brain had evolved into
a fit instrument to respond to the Divine Spark could

---

1   *The Secret Doctrine*, Blavatsky, Vol. II, 170-171.

man become a rational self-conscious being. Until then he was merely a human-animal, begetting his kind according to animal instinct but unable consciously to create according to his will and desire. "He has now a perfectly concrete or compacted body, at first the form of a giant-ape, and now more intelligent, or rather cunning, than spiritual. For, on the downward arc, he has now reached a point where his primordial spirituality is eclipsed and overshadowed by nascent mentality. In the last half of the Third (Race) his gigantic stature decreases and his body improves in texture, and he becomes a more rational being, though still more an ape than a Deva." [1]

The Fourth Race, like the Fourth Globe or Round, is the lowest point of involution, or the turning point. The gift of mind having evolved through all the ages of the Third, and the first part of the Fourth Race, reached its truly human stage about the middle point of the Fourth. "The (hitherto) dumb races acquired our (present) human speech on this Globe, on which, from the Fourth Race, language is perfected and knowledge increases."[2] At that time the psychic powers held sway but were beginning to be dominated by the rapidly developing intellect and will. Under the guidance of his Divine Ancestors man had been taught all the arts and sciences as well as the control and proper use of all the powers within himself and in Nature. When he had grown up as it were, his divine Instructors withdrew leaving him free to use his powers as he would, and of his own free-will put into practice the precepts They had inculcated. But with the exercise of free-will the temptation to use his great knowledge for his own sensuous pleasure and for his selfish aggrandizement was too great and gradually

1   *Ibid*, Vol. I, 211.
2   *Ibid*, Vol. I, 211.

he chose to follow the lure of the senses rather than the call of the Spirit. It was during this period of evolution that the seeds of Karma were sown, whose terrible harvest the world as a whole has been and still is reaping even unto this day. His spiritual Progenitors, seeing the awful results of man's failure, in love and mercy, temporarily removed the greater part of the Race from the scene of its debasement through the great cataclysms which destroyed the continent of Atlantis, a memory of which is recorded in the scriptures of many nations today as the Great Flood.

Many legends are extant concerning the nations of that Fourth or Atlantean Race. And today a new interest in their histories is awakening in the minds of all classes of thinkers, and many theories and even circumstantial accounts are being given out concerning their civilizations. The reason for this is that those Souls who formerly composed the Atlantean Race are now reincarnating in large numbers in the western world where they must re-acquire their former knowledge, redeem the failures of the past, and rise to a higher stage of spirituality than ever before.

The Atlantean Race was the culminating point in the evolution of the physical, mental, and psychic powers. Their intellectual powers had reached as great perfection as their physical and psychic powers, but spirituality was more or less dormant. The result was that they controlled and manipulated the physical and psychic currents of force and dominated both the animal and elemental worlds. They thus reached a stage of civilization in some respects far higher than man has subsequently attained. In our present Race, however, this same degree of perfection must again be attained, but dominated by the higher spiritual evolution. It is this culmination that we are now rapidly attaining and for which the advanced Souls of the former Race are again incarnating. It is the Atlantean civilization which is symbolized by the Tower of Babel, a civilization whose base rested on earth but whose top reached into the higher realms farther than man of that day was entitled to go. By the perversion and debasement of their powers, their impurity and selfishness, they fell into monstrous evils. Striving only for personal power and gratification many became terrible black magicians, misusing and perverting the forces of life.

All, however, were not wicked; some followed the precepts of their divine Teachers and used their great powers for good. Certain of these were gathered together—especially out of the fifth sub-race—and during the sixth and seventh sub-races were taught by the "Sons of God" how to perpetuate the sacred teachings and carry them over the period of the cataclysms which marked the close of the Race. They thus became the teachers and guides of future Races, as symbolized by the *Bible* story of Noah. During the sixth and seventh sub-races all classes were warned of the coming disasters by their spiritual Teachers and were exhorted to repentance and a change of life. All who listened and believed escaped and settled in various distant mountainous regions. This teaching is corroborated by the discovery today, in such widely separated countries as Egypt, India, Central and South America, of similar and even identical hieroglyphics, symbols, architecture, etc. The reign of the black magicians grew worse and worse and the enslavement of their fellow men and the perversion of their forces became more awful until the earth's crust could no longer withstand the perverted currents of force, and after a series of cataclysms lasting through the sixth and seventh sub-races it finally sank beneath the waves. Owing to these cataclysms great numbers emigrated to distant lands and became the seed from which sprang the great masses of the present Race. In fact, the yellow races of Eastern Asia today are their direct descendants.

History repeats itself, and the same thing is happening today. Humanity is being warned through various sources. Prophets today as of old are proclaiming the near approach of catastrophes and cataclysms and the call to repentance, love, and brotherhood is heard in the land. The approaching cataclysms, however, will not be as widespread as those of Atlantis, the close of this cycle being but the close of a sub-race (fifth) instead of a Great Race.

The Fifth Great Race is our present red or white Aryan Race, the characteristic of which is the increasing spiritualization of matter through man. Up to the turning point at the middle of the Fourth Race spirit was being involved into matter, but from that time on matter has been evolving toward Spirit. We have evolved through the sub-races of this Fifth Race until we are now just entering upon its sixth sub-race. During this coming sub-race the seed will be planted of that which will be reaped by the Sixth Great Race, just as the fifth sub-race of the Atlanteans planted the seed of this present Fifth Great Race. This Fifth Race, however, has some sixteen thousand years of its cycle still left ere the close of its seventh sub-race and the great cataclysms which will mark its end.

In the Sixth Great Race the Christ-principle will find its greatest expression, and its greatest power in and over matter, thus spiritualizing and lifting both life and matter on all planes into a higher state. This Race must also witness the culmination and fulfillment through Divine Love of all the efforts put forth during all previous Races. Thus will it usher in the Golden Age. This Race will cover but a short period of time as compared with the earlier Races.

The Seventh Race will bring into manifestation the Golden Age and synthesise all that has been gained, thus becoming the great Fulfillment, the culmination of man's evolution in this Day-period or Round. During this Race the highest attainments of man's evolution will be gathered up preparatory to informing the humanity of a new Globe or Day-period, the Fifth Round.

As in the days of Atlantis, so today. Those whose hearts can respond to the higher note today being imparted to humanity through the various avenues of teaching utilized by the Progenitors of man, will first be prepared then gathered together into a definite Center of civilization where they can have an opportunity to receive the direct teaching and guidance of the same Great Souls who have always prepared for the re-unfoldment of wisdom at certain cyclic intervals. This great Center, however, will not be limited to any one sect, avenue of teaching or any one organization, society, or order, but will be composed of all those symbolized in *Revelation* by the mystic "hundred and forty and four thousand" who stood on Mount Sion "having their Father's name written in their foreheads." In other words, those who have received their mystical name and through the power of The Christ have developed their spiritual perceptions. Every movement which is striving to give out pure spiritual teachings is an avenue used by the Great Ones to reach a certain class of persons, but only those who are ready and have received the mystic mark in their foreheads will be able to enter in.

The Order of the 15, being composed largely of the reincarnated Souls who in the days of ancient Atlantis were entrusted with the task of preparing a place of refuge and promulgating the arcane teachings, must again take up the reincarnated work; for ideas, teachings and movements incarnate as well as Souls. All who at that time responded to its call will naturally be attracted to this particular movement today, and according to their point of development and the work they accomplished then will they be given a special place and a special work to do in the preparation for the coming of the new sub-race. Many who repudiated the teachings in those days and through the resulting suffering have learned their lessons will through this Order be given another opportunity to retrieve the past and take an advanced step in their spiritual life.

CHAPTER XVIII

"Now the serpent was more subtil than any beast of the field which the Lord God had made. And he said unto the woman, Yea, hath God said, Ye shall not eat of every tree of the garden? And the woman said unto the serpent, We may eat of the fruit of the trees of the garden: but of the fruit of the tree which is in the midst of the garden, God hath said, Ye shall not eat of it, neither shall ye touch it, lest ye die. And the serpent said unto the woman, Ye shall not surely die: For God doth know that in the day ye eat thereof, then your eyes shall be opened, and ye shall be as gods, knowing good and evil" *Genesis*, III, 1-5.

In that remote period, during which both sacred and profane history admit the fact that the gods confabulated with infant humanity, the serpent was the symbol of the god Saturn (in Egypt Sat-An, later Saturn), giver of esoteric Wisdom, one of the Elohim, the Sons of God. He is referred to in *Job* as the Great Initiator sent by the Lord to test Job,[1] the whole book of Job being the story of an initiation. From the earliest ages the serpent was recognized as the symbol of Esoteric Wisdom. Many nations worshiped it as the symbol of the Sun, the Giver of Life. Only during the Dark Ages of medieval history was it degraded and limited to signify the force of evil or D-evil. Jesus recognized the serpent as a symbol of good when He admonished His disciples: "Be ye therefore wise as serpents and harmless as doves." The Assyrian priests were called Serpents, as were also the Druid priests. The

---

1   *Job* I, 6.

Masters of Wisdom, and all Initiates into the Sacred
Mysteries, are called *Nagas*, or Serpents of Wisdom,
because, by overcoming temptation they are said to have
cast off their outer skin and to have been "born again,"
thus becoming Sons of Will and Wisdom, and immortal; they have met the Great Initiator and have wrested
from him his Rod of Power. Again the serpent is an old
glyph for the Astral Light, the medium of both white and
black magic, good in its spiritual aspect, but evil in its
lower. "The primitive symbol of the serpent symbolized
divine Wisdom and Perfection, and has always stood
for psychical Regeneration and Immortality."[1] Hermes
called the serpent the most spiritual of all creatures.
Moses, initiated into the wisdom of Hermes, called it,
"More subtil than any beast of the field." "The strange
veneration in which the Ophites held the serpent which
represented Christos may become less perplexing if
the students would but remember that at all ages the
serpent was the symbol of divine wisdom, which kills
in order to resurrect, destroys but to rebuild the better.
Moses is made a descendant of Levi, a serpent-tribe.
Gautama-Buddha is of a serpent-lineage, through the
Naga (serpent) race of kings who reigned in Magadha.
Hermes, or the god Taaut (Thoth), in his snake-symbol
is Tet; and according to the Ophite legends, Jesus or
Christos is born from a snake (divine Wisdom or Holy
Ghost) i.e., he became a Son of God through his initia-
tion into the 'Serpent Science.'[2]

From time immemorial the serpent has symbolized the sex-force, good when lifted up—as Moses

---

1   *The Secret Doctrine*, Blavatsky, Vol. 1, page 102. The Sacred Dragon of
    China and Japan, indicating the divine origin of the rulers, has the same
    significance.

2   *Isis Unveiled*, Blavatsky, Vol. 484.

lifted it up in the wilderness, that all who were suffering and dying from the stings of the poisonous vipers (perversions of the sex-force) might be healed by the vision of Purity revealed by the Brazen Serpent–evil when allowed to crawl in the mire of earth, biting the heel of the woman and placing enmity between her seed and it. It is said that: "Before our globe became egg-shaped — and the Universe also—'a long trail of cosmic dust (or fire-mist) moved and writhed like a serpent in space. ' "[1] Thus our globe was prepared by the serpent-force for the great test humanity came to this planet to experience, *i.e.*, the ability to control the creative power and create "in the image of God," through the spiritualization and perfect blending of the separated sexes. This great lesson when learned will enable man to become "as one of us" or Divine.

After man became involved in matter (as outlined in Chapter XIII) and the androgynous Third Race had gradually evolved through its various stages the separation of the sexes took place. This, however, was not a sudden change affecting the entire Race, but was the result of a gradual evolution lasting through the entire latter half of that Race. This is symbolized by the story of Eve being taken from Adam, *solus*, while he was in a deep sleep, the deep sleep being the *pralaya* or night-period between the Third and Fourth Races, during which the separation was perfected. The word Adam means "red earth" and refers to the Third Race in which the humanity of the Red Ray was first clothed in an earthly body. The Adam and Eve spoken of later as one man and one woman, symbolize the sexes functioning separately in the great

---

1 *The Secret Doctrine*, Vol. I, p. 103. Many ancient people believed that the earth was hatched from a serpent's egg.

Atlantean or Fourth Race. Hence at the dawn of the
Fourth Race the androgynous forms of the early Third
Race had disappeared and only the separated sexual
forms known to us today remained.

In one sense the Garden of Eden symbolizes the pure
and perfect physical body in which infant humanity
was originally clothed. According to the same symbology the Tree which is in the midst of the Garden is the
spinal cord, the sap of which is the *Kundalini-force*[1]
(serpent-force), a dynamic creative power functioning
through the spinal cord, its lower aspect being expressed
through the sex organs, and its higher aspect functioning
through the pineal gland.[2] The Fruit of this Tree is the
spiritual power gained as the result of the opening of
that what is known as the Third Eye. As man, through
experience, gains Wisdom he uses this mystic power
gradually to bring about its higher physical manifestations as well as the psychic and spiritual. It slowly
ascends the spinal cord through the central canal until
it reaches and stimulates into activity the pineal gland,
the functioning of which is called the opening of the
Eye of Wisdom. It is not, however, the physiological
change in this organ which opens man's consciousness
to Divine Wisdom, but—following the biological law
"function makes structure"—it is the attainment of the
higher function which results in the anatomical and
physiological change. Only through the functioning of
this *Kundalini* power can mankind gain the experience
that both good and evil have to teach.

A moment's thought as to these early symbol-

---

1 "The 'power' and the 'World Mother' are names given to the kundalini-one
of the mystic 'Yogi powers'. . . . It is an electro-spiritual force, a creative
power which when aroused into action, can as easily kill as it can create."*The
Voice of the Silence*, Blavatsky. Note to page 9.
2 'The Third Eye, or Seat of the Soul.

isms will show that there is an underlying meaning common to all (Saturn the Initiator, Satan the Tempter, the Astral Light, the Creative Power of sex, et cetera), namely, that it is, in very truth, the power to become "as gods" that is indicated. Being the distinctive heritage of the Fourth Race, this power to create sexually became at one and the same time the great temptation and *the great opportunity*. In fact, it was the one experience for which this globe was created and for which humanity fell into generation and became clothed with "coats of skin."

The infant Race at its outset was confronted by the Initiator, Saturn, the Serpent, who was commissioned to impart, as the crowning gift, the creative power—which humanity only then was prepared to receive. The so-called "temptation" was but a test of man's ability either to use or abuse this divine gift. Ever since that time man and woman, individually, have had to meet the same test. Man created *in the image of God*, and endowed with the God-power of creativeness, must prove his ability to use this power wisely, or, through its abuse, learn the lesson and gain through suffering the experience that physical existence in separated sexes alone can teach. The power was given him not as a temptation but as a step in evolution through which he must pass in perfect purity. Just as in this day a teacher who gives out a new advanced truth is condemned for the evil resulting from its misuse, so Saturn (Satan), has had to bear the responsibility arising from the failure of man to use the creative power in purity and holiness. Man has chosen to become "as gods" knowing the evil through the misuse of this power, but, ere the cycle closes, must become "as gods" to know the good.

The culmination of his degradation was reached by the Atlanteans, who not only used this force for animal gratification, but also perverted it to accomplish their horrible practices of black magic. It was for this sin that the continent of Atlantis and most of its inhabitants were destroyed.[1] While the sinking of Atlantis destroyed much of the dangerous knowledge of how to pervert this force into black magic or evil, yet enough remained to perpetuate evil and misery on earth and make a hell out of what was given to man to be his Paradise. The whole experience, including the sin and suffering which the perversion of this force has created, is an initiation, not only for the Race, but also for the planet, which when successfully passed will make the planet the completion of the octave of this system and the beginning of a new and greater system.

The banishment of Adam and Eve from Eden was due to the fact they could not face the Flaming Sword of Purity, which turned every way and barred them from obtaining the Fruit of the Tree. This banishment meant that man could no longer dwell in the etherealized body (Eden) with his spiritual faculties freely functioning and able to talk face to face with God. Instead, the Immortal Soul is forced to dwell in a body of dense physical matter with the spiritual centers dormant, so that only by the sweat of his brow can he obtain spiritual bread. This means that only by laborious effort can man open the inner doors that communicate with the higher planes and consciously bring to himself the spiritual food upon which his Soul

---

1   The destruction recorded in Babylonian, Chaldean, Hebrew and other Scriptures, in the story of the great flood.

must live. At every attempt to re-enter Eden man is met by the Angel of the Flaming Sword placed by God to guard the Tree of Immortal Life from man's impurity.

"Thou shalt surely die" is usually considered a penalty for man's defilement of Eden, but in reality even this death sentence was but the working of the immutable Law of Divine Love; for immortality under conditions of impurity, sickness and suffering, would be a punishment far surpassing even the medieval conceptions of a physical hell. Only when man can face this Sword of the Spirit and allow it to cleave from him every cloak of impurity and once more enter the Garden naked but not ashamed, can he meet "The Lord God walking in the Garden in the cool of the day." "The cool of the day" refers to the close of the cycle of wandering outside the Garden, the "day-period" the period of stress and strain, of heat and passion, which both the individual and the Race must face and conquer ere they can attain poise or cool, quiet perception, in which state alone they can become aware of the Lord God or the Law of Good manifesting in the garden of their human personality.

The so-called temptation was the act of one of the Sons of God who was the direct channel through which the power to create reached humanity. The giver of this gift, Saturn, or Lucifer, Star of the Morning, is a bright Archangel, who "fell" or descended from heaven to confer this gift of immortality upon man. Saturn or Satan is that aspect of Jehovah which brought humanity its great test, and in this sense may be regarded as its tempter or Initiator, while Lucifer is the aspect of that same force which confers the crown of victory on those who conquer.

There are many passages referring to him as one of the Elohim.

"This personification denominated *Satan* is to be contemplated from three different planes: the *Old Testament*, the Christian Fathers, and the ancient Gentile attitude. He is supposed to have been represented by the Serpent in the Garden of Eden; nevertheless, the epithet of Satan is *nowhere in the Hebrew sacred writings* applied to that or any other form of ophidian."[1] His so-called "fall" was by no means one of sin or failure, but a voluntary descent to earth to bring to man the Creative Fire, the gift of the gods; for only through the mastery and proper use of this force can immortality be obtained. The story of Prometheus is but another expression of this ideograph.

There is no evil outside mankind that can produce a Satan in the orthodox sense of a devil. It is only through terrible perversions of the creative power that it has become the Evil or D-evil. As time passed, by his vile, lustful thoughts on this subject and his misuse of the life-force, man has created a composite thought-form which may be said to be entitized into a living force of evil (commonly called the devil), which, with an army of so called lesser devils, arrayed in serried ranks, continually fights against the power of Good (God). These are the vipers that tormented the Children of Israel, and all other races. This army must be met by Good, and will be annihilated only when thought-forms of Purity are sent forth by man in sufficient numbers and force to overcome the evil creations. Being the creation of man, functioning in his lowest aspect, this evil can be conquered

---

1   *Isis Unveiled*, Blavatsky, Vol. II, 481.

only by man, its creator. The conquering must take the form of a transmutation, *i.e.*, the substitution of vitalized thoughts of love and purity for those of lust and evil.

In the childhood of the Race a great wave of serpent worship, originally intended to symbolize this truth in its purity, spread over the world. This, however, in time became degraded, and the reptile itself was finally worshiped as a god. It was kept in a filthy den and the youth and beauty of the land were thrown to it for prey. It was fed on human beings until it grew fat and the stench of it filled all the Temple, even to the outer courts. Humanity is again walking in the same old paths, according to the law of cycles, and today is but repeating the sad story upon a higher plane (the mental). First, undue exaltation and worship, as witnessed in the days of phallicism, then materialization and consequent defilement, until today the world's idea of the serpent-power (Sex) is that of a monster grown fat upon the youth and beauty of the land.

The teachings in regard to the sex-function have always been held most sacred, and for this reason they have been veiled from humanity in general and revealed only to those whose purity of heart and life permitted them to grasp something of their deeper truths. Because of this veiling of the truth, there have sprung up in the minds of those not instructed in the Mysteries many misconceptions, chief of which is that this great God-given power is in and of itself inherently impure and accursed. This belief has given rise to doctrines which teach man to despise and try to kill out this greatest of gifts. But as long as this serpent of sex is accursed and degraded by man's thought, it is doomed to crawl upon the ground and bring forth its progeny of vipers in darkness and filth, and woman is doomed to conceive and bring forth in pain and suffering instead of Purity and Joy. Woman has suffered the most, but by that suffering she should have developed her spiritual intuition.

The sex-force is considered impure only because the spiritually blind have decreed that it shall be considered impure. They assume that they are wiser and holier than He who created them, He who breathed into them the Living Fire of creative force. Being wiser than the gods, they have decreed that the normal expression of the sex-function (within the married relation) shall be considered vile and that it shall be suppressed. The result is already apparent. Go over the world's history and you will find that, after every period[1] during which the marriage relation, consummated in pure and holy love, was relegated to second place in gaining spiritual development, and the normal sex-function was taught to be inherently impure and calculated to hold back the participants from spiritual growth and final liberation, that it was something to be suppressed and killed out, there invariably followed a wave of licentiousness in which filthy substitutes, practiced for so-called "mere physical relief," were not only condoned, but taught as preferable to the normal relation! and taught in the name of religion! or spiritual development! or "occult" or "esoteric" science!

If such practices were advocated by the outcasts of humanity the world would stand aghast, and societies for the suppression of the vice would quickly spring up. But when such perverted teach-

---

1   Periods during which celibacy was held to be the ideal.

ings are given out under the name of "spiritual" or "esoteric" truth (as though secrecy could make impurity pure!) by those who are well advanced upon the Path, many, many blinded ones forget even the common standards of morality and decency, and eagerly clutch at such an excuse for the gratification of inherent vileness under the cloak of "esoteric teaching" which lends to it an air of respectability. "The greater the height attained the more disastrous the fall." The greater the influence of such a teacher the more serious and far-reaching the effects of the lapse from Purity.

Instead of there being any latitude permitted to those who are advanced upon the Path of Attainment, *the rules are far more strict.* What would be but a slight lapse from virtue in a savage or in the ignorant, becomes a cyclone of iniquity sweeping many before it, in one who has entered the inner degrees of occultism; for upon each inner step every vibration is multiplied a thousand fold. This is why the disciple should absolutely master (gain perfect control of, not suppress) all life-forces ere he attempts to enter the inner degrees, or his failure is foreordained. Let this point be clearly understood, *there can be no spiritual teachings, of any kind, either esoteric of exoteric, that are not founded upon absolute Purity, not only of body but of mind.* The higher and more esoteric the teaching, the more rigid the standard of Purity. All planes interblend, and all acts upon the physical-plane have their correspondences upon all other planes. Therefore, what is impure on the lowest plane is a thousand times more so upon each successive inner plane. If a pilgrim were approaching a sacred shrine he would not knowingly enter with his feet slimed with the mud of the public highway, and hope to leave no stain upon the pure alabaster floor of the inner court, for even the faintest footprint would be more noticeable there than the filth that covered the public highway an inch deep.

This subject has been the greatest stumbling block for many teachers who are otherwise trying to uplift humanity, because it is *the greatest test* of the humanity on this globe. Only when this lesson is learned will others await it under different conditions: But there must be some brave Souls who are willing now to face the world's misconceptions and slander and stand boldly for the uplifting and purifying of this subject. The world must be taught the difference between the wise, *normal use* of this function in perfect purity, in the married relation only, and killing it out or suppressing it. Many talk loudly about "overcoming" and "killing out" this force, but if you could look into their hearts you would see that their "overcoming" is usually but satiety. They have crawled through the filthy places of life and have slimed their impure ideas of sex over everything until they have grown sick. Then they put on monkish habits, and talk loudly about having "outgrown all such animal instincts." Many others have never known anything but the impure side of sex. Their ideals have been so shattered by contact with the world's misconceptions that they, in their natural purity, have put the thought of it from them as something too vile to be considered. This shrinking from the subject is the natural result of the world's attitude. For, alas, even those who set themselves up as teachers on this subject are apt to but stir up the filth and leave things worse than they were before. This is invariably the rule if the world's standards of morality are ruthlessly set aside, especially those pertaining to the legal marriage relation, which is not only a sacred sacrament—a symbol of the Marriage of the Soul, the union with the Higher Self, becoming one with the Father-in-heaven—but is also a bulwark of safety to society that must never, *under any pretext*, be weakened.

As to the final disuse of this function: As long as man has his present anatomical structure and physiological functions he must learn how to bring to perfection, purify and use for its highest purpose the body and functions he now possesses and not waste time speculating on what conditions will obtain in future world-periods. For only when new conditions are given him can he grasp more advanced lessons. "It doth not appear what we shall be: "I shall be satisfied, when I awake, with thy likeness." But we cannot "awake" until we have purified and used every function we possess for the glory of God. Hence *The Order of the 15* desires to teach humanity how to prepare for the future by taking the next step here and now.

The time has come when woman must take her place as the Priestess of the Most High, the Revealer of Purity and Truth to man. She it is who must lift the corner of the veil that hides the face of the Divine Mother, Isis. Isis is called the Divine Mother because hers is the force, both in Nature and humanity, that brings forth. She is spoken of as having seven veils, alluding to the protection thrown around the sacred mysteries connected with the bringing into manifestation of the creative force (God-the-Father) sent out through the masculine expression. The seven veils are the mysteries upon the seven planes of consciousness and manifestation. The first and lowest of these veils, the mystery of physical birth, has never yet been lifted, nor can it be by profane hands. In the ancient Temples of Isis it was death to so much as touch the veil before Her shrine, and on many tablets recently unearthed a carven serpent has been found having seven heads, which symbolizes the same mystery. The Phoenicians are said to have originated the alphabet from the symbols made by the writhing of the sacred serpents. This was another advance (creation) in evolution attributed to the serpent-god Saturn, for letters serve to manifest ideas, and their invention placed man upon a new step in evolution.

Since through the ages woman has been made the plaything of man and taught to use her powers to entice and beguile him, as the only method by which she could attain her ends, in this new woman's era she is confronted with the task which her training makes most difficult, *i.e.*, the facing of herself and her real motives. For she must turn her feminine powers of love, intuition and beauty to the upliftment of the Race instead of to the beguilement of man that she may satisfy her vanity, love of conquest and desire for creature comforts. Although man, being the positive pole upon the earth-plane, by his superior physical powers has throughout the ages enslaved woman, still woman, upon the more subtle plane of desire, has dominated and enslaved man. Hence it is woman who must break the shackles, first of her own desires and then for the Race. This she can never do by playing upon man's chivalry to attain the gratification of her own ends, be those ends love, ambition, vanity, ease and comfort or whatnot. Many otherwise admir-

able women have debased their god-given instincts —
love of home and desire for children — first by awakening
and playing upon man's animal passions to satisfy their
ambition and then, by appealing to his chivalry, forcing
him into what must inevitably prove an unhappy marriage. For quite as many men are blinded and led from
the path of purity because of woman's ambitions and
desires as women are led astray through man's passion.
And until woman awakens to her responsibility and understands her real mission, *i.e.*, her power to play upon
man's heart, stimulate his noblest aspirations and thus
lead him to the heights of spiritual attainment instead of
into mere physical union without love, she will continue
to be the slave she is today in spite of any political or
social liberties she may obtain.

It is woman who must lift up the world's ideas of the
sex-force from the mire and degradation of man's misconceptions and give this great power its proper place in
the Temple of the Living God (the body) as the highest
expression of the Divine in man. Just as it was woman
who gave to man the apple of discord, so must woman
pluck the golden apples that grow at the top of the Tree
of Life and give them to man to eat.

CHAPTER XIX

PURIFICATION VERSUS DEIFICATION

"Hokhmah Wisdom is the Father, and Bina
Understanding is the Mother. When they connect
one with the other, they bring forth and diffuse and
emanate Truth." *Zoahr*, III, 290.

"And the woman was arrayed in purple and scarlet
colour, and decked with gold and precious stones
and pearls, having a golden cup in her hand full
of abominations and filthiness of her fornication."
Revelation XVII, 4.

We have had so many inquiries from earnest students
as to our teachings on the subject of sex, in addition to
those given in former lessons,[1] and as this subject has
been the stumbling block for mankind since its fall into
matter (middle of the Third Race), and as once more
a cyclic wave of the old phallic worship is sweeping
over the earth, it seems necessary that we define our
teachings on this subject so clearly and concisely that
the earnest seeker after truth may have no doubt of the
Path which we point out. Many pupils may feel that the
conditions herein outlined are exaggerated, that this lesson is uncalled for, and is touching a subject it is well
not to mention; but if there are any such, we advise them
to lay this lesson aside and permit us to be the judge of
its necessity and of the great cry from so many hearts to
be shown the straight and narrow way, and have some
clear and sound understanding of this subject.

As we stated in the previous chapter, the fall into

---

1   *Purity; The Symbol of the Serpent; Celibacy; The Meaning of the Cross.*

generation was simply an opportunity given humanity to meet and conquer a new and advanced step; that the temptation by the serpent recorded in *Genesis* was the great test for which the whole scheme of evolution on this planet (the middle or turning point of evolution), and the planet itself was created; that only when man, through the experience reaped by wading through the lower aspects of this problem, had reached a conception of its higher possibilities, could he fulfill the prophecy and become as the gods. Concerning the forbidden fruit the serpent told Eve that "In the day ye eat thereof . . . ye shall become as gods." This is applied to the life-essence or the ripened fruit of the tree. Adam and Eve had been expressly forbidden to eat of the tree until through their enlightened and purified love they had been able to lift up the serpent-force and eat of the fruit with a godlike understanding of its sacredness. Their disobedience was that they plucked and ate the unripened fruit in ignorance and merely for the gratification of their animal appetites. As the sex question is the one great issue of the whole evolution of this planet, he who is misled on this subject takes a path that can lead only to destruction. Many well-meaning teachers as they gain some idea of the sacredness and purity of the interchange of the sex-forces are easily led into giving the subject undue prominence, into tearing down the veil which hangs before the altar of all sacred mysteries, thus throwing themselves open, not only to the world's ridicule and censure, but also to the inrush of the hordes of the world's accumulated impure thoughts of phallic worship. This is inevitably true if their unconquered secret desires tend toward any form of self-indulgence. And very soon we find them permitting their minds to temporize with the world's standard of purity. Then departing little by little from the sacred instincts of purity and the innate modesty implanted in each heart to guide it—unless ruthlessly torn out, smothered or argued down by the high-sounding sophistries so readily furnished by the worshipers at the shrine of sexuality—they at length advocate either secret or semi-public orgies under the guise of spiritual ecstasy or some "advanced" conception of the sacredness of sexual intercourse. Others again make this subject a cloak under which they can revel in licentious thoughts and make their pretended desire an excuse for promiscuous intercourse, claiming to be above the Law, yet all the time in bondage to the "old queen of the world," the most tyrannous and ruthless of all rulers.

There are today many, many entities on the astral plane, some of them literally masters of evil, and others well-meaning but misled and misleading—called astral "guides"—who, taking advantage of this misconception of the symbol, are ready to give the most subtle teachings upon this subject to those who are awakening to the allurements of the astral plane and who think everything that comes from that plane must necessarily be Divine. Hence, there are many well-meaning persons who are today unthinkingly taking the first steps on the downward path by letting their minds dwell continually upon this subject, thus being drawn into vortices of sex-thought which very quickly obsess them so that they can think and talk of little else. They are desirous of doing right but disregard the voice of Intuition and fail to use common-sense and hence are misled on this point. There is nothing that so quickly leads to obsession as the constant dwelling upon the thoughts of sex.

This whole symbol has been grossly misunderstood. The serpent was Saturn the Initiator, and the day spoken of in which the Race should become as the gods has never yet dawned. To eat of the Tree of Life has nothing to do with the degradation of the physical creative act. The promise given to the Third Race—symbolized by Adam and Eve—that has been and still is being fulfilled was "cursed is the ground . . . in sorrow shalt thou bring forth." This was not an unjust punishment, for they were not left in ignorance. It was the willful disobedience of the Third Race acting in spite of the teachings of their Divine Instructors—and brought to its greatest degradation during the Fourth Race—which fastened the curse upon humanity. From the beginning of recorded history, yea, even before recorded history, man has floated on a sea whose motive-power was this force, and whose tides alternated between the lowest depth of degradation and the uplifting and deification of this function under various forms of phallic worship. "It was only in the Fourth Race that man, who had lost all right to be considered Divine, resorted to body worship, in other words, Phallicism."[1]

Whenever there has been an attempt to lift this subject out of the mire, immediately some few have gone to the extreme and have placed it upon a pinnacle for worship. This, however, is even more disastrous to humanity than its degradation. The sex-force is always creative, and, when degraded and perverted from functioning according to the law of generation will create upon the astral-plane monsters which, by

---

1 *The Secret Doctrine*, Blavatsky, Vol. II, p. 297.

their precipitating upon man sickness and disease—especially disorders of the mental and psychic
faculties—will the more quickly bring about his bodily
dissolution. It's deification creates a tempter, who, being
clothed in garments of self-righteousness and absolute
contentment with his own state, is endowed with an immense longevity which the monster does not possess,
and therefore has the power to delude the unwary victim
with plausible sophistry.

This law is graphically illustrated in Richard
Mansfield's version of the drama *Peer Gynt*, in which
he meets his perverted astral creations upon the mountain. These entities follow him and call him father until
his reason totters. All such creations man must face and
redeem either in this or some future incarnation, for like
Peer Gynt he is their father. Their mother is that perverted
feminine force an entitization of which is so graphically
described by Eliphas Levi. "Knowest thou that old queen
of the world who is on the march always and wearies
never? Every uncurbed passion, every selfish pleasure,
every licentious energy of humanity, and all its tyrannous
weakness, go before the sordid mistress of our tearful
valley. . . . That queen is old as time, but her skeleton is
concealed in the wreckage of women's beauty, which
she abstracts from their youth and their love. . . Her livid
and frozen body is clothed in polluted garments and tat-
tered winding sheets. . . . When she goes by, doors open
of themselves; she passes through walls; she penetrates
to the cabinets of kings; she surprises the extortioners
of the poor in their most secret orgies; she sits down at
their board, pours out their wine, grins at their songs with
her gumless teeth, takes the place of the lecherous cour-
tesan hidden behind their curtains. She delights in the

vicinity of sleeping voluptuaries; she seeks their caresses as if she hoped to grow warm in their embrace, but she freezes all those whom she touches and herself never kindles."[1] This seemingly fanciful picture refers to a great reality, for there is an entitized thought-form, born of man's lustful imaginings and woman's desires, which casts a glamour of youth and loveliness over man and appears in his dreams in the form of his most cherished ideal of womanhood to tempt him and draw from him the creative life-force upon which she lives. She appears especially to test those who are striving to purify their lives and conquer sex desire. If she is resisted and foiled in her purpose the glamour disappears and she is revealed as she is, the Ancient One, the Old Hag.

To get at the truth underlying this question we must separate the Divine Creative Essence entirely from its physical vehicles and get away from all its lower manifestations. Up to the middle of the Third Race humanity was androgynous, but soon after the separation of the sexes the early Atlanteans made their first departure from right living by worshiping form, or the human body and its functions. This period is alluded to in the *Bible*,[2] where it says that "The Sons of God saw the daughters of men that they were fair; and they took them wives of all which they chose."[3] Those called "sons of God" were the descendants of the first great spiritual Teachers (Rishis), while "the daughters of men" were what history refers to as the pre-Adamite races, which in the *Bible* were embraced under the symbol of Lillith. They were the mindless Races or the Races which had not yet received the divine spark from the Mind-

---

1   *Transcendental Magic*, Levi.
2   *Genesis* VI, 1-4.
3   See also "The Death of Lillis" in Thomas Moore's *The Loves of the Angels*.

Born. To bring the spark of mind to the mindless Races by taking them to wife was the duty of the "Sons of God." The sin was in using the power of mind to enhance the pleasures of mere sex contact. This was the beginning of the perversion and worship of sex. "The Demon of Pride, Lust, Rebellion and Hatred, had no being *before* the appearance of physical conscious man. It is man who has begotten and nurtured the fiend, and allowed it to develop in his heart; it is he, again, who has contaminated the Indwelling God in himself, by linking the pure Spirit with the impure Demon of Matter."[1] Since that early day, with every attempt to reform the thought of humanity on the sex question, there comes up this old mistake of man's deification of matter in his worship of the mere physical expression rather than the Divine Creative Force. But such attempts to reform are necessary, for only by a right understanding of this vital problem can man attain the ultimate goal of his evolution.

Therefore we wish to make it very clear to our students that, although the world is wrong in its attitude of looking upon this whole relationship as vile and wicked, and while we most ardently desire to purify the world's polluted stream of thought on this subject, still it is nevertheless true that the world's rules of conduct, established as a minimum after ages of experience, must be observed. Underneath every law of morality and every convention of society there stands a Divine Truth from which the law or conventionality has grown. Nothing can endure from generation to generation which is not rooted in Truth, although much evil may be grafted upon this root. Although from time to time, through

---

1   The Secret Doctrine, Blavatsky, Vol. II, p. 287.

the rebellion of great reformers against conventions and man-made laws, humanity has advanced, still in every such instance the rebellion was not so much against the convention or law itself as against the abuses and evils which were grafted upon it.

All that pertains to the sex relations belongs to the deep, mysterious workings of Divinity and is not to be brought publicly before the world. Humanity must travel the path of generation, until by conquering — which means learning all its lessons — it finds the gate of regeneration. Just as this was symbolized by Noah's ark, into which the animals went two by two, so must humanity enter the Ark of Safety — the Temple not made with hands, the ark built after the pattern given by God, the only thing that can ride the tempestuous sea of humanity — two by two, male and female. Until these twain, whom only God can make one flesh have literally deified, not the physical organs of generation, but the Divine Creative Force and by together learning the lessons of love and sacrifice, have discovered that there is Something apart, above and beyond mere physical union which can be brought forth only by the twain, and that this Something can never be brought down into matter, they can never say "It is finished." The very thought of opening the door of the sanctuary where this holy Something shines above the tabernacle, to an outsider or to a third party, let alone the gaze of the multitude, absolutely destroys it; for this Something is an emanation from the Omnipotent Creative Force of Divinity making the twain one in heaven although on earth they still manifest as two. It is this Divine Force which completes the Trinity; for that which completes the Trinity must always be Divine, never human. The top of the triangle must always be pointing up with the flame of the Divine Creative Force rising from its apex. To debase this symbol and try to represent it in matter by three human personalities; to permit any but the twain to enter the ark, is to point the apex of the triangle toward earth. In such a case the Divine Flame or the Fire of the Lord at once becomes the burning, consuming fire of passion which destroys the false worshipers. In other words, if through sexual excesses indulged in under the name of worship an attempt is made to create earthly fires, *i.e.*, sex-passion, upon the altar, you are like the priests of the false Baal—worshipers of perverted sex-force—unable to call down the Fire of the Lord to consume your sacrifice; but if, through devotion, pure love, and in the sanctity of *absolute privacy*, two Souls reach up to heaven and ask the divine blessing upon their union the Fire of the Lord descends and makes their sacrifice complete.

These departures from Purity—which, alas, almost everyone who has had much experience among socalled occult teachings has no doubt met with to a greater or lesser degree—do not take place all at once; they are insidious. The evil astral entities having once gained an entrance to the aura of the pupils, usually over the line of ambition, vanity, etc., at first flatter them with the idea that they are chosen to be great world-leaders or teachers, then their animal nature is stirred up and its manifestations disguised with high-sounding terms; or perhaps some mysterious relationship is hinted at to make the first departure from Purity seem natural and necessary, such as dual personalities requiring more than one vehicle to express the same Soul, etc. But no matter how brought about, the end is as sure as it is pitiful,

pitiful because the deluded one thinks the guidance is Divine. Such entities, animated by their own designs and given increased power by the perversion of the victims' sex-forces, teach them that there is some special reason why *they* are exempt from laws that are well enough for less evolved humanity; that true "freedom" includes freedom in sex relations, even that such sexual excesses are the only path to the heights of spiritual attainment. The instant such a departure from the one Law of Purity takes place the Divine Triangle is pointed downward; they have attempted to confine Spirit in matter, and like a consuming fire it will spread and will feed upon, first their higher ideals, then upon all their principles of right thought and conduct, until all that was beautiful in their natures is consumed, leaving only their gross and material nature which, no matter how they cloak it with the garments of sanctity and hypocrisy, the world will have no difficulty in recognizing. If the physical body of such a victim is coarse and strong its grossness becomes more and more apparent, but if the body is sensitive and finely organized such practices quickly bring about various nervous and mental affections, especially epilepsy, and in some cases insanity.

This brings us to one of our fundamental teachings which we repeat and emphasize here, namely, *no matter what the apparent source of any teaching and no matter how beautiful the language used*, DO NOT ACCEPT IT UNLESS IT MEETS THE TEST OF PURITY AND COMMON-SENSE,—*does not violate the moral code and is confirmed by the Intuition of your own Soul*. It is only common-sense to demand that teachings which profess a *higher* standard of purity than that of the world *must at least include* what the experience of the world holds as essential.

The woman referred to in our opening text symbolizes the mother-force or sex-force degraded. The cup of pure gold which she holds symbolizes something sacred which through her impurity is defiled and filled with abominations. In this case the cup symbolizes the place of generation through which the Divine Creative Force should manifest as regeneration, but which instead is filled with the abominations of man's own imaginings. She was ultimately consumed by the karmic fires spoken of above. [1]

As to our definite teachings on this subject we would say to our pupils USE COMMON-SENSE. Avoid both the *Scylla* of degradation and the *Charybdis* of undue exaltation of this force. Obey what the world calls the moral code, but infuse into the dead-letter of that code the Spirit of Divine Love. Realize that physical marriage is but the gross and earthly counterpart of the Divine Marriage of the Soul and that mistaken marriages which are not marriages of the Soul can be avoided if you will prayerfully listen to the Voice of Intuition and are not carried away by emotion, passion or desire for worldly gain. Above all examine your own heart and drive out all lustful desires and imaginings, for only the pure in heart shall see God. Purity of heart and mind will be a shield and buckler to protect you in the hour of temptation and guide your feet in safety over the narrow bridge which separates animal desire from spiritual ecstasy.

Sexual union is but the physical expression of man's ability to reach up to Divinity. For in the union of perfectly affinitized Souls there is a force brought into

---

1   *Revelation*, XVII, 16.

action which is greater than the physical senses can express, the senses are transcended and the Souls are lifted from human into Divine Love. This is the point where Divine Love touches and overlaps human love, but only when human love has grown so pure and sacred and holy that nothing human can express it, because it transcends the powers of the human mind to grasp. Only then is a new force brought into manifestation, a force which is the vehicle for a direct manifestation of the Divine. This force at one end unites into one flesh the twain, and at the other end unites them to the Godhead, or their mutual Father-in-heaven, thus making the perfect triangle. In such a union God is manifested through perfected and purified human love.

Let no one, however, be discouraged or think the day of attainment so far distant that there is no use trying, for the first step is right thinking on this subject; and the next is so to live as to be ready and worthy, for literally ye know neither the day nor the hour when the Son of Man cometh in His glory. The glory is the illumination which comes to every Soul who reaches this ideal conception of love, where the Divine overlaps and perfects the human. Some, having taken steps on this Path in past incarnations, have now to learn certain minor parts of the Law. They may find themselves compelled to learn these lessons alone, without an earthly companion to help them, but this does not prevent them from learning the lessons. If karmic Law has brought some close to the borderland between the human and the Divine through suffering, disappointment or ideal love trampled in the mire, nevertheless they can learn their lessons and often learn them more thoroughly than those more blessed, although forced to seek love only in the Divine because the human has failed them. There will come an incarnation when each Soul must step over the threshold between ideal mortal love and Divine Love hand in hand with the companion best fitted to make that correlation perfect. Nothing can be gained, however, by fretting or chafing at the Law, for what is really yours can only come to you when both are ready to receive.

Each can help himself best by helping all humanity; for, as Nature abhors a vacuum, the more love and purity you pour out for humanity the more rushes in to take its place. Help by spreading the thought of Purity regarding this subject; by giving this subject its proper place, for it was never intended to be considered publicly or mentioned lightly. True love must be nurtured in modesty and privacy, fed on the unseen forces from Divinity and grow naturally. It must be the culmination of natural development rather than the point from which development starts.

It is not possible in this age for all to reach this point of spiritual as well as physical union, for, alas, too many have walked in the world's by-paths until their garments (bodies and minds) are polluted with the vileness which man has created around this holy function. Therefore such must willingly stand still in the burnings of karmic Law until all that is impure is consumed, and until their own true companion, who is also being purified, is brought to them in fulfillment of the law of exact Justice, that they two, hand in hand, having faced and successfully passed the Angel of the Flaming Sword, may enter into the Garden and there meet the Lord face to face.

CHAPTER XX

THE MEMORY OF PAST LIVES

"Both thou and I have passed through many births.
... Mine are known unto me, but thou knowest not
of thine." *The Bhagavad-Gita, Chapter iv*.

"Tell him, O Aspirant, that true devotion may
bring him back the knowledge, that knowledge
which was his in former births." *The Voice of the
Silence*, Blavatsky, Fragment II.

The memory of past lives is given not for amusement,
nor to satisfy vain curiosity, but to inculcate a needed
lesson. As we stated in the chapter on Karma, the destiny of each Soul is ultimately to take its proper place in
the Divine Plan. While the Soul may spend many lives
in perfecting its powers and working out minor Karma,
still at certain cycles—usually every seventh life—the
destiny of the Soul will be its main task, retarded or
accelerated according to the Karma to be worked out,
just as the seventh wave of the sea rises higher on the
shore than the other six. When a person is ready to take
a decided step in his work of destiny he must see what
he has accomplished toward it in the past, and how to
avoid the mistakes and side issues that led him astray
in former lives. He may not remember all the details,
but, step by step as he needs them, the main lessons
will be revealed to him. If he is about to repeat a previous blunder, the memory of it will be given him, often
in a dream or vision. And if he is not carried away by
the mere remembering, or does not push it aside as a
fantasy or delusion, and if he sincerely desires light

and help, and is striving to follow his intuitions, he will see the lesson and understand its application to his present condition. There is no chance remembering. All follows an exact law. It comes when the Higher Self sees that the personality is ready—when the physical brain has been trained to vibrate to some extent in response to the will of the Higher Self.

Many ask, "Why is not the memory of past lives more common?" There is a deep reason for this. In our evolution we have passed through many sad and embittering experiences which, if remembered, would so depress our spirits, so discourage and hamper us that we would make little progress. Also, did we remember who we were and who our present companions were, in many cases we would find it so hard to forgive the injuries, so hard to forget the troubles we had passed through in connection with them that our spiritual growth would be retarded. Since the Law, acting as Karma, demands perfect compensation or adjustment, one great object in each new life is to readjust the mistakes of the past. When an opportunity to do so comes to us in this life, if we could remember all that had passed it would be far harder to "Love your enemies, do good to them which hate you, bless them that curse you, and pray for them which despitefully use you." Hence it is in love and wisdom that the knowledge of past lives is withheld.

Many think that could they remember who they were in the past it would be all joy and wonder, but in the majority of cases it would be a bitter disappointment and a sad and depressing remembering. Therefore we will never be permitted to remember our past lives until we have advanced beyond the point where the grief's, the ills and the unkindness's done us can affect us, make us worry or become discouraged and thus retard our progress. We will not remember until we have gained that poise which nothing can disturb; until we have become centered in the thought that to manifest Divine Love is all there is worth striving for.

Most Souls find the memory of the trials and sorrows of one life as much as the personality can bear, therefore the complete remembrance of all it had endured in its many lives would tend to crush it. It is memory that haunts; that drives to insanity. No one day can hold enough sorrow to dishearten utterly the personality; it is the accumulated burden that overwhelms. A most important lesson to learn is to put from you all that is past. Live in the present. "Let the dead past bury its dead." Until the Soul has learned that what is passed is registered within the Real Self as a lesson learned—a needed experience gained—and can let it go and not be crushed by its memory; until the personality shows its strength of character by not brooding over mistakes; until it has exemplified this stability in its present life, its Heavenly Father, in loving mercy, draws a veil over the memory of previous incarnations. When it can bear without flinching or shrinking, the memory of the sorrows of one life it will be ready to bear a more extended memory.

Another reason why we do not remember is that at each incarnation the Soul clothes itself in a new body, the brain cells of which have never responded to the past conditions, and only when the brain is capable of responding to the memory stored up in the Higher Self, can that memory be impressed upon the waking consciousness. In other words, the personality, *per se*, cannot remember the past because it has experienced but the present life. Another reason is that many, many of our lives have been so common-place or trivial that they have registered little of value in the Real Self, hence have little of importance to remember. For out of each life it is only those experiences and those lessons which have made for Soul growth that are immortalized by being registered in the Real Self. Only good is immortal; evil is but transitory.

The memory of a past life is often awakened by reading about or seeing the picture of some historical character. This arouses a consciousness of having lived at that time or in that place, or perhaps, that the reader was himself the character mentioned. This is apt to give rise to ridicule, for many upon whom the memory of past lives is dawning seem never to have been anything but kings and queens, or notable characters in history. There is a reason for this, for, like most mistakes, it is rather a misunderstanding or misapplication of the remembrance than a deliberate attempt to deceive. It is a result of ignorance of the Law. In such a case the probability is that the person did live at the period remembered, and perhaps took a prominent part in the events enacted, but he was not necessarily the principal character. The feeling of peculiar sympathy or aversion that one feels in such a case is precisely what he felt at the time of the event. In the past he may have been deeply interested in the characters under consideration, and fond of imagining himself in their place. Thus, when the attention is turned to those old times it awakens the old currents of feeling, and he thinks he actually was what in the past he had wished to be. Often there is another explanation. The noted personage may have stood out as the key-note of his time, and the circumstances that produced his eminence were lessons that many other Souls learned. In fact, the leading character enacted the drama for all the lesser personalities belonging to the same group, and all learned the lesson through the one.

The great body of humanity is like the physical body, composed of cells and organs, each with its center of force (nucleus) which takes up impressions and transmits them to all the atoms composing that center or organ. The hand learns to execute a certain movement and every cell of each finger retains the impress or latent memory of its share in that movement. So the cells of every organ learn their lessons not so much as separate cells, but all together as an organ, viz., a hand, a foot, a head, a heart, et cetera. For example, through the action of Abraham Lincoln the whole nation learned that slavery should be and could be abolished, and the lesson was impressed more or less deeply on each Soul according to its sympathy or activity in the matter; but only Abraham Lincoln actually freed the slaves. He could not have done this, however, without the aid of the thought-force of the nation. He was the executor of the will of those who thought freedom.

Every character in history had many persons who belonged to the same group—to the same nation—who were carried along in evolution by the same current; who learned by the failure or profited by the success of that character. As the Soul at first remembers only the most important events, personages and lessons impressed upon its consciousness, when that memory begins to be awakened it is natural for it to think it was the central figure.

Many psychics receive messages which they interpret to mean that they were the Virgin Mother, St. John, John the Baptist, Elijah, Moses, or some other noted *Bible* character, and find to their dismay that many others have been told the same. Since they are unable to conceive how all could have been the one character, much confusion and loss of faith in their guidance results. The true explanation is that all such personages were types, or expressions, of some of the cosmic Rays—differing phases of experience through which their Father had passed in His evolution. When a disciple is told, for instance, that she was the Virgin Mary, it means that she belongs to that expression of the Father Ray, *i.e.*, was emanated and started on her earthly evolution during the period when the Father was correlating with the Virgin Mother principle, when He was experiencing the lessons of the Great Mother, Isis. And so on through the whole list of characters.

There are hundreds who are sure they were Mary, Queen of Scots; hundreds who were Martin Luther, Julius Cæsar, Cleopatra, Helen of Troy, et cetera. If they understood the Law, however, it would be quite easy to determine whether or not they were great personages whose names are given. A careful study of the character, giving due consideration to the three streams of evolution,[1] (physical, mental and spiritual) will readily determine this. Study their mistakes and

---

1 See Chapter XIII.

successes and try to calculate what would be needed, according to the Law of Compensation (Karma), to overcome the mistakes or reap the rewards. Study their mentality and your own, and know well there is no retrogression. There are ups and downs that may seem like retrogression but they are like the ups and downs of a gravity railway; the downs are always above the level of the starting point. A personage of historical prominence may at this time be incarnated in a very lowly station, but he will still have the same characteristics that made him great. He may be placed in a lowly station to learn lessons of patience and humility, but his character will still be great, and the important lesson learned in the prominent life will be indelibly impressed upon his present personality. If he were the central figure of the group, either for good or evil, he will always be a central figure, no matter in what walk of life he may incarnate. An Abraham Lincoln might incarnate as a plough-boy where conditions made education and culture almost impossible, but he would always have the ability of a Lincoln to master conditions.

Many declare they find it impossible to live out their true selves; but the inner development will always manifest, no matter what the environment. If a Soul fails to demonstrate that it is spiritually advanced it simply means that it has not attained to or created the state it desires to manifest. The pilgrimage of the Soul is like an earthly journey. We may see the distant goal yet may have many sad experiences and much weary travel ere we reach it. If one is absorbed in petty cares, to the exclusion of higher aims, it means that he has not

outgrown petty conditions; for if he had he would find
time to follow the higher leadings and manifest them
in his life. Abraham Lincoln found time to study law
while splitting rails; Isaac Watt discovered the force of
steam while apparently absorbed in the petty care of
minding the baby. Although environment does modify
the expression, still the real inner development will
always manifest, no matter what the environment.
Accomplishment in spite of difficulties is the best proof
of inner development and strength; for difficulties only
spur us on to express the powers we have won.

The general rule is that, after one has cultivated his
mental faculties and developed his brain to a high degree, he passes through an incarnation devoid of all
chance for education. This is, firstly, to give him an opportunity to develop his heart qualities; and, secondly,
to prove how much of the former culture he has really
assimilated. No one can prove his character unless he
is forced to depend on his real inner powers. Hence,
no matter what the gain has been in the past, whether
toward physical, intellectual or spiritual perfection, he
must, of necessity, pass an incarnation where all outward
helps toward the things attained are lacking, that he may
prove himself.

When one is told that in the past he was some great
personage, it is wise to look up the history and customs
of the time indicated, and search for any glaring discrepancies between his own character and the character
of the person under consideration. If discrepancies are
found they indicate error somewhere. For example, if a
woman is told that she was an Egyptian Priestess, or if a
man is told that he was beheaded while King of Egypt,

a glance at history will show that the Egyptians carefully excluded women from participating in the Mysteries, hence there were no Egyptian Priestesses. History will also show that the Egyptians had a superstitious horror of any sort of mutilation of the body; this was inculcated by the fundamental tenets of their religion. Under no circumstances was a king or even a person of common social rank mutilated either before or after death. The worst possible punishment for the lowest criminal was the cutting off of his ears. Therefore this would most convincingly point to an error in such a message. In this instance we find that Egypt was once overrun with foreigners, much as it is at the present time. Some of them were kings and queens who followed the customs and religions of their own country. There were also numerous cities whose names have long been lost to history which while paying tribute to Egypt and inhabited largely by Egyptians, nevertheless followed their own customs. Thus a woman might have been a Priestess or a king might have been beheaded while in Egypt and yet not be Egyptians. This will show how easily psychic messages can be confused and how absurd it makes one to repeat them without verifying them. While such discrepancies do not always mean that the one giving the information has misled him, yet, under such circumstances, a careful investigation of the message, and a consideration of its source, is advisable. It may be, however, that he has misinterpreted the message; his brain may have given it a twist in accord with his personal bias. A careful study of history, together with a sincere prayer for light and help, will generally straighten the matter out.

It has become the custom for untrained or pseudo psychics to flatter their friends or sitters by telling them they
were great personages in the past. In this connection it is
a good plan never to believe such tales unless confirmed
by your own Soul or by history. For all must come under
the law of probability and common-sense.

The whole object of rebirth is for each Soul to attain all-around Soul-perfection, learn all the lessons life
can teach, and thus be prepared to do its work in the
Grand Plan. Even if it were possible for a man to gain
all knowledge and have all experience in one life, nevertheless the stupendous task of evolution, from an atom
to a God, would require incalculable aeons. Comparing
our life period to a day, as well might we expect a child
to acquire the experience and wisdom of a life-time
between sunrise and sunset. If such a prodigy were possible, evolution would still be unsatisfied, for the child
would have neither the ability nor the organism whereby
to utilize the knowledge and do the work of a man; for it
would not have reached man's estate. Perfection could
not be attained in one life.

When a student is earnestly and sincerely seeking for
light, and is striving toward self-mastery, he frequently
gets a strong impression that he has a special work to
do. This is generally the first glimmerings of a bona fide
memory of the past and of his Soul destiny. It is frequently
given in dreams, and perhaps is remembered in the waking consciousness only as an intangible impression. Many
wonder why they must grope so long in the dark. But here
again there is a reason. The Soul must struggle toward
the light alone, just as a plant by its struggles gains the

strength to push up through the earth to the sunlight.

One may be given the outline of the work which he, both karmicly and constitutionally, is destined to accomplish, but the exact manner of its fulfillment is always left to his own judgment. He is helped to think and use his own powers of judgment to decide wisely. He is shown the Goal and the Path, then is left to his own devices as to the best manner of following it. His judgment may be at fault, and he may make mistakes, but if he is working in sincerity and love for his fellow men, the One guiding him must let him experiment. The Masters dare not interfere, for They know that strength and wisdom come from learning lessons, and if the pupil is doing the best he can it will be but a matter of time ere he will reach the end of his mistaken line of activity.

If a memory of a past mistake is necessary it will be given him, but if the exact step in his future work were mapped out for him he would become a mere puppet— the executor of another's will—and not a free agent. Perhaps when the outline of this work is given him, the pupil makes the mistake of thinking that he is ready to begin at once. In reality the command is to begin the work of *preparation*. Such a disciple is in the position of a child who heedlessly rushes off before he has heard what his father really desires, or how he must prepare himself for the task; he hears the command "work" but does not wait for the end of the sentence. *No one is ever required to do work for which he is not prepared.* A teacher would not teach advanced subjects without special training; a physician would not prescribe without years of technical study; a man would not be placed in charge of a bank or business

concern without long years of special training for such
work; and yet many a psychic who hears the cry: "Son,
go work today in my vineyard," never stops to hear
more, nor dreams that any preparation is necessary. In
fact, such usually take great pride in their attitude of
trust, that *they* have no need of preparation or special
knowledge; that their Heavenly Father will guide and
teach them *in all things*. While it is true that they will
be guided and helped, yet there is an old axiom which
says: "God helps him who helps himself," which, being
interpreted, means that he who uses common-sense, and
places himself in the current, or trains his brain mind so
it can receive and comprehend the higher truths, makes
intelligent help a possibility, while he who depends entirely upon astral communications must make himself so
negative that his mind is a fertile field for the sowing of
tares by the enemy who is always waiting to sow them
among the wheat while the husbandmen sleep.

There is no royal road to Divine Wisdom. There is,
however, a straight and narrow Path to spiritual unfoldment. It is found only by wedding Knowledge to
Understanding and Love to Wisdom. It must be trodden
step by step, often in weariness and with bleeding feet.
Even Jesus, although His mission was announced both at
his birth and at His baptism, spent over thirty years studying with the teachers, adepts and Masters, before His
brain mind was capable of correlating with the Divine
Wisdom of which His Soul was fully cognizant. While
book-learning is in no way necessary for spiritual development, yet it is necessary if one is to be a teacher of the
higher laws and the higher philosophy, or is to be a leader
in spiritual thought, to perfect the instrument (brain)

through which the Divine inspiration is seeking expression.

The astral world is full of false teachers who promise many wonderful things and seek to gain your attention by telling you how great or how good you are; hence discrimination is the first faculty that must be perfected. It can only be gained by careful training and a thorough understanding of the Law. The astral-plane is called the "Hall of Learning," but the pupil is warned that "In it thy soul will find the blossoms of life, but under every flower a serpent coiled."[1] No purity of heart or desire for truth can protect from this serpent's sting those who *willfully* neglect to cultivate their minds and familiarize themselves with the laws of that plane.

If a person has not the opportunity to carry on a study of the laws and philosophy of the Higher Life this is proof positive that such an one is not yet ready to teach. He may be selected as a teacher, but for the time he is being prepared along a particular line. For the training of the heart, or the love-nature for obedience and for ardor and for love for humanity, and the perfecting of patience by the cheerful performance of daily tasks, has first to be developed in the character. When the pupil is considered by the Master to be a fit instrument in these respects (obedience, love, sympathy, patience, etc.) then will he be brought into an environment which will give him the opportunity to acquire a knowledge of the spiritual laws and the philosophy. *The pupil is never asked to leave a plain duty undone to take up the work of teacher*; for just so long as a duty confronts him which would prevent him from beginning the work, he should know that his preparation is not complete.

---

1   *The Voice of the Silence,* Blavatsky, Fragment I.

Instead of chafing at the confining bonds he should
cheerfully go ahead preparing himself in body, mind
and Soul, remembering that he has all eternity before
him, and that it is much easier to make up for delay than
to rectify a vital mistake made through precipitation.
When he perceives the outline of a work to be done, let
him prepare himself to do it to the best of his ability. But
let him be humble and be ready to see and acknowledge
his shortcomings but without exaggerating them and the
Guiding Hand will not let him stray far from the Path.

Pupils should, therefore, study most carefully the
law of all spiritual unfoldment. Never does the Higher
Self make a mere automaton of a pupil, nor sow the
seed of final failure by flattering him or by appeals to
his ambition. On the contrary his earliest memories are
more apt to be of mistakes than of triumphs, and the first
lessons given will be those which will inculcate humility. His training is a process of guiding, overshadowing
and the awakening of all dormant faculties. And once
awakened each faculty must be put to the most severe
tests ere the pupil is ready to be used. Only thus can
he raise his vibrations to the spiritual key-note. *Never
is the pupil told to do this or do that blindly.* He may
be the victim of the arbitrary commands of some entity who is taking advantage of his lack of training and
discrimination to use him as a catspaw. If so, he will
find that obedience will lead him to violate common-
sense and bring him into all kinds of trouble. When
such commands are received interiorly the pupil must
consider them with the gravest doubt, and is perfectly
justified in refusing to obey; for *arbitrary commands
are against the whole law of evolution*, and are there-

fore *never given by the Higher Self or by the Masters of the Great White Lodge.*

Absolute obedience to the Higher Guidance is required of all who would do the Master's work, but such guidance never violates common-sense, and even the vow of obedience is never required until the pupil through repeated experiences has learned to have implicit faith in his Guidance.

CHAPTER XXI

THE CYCLE OF NECESSITY

"I and my Father are one."

The Higher Self is the Father-in-heaven who is continually striving to lead and guide the human personality (the son) among the rocks and quick-sands of physical existence, called "the cycle of necessity," back to conscious oneness with Him. Until the personality can consciously receive its teachings direct, through The Voice of The Silence, the Higher Self must take advantage of every opportunity and event in the earth-life to impress upon the physical brain cells of the personality, the main lesson which the incarnation is intended to teach. For every earth-life is carefully chosen by the reincarnating Ego, and is brought about under the best conditions and in the best environment possible, under the limitations of karmic law, to learn a certain great lesson necessary for the next step in experience. That is, the environment chosen is not the easiest or most pleasant for the personality, but the one which through its temptations and trials the omniscience of the Higher Self deems best calculated to develop the Soul-qualities necessary for spiritual advance. Often the personality, owing to the denseness and sluggishness of the particles of its physical brain centers, fails to respond to the vibrations of this higher Intelligence and cannot understand the guidance, hence ignorantly places karmic barriers between itself and the desired end. In such cases life itself must be the teacher. Indeed, life after life is often spent in learning one great lesson.

Since the personality has free-will, within certain karmic limits, it cannot be coerced into following its Divine
Guidance, hence if like a boy playing truant from school
it refuses to learn its lessons it must return day after
day (life after life) to the same lesson until the lesson is
built into the character as a Soul-quality. Therefore it is
of the greatest importance for all students of the higher
life to at least begin to learn how to control the higher
centers of their physical brains and render them capable of registering the vibrations sent them from higher
Intelligences. Like wireless telegraphy, no matter how
perfectly the messages are sent, unless the receiving
apparatus is attuned to the key-note of the sender the
messages cannot be intelligently received.

As all Souls are but differing expressions of the One
Life, each must bring back into the One Life a special
experience. Unity does not mean an everlasting recur-
rence of one experience for all, but all experiences in
the One. As each different part of the body has its own
function, the experience of which is subject to and is
registered in the brain—the sum total of the experiences
of all organs and parts being necessary to complete a
Man—so are all Soul-experiences comprised in the One
Life. Thus is personality transmuted into Individuality.
Individuality is never lost; it grows more complete as
it finds the complementary phases of individuality in
all the units of the One. The more a man individual-
izes the use of his hands, feet or brain, the more perfect
a man is he; for if the hands or feet or brain are left
to follow their own subconscious (animal) instincts,
the man remains but a clod. Only man has the power
to individualize himself, and the urge toward this advance is imparted from the Higher Self or Real Ego. A

Master is one who has trained all parts and functions of his body to their highest possible individual development and holds them all subject to his will. Animals are subject to the will of man and can only gain what is called "higher intelligence" in an animal, through the emanations of man's thought and will. Some animals can respond readily to man and some cannot. Some men can easily respond to the Higher Self and learn, while others less evolved cannot respond so readily. Yet all Souls bring their individual contribution of experiences into the One Life.

Animals seem to follow more perfectly than man the laws of the One Life and are less rebellious than man. The reason for this is that animals lack freewill and blindly and obediently follow the Group soul of the species. Thus all wolves have the same instincts, all serpents the same characteristics, etc.[1] Hence you know what to expect from any animal of a given species under similar conditions.

In the beginning each Soul is given its particular work and place in the Grand Plan, and the experience necessary to attain this end must be gained by clothing itself in various personalities. The faults and drawbacks which prevent this attainment loom so darkly before the Soul that paths are chosen which, no matter what the suffering involved may be, will correct the faults and remove the barriers to the fulfillment of that Soul's destiny. Perhaps the destiny of the Soul is to be an important worker for the upliftment of humanity, with a definite place in that work. Such a Soul may begin the work, or at least lay the foundations, in the earlier incarnations when the Soul is young (in experience) and has not gone far from the sheltering love of the Father's house, but later, the

1   See *Letters From the Teacher*, Curtiss, Chapter X.

various personalities built up life after life by the Soul to use as instruments, may become rebellious, stray from the Path and set up side-issues, either as desires or complications—all of which must later be experienced and their essence of wisdom and power assimilated. For there must be free-will. The personality must be free to choose its path, to follow or not to follow its Divine Guidance. Man alone, of all the animals, can choose whether he will or will not listen and obey.

The Father (the Higher Self) gives to each son (the personality) the portion of goods belonging to him; that out of which he must weave his destiny. The son then departs into the far country of physical existence. Each son has his own portion—the portion belonging to him by right. If by karmic action he has earned a pleasant portion—wealth, position, and love of friends—with these he must cultivate Soul growth and bring back to his Father's house the greatest experiences and the deepest lessons of Divine Love that it is possible to garner through those earthly blessings. If he has earned or chosen as his portion poverty, loneliness, sorrow and sickness he must garner the golden grains of wisdom from these experiences also, for all experiences are necessary. But the Soul who can learn from another's experience need not pass that way itself. The personality must learn, either by actual experience or by observation and sympathy with others, that the side-issues are not what the Higher Self desires it to experience. And it must ultimately learn the great lesson, attain the position and do the work mapped out for it from the beginning.

After eons of time and myriads of incarnations the Soul gradually gains more and more power over the

various personalities through which it functions, and,
center by center, subjects their physical matter to its
own vibrations. The Soul thus learns by experience how
to manipulate matter and how better to express itself
through a physical instrument—the body. When the Ego
has succeeded in building up an instrument into whose
physical brain-centers a sufficient number of spiritualized atoms which vibrate in harmony with the Higher
Self are emplanted, the instrument or personality may
be said to be unfolding its inner faculties. At this stage
of evolution the greatest care is needed; for, as indicated
in a previous chapter,[1] there are many enemies waiting
for the opportunity to push back into the darkness, or
mislead for their own personal ends, the one who has la-
bored so long and patiently to reach this advanced point.
Let us suppose that one has reached this point and has
kept the "door" of his heart, and is conscious of the loving guidance of his Father-in-heaven. The great danger
at this stage makes a careful study of the philosophy and
laws of Being essential. The Voice of The Silence has
to penetrate into, triumph over prejudice—the result of
false education—and act through a physical brain. Since
a physical brain can only register that which vibrates
in harmony with its capacity, and since through all the
years of its life it has been trained to vibrate only to
physical stimuli, it must be gradually regenerated or, being the medium through which the message must pass to
reach the brain consciousness of the personality, all that
is passed through it will necessarily be colored by something of its personal characteristics and prejudices. In
other words, a message received from the Higher Self or
from a Master of Wisdom can be interpreted only in the

---

1   *Narcotics, Alcohol and Psychism.*

terms afforded by the knowledge, training and capacity of the physical brain of the personality. Thus, without special training, misunderstanding and misapplication of the message is more than probable. Many psychics blunder and subject themselves to ridicule and suffering by blindly accepting as literal the interpretation made by their untrained brains of messages which they know come from a true source. If this interpretation proves misleading, they are made miserable and perhaps turn away from the guiding Voice which is trying so hard to help them. In such cases the following rules should be strictly adhered to:

First, by spiritual aspiration (prayer, uttered or unuttered), meditation and above all by love for all mankind as shown in the daily life, raise the vibrations of all the particles composing the brain-centers.

Second, by a careful study of proper books, and by a close observation of Nature, strive to familiarize the physical brain with the laws governing *independent* psychic and spiritual communication.

Third, carefully write out any message received, but do not talk about it to others. Then, before showing it to anyone, go over it again and again, bringing to bear all your powers of logic and common-sense to get its most probable application to your own life; for all messages from a proper source are in accord with the law of absolute justice. No true Master ever tells a pupil to do anything that will in any way infringe upon the rights of another. Messages that cannot stand the test of love, compassion and justice are either mistakes of understanding or deliberate attempts to mislead; for it must be remembered that there are masters of darkness ever watching and waiting to take advantage of those whose inner faculties are unfolding. Such perverted entities, under-

standing the laws of communication, are able to reach
the student at an earlier period of his development than
are the Masters of Light, because their vibrations are
more nearly akin to the earth-plane. For instance, the
Teachers and Masters of the Great White Lodge can
communicate with a pupil only over waves of selfless
love, high aspiration, compassion, purity and humility,
while those of "the left hand path" can use vibrations
of ambition, self-seeking, pride and vanity. But their
messages, while apparently lofty and pure, especially at
first, have always the germ of some great personal power
or reward to be gained by the pupil. *Subtle flattery is always a feature of their instruction*, while those from the
White Lodge carefully point out the pupil's faults and
tell him how to conquer them. The story of Dr. Faustus
is a materialized dramatization of the method used by
such masters of evil.

Until the pupil has cleansed his heart of all self-seeking he is open to attacks from the first mentioned source.
You are never safe if the Devil—the power of all that
works against God or good—can find a single vibration
of ambition or selfishness over which he can enter. As
the Higher Self can communicate only over vibrations
akin to Himself, so the Devil can tempt, but can lead
astray and deceive only over vibrations similar to his
own. Hence to protect yourself, send out vibrations of
selfless love and compassion to all humanity.

Each Soul has an evil genius created by it during its long
pilgrimage through matter. This is fully recognized and
plainly taught in the temptations of the man Jesus. For ere
He could gain mastery and enter on His earthly ministry, He
was led by the Spirit into the Wilderness to be tempted. Every

neophyte is led by the Spirit—the Higher Self—into a
mental wilderness where, alone in the dreary wastes of
physical experience, he is tempted by the devil of his
own creation. The fasting for forty days is that period
during which he must abstain from his old thoughts
and habits, must cease to seek for outward help and
learn to seek within; must turn to his Father-in-heaven,
listen to the voice of his Higher Self and refuse longer
to be guided by physical vibrations. It is a period during
which the neophyte is left without spiritual food and
hence must fast; when it seems that no help can reach
him. Only after this prolonged fast in the mental wilderness does the Devil come to tempt him. In the parable
of the Prodigal Son this is the period of his homeward
journey, when he has refused to eat the husks and has
not yet reached his Father's house. It is always here that
the Devil meets each Soul and tempts. In other words,
long ere he has really found that perfect vibration of
love through which alone he can hear his Higher Self
speak, the evil genius, or those akin to him—the masters
of the shadow—can speak and tempt over vibrations of
selfishness. This selfishness and ambition often require
a long time to be transmuted into love for others, for
they have a way of hiding behind all sorts of sophistries.

Up to this point the pupil has had to contend with
but petty temptations and appetites, but now, having
consciously taken an advanced step, through prayer and
fasting he has deliberately entered the Wilderness to be
tempted. The first temptation coming from the side of evil
is generally that of Power. "Command that these stones
be made bread." The Devil says: "Command and demand
all that you need. You are not sick or hungry. You are The

Christ, therefore command that the earth (which karmic law has bereft of Soul-nourishment and spiritual
satisfaction) shall be turned into bread to satisfy your
physical wants," even though the very eating thereof
binds you tighter to the wheel of physical existence. The
second temptation comes in the form of self-righteousness. The Devil takes the hungry Soul up into a high
place, upon the very pinnacle of the Temple (the body),
and there showeth how the Soul has conquered the flesh,
growing holier than others by the control of the lower
appetites, how it has reached the gates of the Holy City
and has become a guide and example for many less holy
and less pure followers. Then the Devil declares: "Thou,
if thou be the Son of God (or if thou be The Christ as you
have affirmed), cast thyself down; for you can do what a
lesser Soul could not do without sin. That which would
be sin in one not placed upon so high a pinnacle of the
Temple within the Holy City is for you but a certain
license earned because of your holiness. 'He shall give
his angels charge concerning thee lest at any time thou
shalt dash thy foot against a stone.' Therefore you can
do that which would be sin in others."

The third temptation is one of Ambition. This only
comes to the Soul who has reached the mountains
of spiritual understanding. The neophyte has pain-
fully climbed the mountain, has entered the Silence,
has heard the Voice and seen with his spiritual eyes.
He has gained certain psychic powers, and lo! all the
kingdoms of the world and the glory thereof are spread
before his sight. His evil genius points out that by his
awakened psychic powers he can gain the whole world;

that men will bow down to him and give him fame and glory because he is a little in advance of the average; that he can charge large sums for interviews, psychic readings, etc.; can be feted and honored and listened to by the multitude; can be heralded from place to place, be interviewed by the newspapers and receive much public acclaim. All of which is a very real and terrible temptation, and one which only those who have actually stood upon the "exceeding high mountain" and in their Soul vision have actually seen the kingdoms of the world at their feet, who have heard the tempter say: "All these things will I give thee if thou wilt fall down and worship me," can understand or appreciate. For this temptation cannot come until the neophyte has approached the mountain's top.

An understanding of these temptations should make each judge leniently the shortcomings and failures of those who have stood upon the heights, but who have fallen down to worship either the Beast, the Dragon or the Anti-Christ. Let every one cultivate in his own garden the fruits of the Spirit, namely, love, joy, peace, gentleness, goodness, faith, meekness and temperance. Every time you stop to censure or condemn another an enemy (your evil genius) comes while you sleep and sows vile weeds in the garden of your Soul; weeds which will grow apace and which must be rooted up ere the fruits of the Spirit can be garnered. Every time you indulge in thoughts of evil you are filling your garden with all sorts of predatory creatures, all of which must be driven out ere you can become one with your Father and sit down at His table to eat of the fruits of the Spirit.

The cultivation of the fruits of the Spirit will leave you no time to see the shortcomings of others. To eat of these fruits will be to sit down at your Father's table and sup with Him. "And they shall see His face, and His name shall be in their foreheads."

CHAPTER XXII

THE PATH

"Thou wilt show me the path of life." *Psalms*, XVI, 11.

"Now for the fourth prepare, the portal of temptations which do ensnare the *inner* man." . . . "Man is a crystal ray; a beam of light immaculate within, a form of clay material upon the lower surface. That beam is thy life-guide and thy true Self, the Watcher and the silent Thinker, the victim of thy lower Self." *The Voice of the Silence*, Blavatsky, Fragment III.

Every student who has earnestly sought association with this Order has done so because of an inner urge, which, whether verbally expressed or not, manifests as a determination to set out in earnest upon the Path of Discipleship which leads to the goal of final liberation. Yet few there be who are aware of the many snares and delusions and the many requirements necessary to attain that great end. Many think this Path but a figure of speech, and that all that is necessary is to live an average life, to have good intentions, to be honest whenever circumstances permit, to be true whenever it seems to pay, saying with a shrug of the shoulders "No one is perfect and I am doing the best I can under the circumstances." Such persons have not only not entered the Path but have no conception of what the Path is.

How many, many there are who earnestly and sincerely believe they have entered the Path, yet who after years of earth-life, years of striving and study and meditation, find themselves apparently no further advanced than when they set out. Hence, many become discouraged and turn back, saying it is a hopeless task, or that only after many lives—some say at least seven more—they may begin to attain. But the truth is that unless you begin to attain today, this present moment, you have not entered the Path; for this Path is made up of regular steps, each one a definite attainment. These attainments are not mystical dreams of a far-away perfection to be attained in the dim future, but something that belongs to your every-day life. The first step in Mastery must be taken now, in a definite practical way; for until this is done the greater steps will forever remain untaken.

The Path is the Path of Renunciation, yet it is also a Path of glorious achievement. Upon it you will find many things to comfort you during the long nights of darkness and the days of combat, many resting-places, many joys. The renunciation does not mean the renunciation of all human sympathy, all natural human traits; for you must be "all things unto all men," and this you cannot be if you become what the world calls a "crank." The renunciation must be the renunciation of the dominion of the lower self and the disciplining and training of its desires and appetites; the self you have built up out of false conceptions of the events through which you have gained the experience which entitles you to enter upon this definite step. Those who have chosen this step are like soldiers who have donned their armor and are waiting to go forth to victory.

The goal is reached through definite attainments, spoken of as Gates opening into new stages of the journey. These Gates are definite attainments here and now in this present life. Each step means a struggle, a literal shaping of every act and thought toward a definite end which is fully outlined in the mind and made the objective point of the life. The first Gate to be passed is the attainment of Charity, and Tolerance for all, a realization of Divine Love and an earnest desire to become one with The Christ-force which is manifesting in your fellow man. This is the first Gate to be entered because intolerance is a bar to further progress. Hence while there is the least intolerance in your heart this barred Gate will shut off even a vista of the Path. To conquer intolerance realize Divine Love as a white light which can only manifest on earth through its many prismatic colors, and that each color, if true and undefiled, has its place in the heart of the pure white light, for the white light could not be complete if one color ray was missing. The color rays symbolize the seven great types or classes of humanity with their various idiosyncrasies. To attain true tolerance realize that your brothers and sisters, with all their differences of opinion and various ways of looking at divine Truth, are nevertheless necessary parts of the Grand Plan, and that without them you would lack. Only a realization of the oneness of all and their necessity for the completion of the whole can bring true tolerance. You may talk of loving your brother as yourself, but not until you have at least a mental grasp of the truth that your brother is necessary to your own growth, can you really manifest it. As long as you look upon yourself as separate and aloof from your brother this great bar of intolerance will remain across the entrance to the Path.

In the above we have emphasized the constructive idea of tolerance. For many think tolerance means so vague and indefinite an idea of what you yourself believe that you are willing to follow the teaching of every phase of Truth anyone may expound to you. But such a course is merely confusing, for you cannot be truly tolerant until you are quite sure which avenue of teaching best suits your Soul needs. Seek earnestly for the particular line of teaching which most appeals to you and which proves most helpful to your spiritual growth, then, while recognizing the good in all others and being tolerant of all divergent views, be well grounded in your chosen teaching, so that you cannot be misled or carried away by sophistry but will remain unmoved as long as the teaching feeds your spiritual hunger. Only thus can you take your place as a shining beam in your own color ray or avenue of teaching. It is like a military evolution; the figure is perfect only when each individual is in his own place in his own company and is paying no attention to the others except to recognize their part in the evolution and work harmoniously with them.

Charity is that all-embracing Love which seeks for the good in all. It does not mean that you are to condone evil, for to do so is to spread it. It means that while you are never to condemn a personality for his or her failings, you are to stand firm for the principles of right, truth, justice and purity whenever you are tempted or see them violated, so that there can be no misunderstanding as to the principles you uphold.

The second Gate consists of the attainment of Harmony, both within yourself and also with your surroundings, or the power to be so harmonized to

Divinity that you pass through the turmoil and inharmony of life without permitting them to upset you.

At this Gate you must conquer fear, for this is a necessary part of the attainment of harmony, for only perfect love casteth out fear. Many pupils knock a long time at this Gate and wonder why it does not open to them. They desire harmony above all else and cry out continually that they are sending out nothing but love to their fellow men yet receive in return inharmony, unkindness and cruelty. If such candidates would look within themselves instead of around them for the harmony they seek they would find that the great specter Fear held them enthralled. They fear a thousand things, chiefly that the world does not understand what they are striving to manifest, for if it did it could not send back so much inharmony. They fear the opinions of friends, poverty, sickness, death. In fact their fears are too numerous to mention and in their hearts, although the beautiful flower of love has been planted, yet the many noxious weeds of fear have sprung up so thickly that the plant is unable to bloom and send out its perfume to harmonize the conditions in which it grows. Therefore they will knock at this Gate in vain until they have vanquished fear or until they have learned to trust and believe in the divine overshadowing Love which casteth out fear. When this is attained they will awaken to find the Gate of Harmony already ajar.

This specter, Fear, while it seems a giant is in reality but a shadow of the night. Let the candidate realize the divinity of his Real Self, that it is deathless, immortal and cannot be harmed. Let him repeat constantly "I am fearless because my Real Self

is divine and there is nothing to fear. Divine Love is
the law of my being and I can trust in this great Law to
conquer all conditions. With it I am strong, powerful,
forceful. Manifesting this love I cannot be discouraged,
frightened, or turned aside from the Path of spiritual attainment." As he permits his consciousness to dwell in
this thought there will grow up in him the strength and
power to conquer. Then ere he knows it he will find this
Gate standing wide and the light of its portal flooding
his whole life with the glory of its Love and Harmony.

The Third Gate is that of Patience, *i.e.*, having earnestly
cultivated Divine Love in your heart, and Tolerance and
Charity for all; having harmonized yourself to The Christ
and to your surroundings, and having conquered fear,
there must ensue a longer or shorter period in which
you wait for you scarce know what. This is beautifully
expressed by the Psalmist: "My soul waiteth for the Lord
more than they that watch for the morning."[1] And again,
the heart cries out: "And now, Lord, what wait I for? my
hope is in Thee. Deliver me from all my transgressions."[2]
You are waiting for the Divine Law to bring to you the
result of your attainments. This is a very trying period in
your life, because, feeling that you have attained to Love,
Harmony, Charity, Tolerance, etc., you cannot understand why you must tarry so long at this Third Gate. Yet
there is a great necessity that it should be so, for without
the virtues of Patience and Trust, and Confidence that
whatever comes is best, you would be utterly unable to
cope with the more active trials and temptations that will
assail you when you reach the Fourth Gate. This waiting

---

1   *Psalms* CXXX, 6.
2   *Psalms* XXXIX, 7-8.

develops the Patience which affords the Soul a chance to learn the great lesson *Keep Silent*, also how to enter into the Silence and become one with it. For you have not mastered Patience until you have learned to quiet the mentality, enter the Silence and realize the meaning of the text "Be still and know that I (the great Law of Love) am God."

When you have consciously sought membership in *The Order of the 15* you are supposed to have passed, in a measure at least, the first three of these Gates, and are now knocking at the Fourth; the Gate which opens to your consciousness the Path itself. You are now ready to obey the voice of your Higher Self which is urging upon you a conscious and persistent effort toward Mastery, instead of drifting aimlessly as heretofore on the sea of life. The entrance to this Fourth Gate is a most momentous event, for it marks the end of the first great cycle of your spiritual growth. Since from an occult standpoint the 4 contains the potency of the 10 (1+2+3+4=10), and since 4 or the square is the most perfect earthly figure, at this point you must square yourself as it were with earthly conditions as you find them; for at this step you face the fourth dimension in which all things interpenetrate. At this point you must face yourself, for over this Gate is written the Pythagorian precept: "Man, know thyself." When you strive to obey this precept you will become aware that there is at least one great iron bar which closes this Gate to you. But within yourself you can find the power to lift this bar and permit the Gate to swing open. No one can recognize and lift this bar but yourself.

Until this Fourth Gate is reached, your life has been
a more or less unconscious growth in Love, Charity,
Tolerance, Harmony, Fearlessness, and Patience, but
now you face a serious conscious struggle. You must
now begin to take account of yourself *within* as well
as without. You have been able largely to control your
actions and your words. You now become responsible
for your own creations, the children of your thoughts,
and must "To the Silent Thinker be united." This Silent
Thinker is not that which is known as the Voice of the
Silence, but that silent undercurrent of thought which
is continually penetrating your brain, although what
might be called the active thoughts may, like ripples
on the surface, make you unaware of what is transpiring in the depths. The instant you begin self analysis
you will find there are many deep thoughts which come
into your mind without your volition and seem to think
themselves. These are of two kinds; if they are uplifting, grand or beyond the power of the physical brain
to express, they come from the Silent Thinker; if they
are frivolous, contemptible, or vile, they are but the reflection of the world's current of thought to which you
have united yourself and permitted to flow through you,
"the children of your thoughts, unseen, impalpable, that
swarm around human-kind." But of whatever character
they may be, they are the index of the self you are to
study and to conquer. For to "know thyself" means to
go down deep into the sources of selfhood and decide
just what the great motives are which are determin-
ing your character and prompting your actions. These
motives can be determined by careful study of the impalpable thoughts which intrude themselves upon you

against your volition. Thoughts are things, and man in the aggregate during his evolution has thrown off thoughts of all kinds, and these accumulated thought-forms have become great vortices of force into which each Soul is naturally drawn, according to its affinity with the one or the other type. In other words, you permit your mind to be so filled with the currents of the world-thought surrounding you that your brain becomes a fit vehicle for, and develops within it definite channels through which certain classes of thought-currents naturally flow, just as a stream automatically follows a channel dug for it; and the longer it flows in one channel the broader and deeper the channel becomes, and the more difficult it is to change the stream. It is well known that the brain of a thinker differs from that of a savage not so much in size and weight as in the number and depth of its convolutions, which convolutions are developed by the functioning of the centers they contain.

Another means of self-analysis is carefully and fearlessly to interpret your dreams and visions. For the Silent Thinker is continually guiding and warning you by means of such experiences. Dreams are of three general classes: first, confused incoherent ideas more or less imperfectly remembered, the result of inharmonious physical or mental conditions which keep the lower mind more or less active yet uncontrolled by the presence of the Ego; second, the experiences of the human-mind wandering uncontrolled in the lower astral world; third, the symbolic dreams and visions, coherent and usually clearly remembered, the result of the personality doing the best it can, by using the thought materials of the waking consciousness, to illustrate

the spiritual truths or lessons given by its Higher Self
during the sleep of the body. Hence a careful analysis
of dreams will show what general stage of development
the candidate has reached and what general problems he
must face and conquer. You do not have to experience
the two lower classes of dreams if you train your brain
mind to refuse to accept such experiences. When this
training is accomplished you will dream only when your
Higher Self desires to give you a lesson or a warning.

It is with these inner thought-currents that the candidate who knocks at the Fourth Gate must determinately
grapple; first recognize, and then control. No thought-
currents coming from your Higher Self or from the
Masters of Wisdom can flow into your consciousness
until, by determined conscious effort, you have swept
away all trifling thoughts and have prepared channels
for higher thoughts. At this step you become responsible
for the effect of every outside influence that impinges
upon your consciousness. You become responsible not
only for all the emanations which you send out to interpenetrate all space and impinge upon every other human
being but also responsible for every thought you permit
to enter your consciousness from any source.

While you cannot expect to conquer all at once and
absolutely shut out every undesirable thought, still *you
can refuse to dwell upon* a thought and can determinately
think some constructive thought which will ultimately
create a channel through which like thoughts will naturally flow. In other words, you must be the Chooser,
the Willer, the Master of your thoughts. And you will

remain before this Gate until you carve out new channels through which the currents of thought from the Silent Thinker can flow into your consciousness. Hence, Patience is the supreme quality to be cultivated at this Gate.

There are many barriers which hold you back at this point—until you can recognize that there is nothing in all the universe that is important enough to stop your onward march; that the Silent Thinker is your True Self, one with Divinity. When these barriers are reached, so many, many cry out: "What shall I do? How shall I conquer? Give me some definite step to take that I may know I have really entered the Path." Why this questioning? When through all the ages "Wisdom crieth without; she uttereth her voice in the streets; she crieth in the chief place of the concourse, in the openings of the gates."[1]

The first step is plainly set forth in *The Voice of Tue Silence*:[2] "Before the Soul can comprehend and may remember, she must unto the Silent Speaker be united, just as the form to which the clay is modeled is first united with the potter's mind." Here you find the first step, the great step, pointed out. Indeed, this step is the beginning and the end, for only as you strive for and accomplish this feat can you truly enter the Fourth Gate and win final victory. How can you get from this injunction the help your heart longs for? the definite step that shall make you something different, something greater, better, higher; that shall give you power? While we do not countenance attempts to cultivate abnormal powers, we are told again and again that if you are a child of the Father and are doing the works of

---

1   *Proverbs*, I, 20-21
2   Page 2.

the Father, then you will have the powers of the Father abiding in you.

How is this to be accomplished? Just as clay is united to the potter's mind. When a potter starts to make a wonderful vase—a marvel of beauty, a poem of symbology, a lesson for all who look—he does not copy something another mind has brought forth. Such a production would be spurious. The true potter, the artist, is original. Long before one stroke is made, even before the clay is moistened, his mind has created every detail of the vase. This is an illustration of how you must go to work. Unite yourself with the mind of the Great Potter, the Great Over-Soul, the Thinker, Him of whom you desire to become an expression, for to you He must first become the Silent Thinker ere He becomes the Speaker. Before you can remodel your life you must catch a glimpse of the Divine Plan in the mind of the Silent Thinker. Tolerate no defect, see a vision of the perfection you desire to reach and work consciously in harmony with it. This cannot be accomplished until you have realized the possibility of closing the door of your mind to all undesirable thoughts. To do this, practice making your mind a blank and shutting out all thought and when this has been accomplished in a measure you will be ready to open the door to such thoughts as you desire.

As long as thoughts of discouragement, impatience, self-depreciation, or other similar thoughts can fill your mind against your will to the exclusion of the thoughts you have chosen, you have not united yourself to the Silent Thinker and cannot hear the voice of the Silent Speaker. Therefore, while the task is arduous it is not hopeless. As we said in the beginning, there are many joys along the Path, chief of which is the consciousness of your Divine Guidance and the realization that you are but following in the steps of every Great Soul who has attained Mastery. And the very fact of determinately facing this Fourth Gate brings you into a thought-current, which has been both created and strengthened by the many pilgrims who have passed this way, so that it may be said that they have left behind landmarks and guideposts for your direction. There is scarcely a temptation that can assail you that many of the loving Elder Brothers have not passed through and conquered, hence They are stretching out guiding hands to help you. The very force with which They conquered remains as a sacred aura around this Gate; in fact, the thoughts They have left behind might be compared to a golden thread reaching all the way. And as long as you hold to this thread you cannot lose your way.

"Ere thou canst near that goal, before thine hand is lifted to upraise the fourth gate's latch, thou must have mastered all the mental changes in thy Self, and slain the army of the thought sensations that, subtle and insidious, creep unasked within the Soul's bright shrine. . . . Strive with thy thoughts unclean before they overpower thee. Use them as they will use thee, for if thou sparest them and they take root and grow, know well these thoughts will overpower and kill thee. . . . O fearless Aspirant, look deep within the well of thine own heart, and answer. Knowest thou of Self the powers, O thou perceiver of external shadows? For, on Path fourth, the lightest breeze of passion or desire will stir the steady light upon the pure white walls of Soul."[1]

---

1   *The Voice of The Silence*, Blavatsky, Fragment I. (Carefully re-study the chapter on Purity.)

CHAPTER XXIII

EARTH'S FINER FORCES

"Earth my mother bid me learn Truth in darkness
to discern; Like thy forces, silently, Work in true
humility." Hymns of *The Order of the 15*.

In the Orient the foot is held in high esteem for its
symbology—spiritual understanding—as well as for its
beauty and symmetry. And frequent ceremonial wash-
ings are enjoined both by religion and hospitality. Shoes
are worn only for protection, it being a breach of eti-
quette to enter the presence of a high dignitary with the
feet covered. In places of worship the shoes are left at
the door, the devotee entering the holy place barefooted.
Moreover, oriental temples are seldom found with any
floor but Mother Earth. The pious Moslem sprinkles
fresh earth in his shoes so that when compelled to wear
them he will still have his feet upon the earth; for he
knows that it is through the soles of the feet that the
nourishing magnetism of Mother Earth enters the body
to give life and health to her children.

The *Yogies* of the East go barefooted in compliance
with this law, and their habit of sitting upon a mat of
rushes spread upon the bare ground is to gain the valued
aid of the earth-forces in their spiritual development. The
magnetic forces that enter at the feet pass out at the head,
therefore the yogi covers his head with a silk turban. Silk,
being a non-conductor, prevents the escape of the earth-

forces and stores them up in his body to be utilized for his further development. To wear silk upon the feet insulates the body from the earth-forces and impedes the flow of the currents of your personal magnetism back to the earth in perfect equilibrium. As the magnetism is the force upon which obsessing or controlling entities feed, persons receiving communications from the astral-plane are frequently advised by their controls to wear silk upon the feet, thus interfering with the normal exchange of forces and storing up the personal magnetism for the use of the controlling entity. Naturally such practices belong to the destructive method of psychic communication and hence are to be avoided.

To obtain power and enter into close touch with Nature it is desirable at certain times to put off your shoes, and, after rubbing the feet with a little vegetable oil, walk barefooted while the dew is still upon the grass. While helpful and advisable this practice is by no means the most important factor, for true spiritual development is the result of manifesting The Christ-force in the heart, and all external forces are but secondary. Without the spiritual growth no amount of magnetic forces can produce spirituality. Walking barefoot in the dew is practiced in many of the occult schools of the East as well as by the Barefoot Friars of the Christian era.

Very early in the morning the earth is giving forth its magnetism most abundantly. The forces with which the sun has filled the earth during the previous day have germinated in the darkness (as all life must), and in the morning are breathed out by Mother Earth in sufficient quantity to sustain her children through the day. While the sun rules the day, and by its creative power causes all life to germinate, still it is only the masculine force—the Father—and alone it cannot create; but when it is joined with the air, its expression,[1] and commingled with water—the feminine force—deep within the bosom of the earth a wonderful alchemical change, called creation, takes place. It is thus that moist earth (the Mother) when fecundated by the sun (the Father) expressing himself through air, brings forth. When the earth is parched and dry the magnetic rays from the sun cannot penetrate it but are deflected and dissipated, so that instead of fecundating they wither and burn the vegetation.

It is through Mother Earth that the life-forces are incubated and brought forth, not only for Nature, but for mankind. After the magnetic rays from the sun have fecundated the germs of physical life they are developed and given forth by the breath of the earth. Well has the earth been called our Mother, for only through the dual forces generated in the earth is life manifested and nourished. It is not sunshine alone that gives life, but it is sunshine *absorbed, fecundated and sent forth* by the earth, assimilated by all vegetation through its roots and by all animal life through the soles of its feet, that gives the magnetic nourishment of the dual forces which perfect life and health. Modern medicine has accepted this fact, under the name of Kneipp[2] treatment, without knowing its rationale. Walking barefooted is now prescribed throughout

---

1 The sun force cannot express itself on the earth without air, i.e., fire cannot burn without oxygen.
2 Father Sebastian Kneipp, a Bavarian priest, son of a poor weaver. He cured himself and a fellow student of nervous prostration by a system of nature cure, and later founded a large sanitarium for nature cure at Woerishofen. Walking barefooted is a marked feature of the treatment.

Europe and at many sanitariums in this country as a part of various nature-cure procedures.

In the ancient Schools of the Prophets, and among the pupils of all the great teachers of the Mysteries, great attention was given to the study of Nature. The disciples, being separated from the world, were required to spend much time in meditation close to Mother Earth, always with their feet bare and their heads covered. The earth-forces, if allowed uninterrupted play through man's body, bring to him, just as they do to the plants, the kind of magnetic nourishment suited to his requirements, in exact accord with his capacity to utilize it, to reach perfection on all planes. As well might we expect a rose to grow to perfection and bloom with its roots suspended above the earth as for man to develop without contact with the earth. For not only does he draw health for his physical body from the earth, but also a power which aids in unfolding his inner faculties. We might give the rose sunlight, air and water, and might tend it with all care, but unless Mother Earth was permitted to first imbibe the forces of the sun, air and rain and by her wonderful alchemical power transmute them into life-force, the rose could not grow. In a similar manner a mother eats and drinks and breathes, and by transmuting all the constituents of nourishment, brings forth their essence in the sustaining life-force in the milk with which she feeds her babe.

The prophet Isaiah says, "How beautiful upon the mountain are the feet of him that bringeth good tidings, that publisheth peace."[1] The earth breathes, the mountains acting as her lungs. They are upheaved by her efforts to throw off in greater

---

1 *Isaiah*, LII, 7.

abundance the magnetic life-force. While in the human body impurities are breathed out and fresh air is breathed in, just the opposite takes place in the case of the earth entity; impurities sink into the earth and are indrawn and purified and are then breathed out as pure, magnetic currents of life-force. Hence upon a mountain the currents would be felt most strongly and a disciple dwelling there, if it all developed, would thus be enabled to carry the good tidings and publish peace with greater power. It is not mere elevation that permits this action but the porosity and character of the rock formations.

Each portion of the earth's surface gives out its particular and characteristic force which influences not only the climate and vegetation but also the mentality and nervous system of its inhabitants. In a general way the force thrown out by mountains is the masculine or Father-force, corresponding to Will. It is a hardening force which is exhilarating yet which makes for ruggedness and stability and gives the power to endure. For instance, the Rocky Mountains may be considered the backbone of this continent. They form a great wall or barrier which is continually being strengthened so that when the cyclic cataclysms occur—as they must not only at the end of the Root Race (Fifth), but also in a minor degree at the end of its fifth sub-race—the Rockies will indeed be a backbone that shall preserve that portion of the continent which is destined to survive. Hence, while excellent for hardy pioneer types, barren and rugged mountains send out a force which is very hard for a spiritually advanced or sensitive person to withstand or correlate with. Nevertheless from them should be gained the power to endure, the power of stability and perseverance. Only those advanced Souls who have mastered or correlated with these forces or persons whose centers are not developed to respond to them, can endure a lengthy sojourn in high mountains.

On the other hand the characteristic of the seacoast, especially in southern or tropical countries, is the Mother-force, the power to bring forth, corresponding to Love. This force is typified by gentle moist breezes, fresh warm air and golden sunshine. The characteristic of southern regions near the sea coast is growth. And just as they produce prolific vegetation, so will they tend to bring forth in the spiritual life. The dangers to be encountered and the trials to be met will also be characteristic of these regions. Instead of the over-exhilaration of the mountain regions there will be a tendency to lassitude and languor and to put forth little effort toward the spiritual life. Instead of the depression of rocks and barrenness there will be the depressing influence of fogs, marshes and excessive rainfall. The daily trials will be comparable to the many stinging insects, the prickly cactus and other thorny forms of vegetation. Moreover, the weeds, *i.e.*, pseudo forms of occult or spiritual growth, will grow apace and tend to choke out the true seed.

In the air from the mountains the Father-force predominates, while the air that sweeps across the sea gathers up the Mother-force which has been purified by the action of the salt. Hence, from an occult standpoint, the most favorable outward conditions for spiritual growth should be found in regions where the breath of the mountains meets that of the sea, and far enough South to avoid using up a large part of your life-forces overcoming the rigors of the climate.

You may thus find an explanation of many of your trials in the character of the region you inhabit, for the inhabitants of a region are subject to the earth's Karma in that region. But remember that wherever you find yourself you are there because you need the lessons of just those conditions. And until you have mastered them and the Law in a natural way takes you elsewhere, it is useless to try to escape them; for if you run away they will meet you in other and perhaps more trying forms until conquered. Once understand what each factor in your environment corresponds to symbolically in your personal life and you have the key to its mastery. Just as Nature conquers and overcomes all difficulties arising from the environment by adapting herself to them, so must you. Each region has special advantages which compensate in a measure for its drawbacks. The luxuriance of growth which is denied to a rugged climate is compensated for by the greater fragrance of its flowers, the superior flavor of its fruits and the greater energy of its inhabitants. So if your spiritual growth seems hampered or dwarfed by an uncongenial environment, remember that you must compensate for this lack by giving forth greater perfume.

If your conditions permit the development of many higher faculties and luxuriant spiritual growth, do not forget to send forth the subtle perfume of love and attractiveness for which no amount of mere growth, mere knowledge, mere intellectual attaintments can ever compensate. The perfume will arise from your rose of life in proportion as you conquer the factors in your life which hold you back.

When the Angel of the Lord spake to Moses out of the burning bush he said unto him, "Put off thy shoes from off thy feet, for the place where on thou standeth is holy ground."[1] While this might have a literal meaning in connection with the magnetic forces of that particular spot, it has an inner significance applicable to all disciples who can hear the Angel of the Lord. It refers to an initiation. The "bush" is the same thing often spoken of as a Tree, the Tree of Life, the Tree of Knowledge of Good and Evil, etc. The tree is the spinal cord, whose sap is the *Kundalini* force. It is the Tree of Life and Death, until, by conscious power, this force is lifted up and made to function in the central canal of the spinal cord. Then it becomes the Tree of Life in the midst of the Garden. To attempt to force the development of this power or to strive to awaken it without a personal teacher who has mastered it, is to invite undreamed of disasters on all planes and in all bodies. It should develop only as the result of natural growth. The whole story is most simple if looked at as an allegory meant to symbolize an important initiation.

We read that "Moses kept the flock," and lead them into the desert, *i.e.*, he kept the flocks of thoughts, inherited tendencies, passions and desires, the portion of goods delivered to him by his Higher Self to keep and control. "And he led the flock to the backside of the desert and came to the mountain of God." As all students, who have truly undertaken to lead and guide the flocks belonging to their lower personality, can verify, the first effect of the attempt at control is to turn life into a lonesome desert. How often do we hear the student

---

1 Exodus, III, 1-5.

complain that this period of sadness and depression is as though he were forsaken and left alone in a desert! Just as the shepherd, alone in the desert, must fight off wild beasts, shield his flock from the elements, find pasturage for them and keep them from straying, so the neophyte must fight the lonely battle with his lower personality in this desert of depression that seems to have enwrapped him. But when he reaches the darkest point—the back-side of the desert—he finds the Mountain of God. He can only reach this Mount by fearlessly entering the desert and conquering its terrors. Here "The Angel of the Lord[1] appeared unto him in a flame of fire out of the midst of a bush; and he looked, and, behold, the bush burned with fire and the bush was not consumed." He had met with a realization of the fire of Divine Love; the sun of Righteousness had illumined his heart; he had arisen and met the Lord. This point is reached when the pupil is able to hear the voice of the Master. When the *Kundalini* force has passed up through the spine and touched the pineal gland[2]—opened the third eye—the disciple is able to see "the glory of the Lord" surrounding him.

This is a physical effect which always accompanies spiritual illumination and is comparable to a fire which burns without consuming. But while this is a physical effect accompanying illumination, remember it is not the cause of illumination, merely an effect. And out of the midst of the bush he will hear the voice of his Lord. But first comes the summons "put off thy shoes from off thy feet." As the feet symbolize spiritual understand-

---

1 The Angel of the Resurrection.
2 An organ in the brain whose function is unknown to physical science. It is the organ of spiritual sight.

ing, so the shoes symbolize a Conception of Truth which has been moulded and adapted to the understanding. Before the student can receive spiritual illumination all old conceptions or coverings to his understanding must be put off or laid aside that the understanding may receive the Light direct. It is not that the old conceptions must be despised, for we do not despise our shoes when we take them off, but that the understanding must be absolutely unhampered before spiritual illumination can come.

The Law back of this manifests equally in the outer world. The pioneer in any plane of activity must turn aside from the path marked out by the dictum of others. No doctor, scientist, or explorer ever makes a great discovery until he metaphorically puts off his shoes or drops the limitations imposed by authority and strikes out into the unknown, untrammeled and free, even though he reach his starting point over a beaten pathway. When the disciple does this he has reached a point where he can receive definite instructions from the Master, and the operation of natural forces and how to control them and correlate with them in accord with the divine Law of Harmony, is one of the first lessons given.

Again we read, "He brought me up also out of a horrible pit, out of the miry clay, and set my feet upon a rock, and established my goings."[1] Miry clay being nonporous, is the least magnetic, and precludes the escape of the life-force from the earth, while rocks, high hills and mountains are distinctly advantageous.

Science is beginning to discover that it is the earth itself that brings forth rather than the rain, or even the sun. They have discovered that far

---

1 *Psalms*, XL, 2.

better crops can be raised when the top soil is kept loose and pervious to the magnetic forces. In reaching these results, however, it has not fully understood the cause. The wonderful results secured in the arid land of the West without irrigation, by the process called "dry farming,"[1] is only proof that Mother Earth holds within her bosom all the nourishment needed to bring forth to perfection, if she is given conditions under which she can absorb the Father-force and transmute it within her womb. In the process of dry farming the ground is ploughed deeply, the subsoil packed firmly and the surface pulverized, and kept loose *and porous* by frequent harrowing. Phenomenal crops have been raised where the rainfall was slight, and on ground considered for generations as arid and forever unproductive, owing to the impossibility of irrigation.

Science, while obtaining results, has only partially solved the problem. It is not alone because this method conserves the little rain that falls, for that of itself would be inadequate to produce the wonderful crops obtained. It is because the loose, porous soil permits the absorption and out-breathing of the forces to go on uninterruptedly, and the vital forces from the sun, after being fecundated, can be sent forth freely and in abundance. Those who have never investigated this new process of farming will marvel at the result, for it is real magic, the magic of Mother Earth. It is the alchemy of the mother transmuting the sand of the desert into gold—golden grain for her children's sustenance.

It is early in the morning, just before sunrise, that the magnetic forces are flowing most strongly upward. This upward flow gradually decreases until

---

1   See U. S. Experiment Station Bulletins on *"Dry Land Farming."*
   Cambell's, *"Soil Culture Manual."* H. W. Cambell, Lincoln, Neb.

at high noon the forces are equalized and then begin to be indrawn again; the Mother is drinking in the power of her Lord, the Sun. Precisely the same action is taking place at noon between the earth and the sun, as takes place at the time of union between man and woman. The Sun (masculine) is giving, pouring out, and the earth (feminine) is receiving and drawing into her womb the force that shall fecundate and bring forth physical life. The very first step in practical occultism is acquiring a knowledge of how Mother Earth works her miracles, and by what means the Divine Creative Force of the Father combines with and fructifies the force of the Mother, for "As above, so below."

Since at noon all the forces of Nature and man are focused on the earth-plane it is wisest to have the principal meal of the day at noon, for then the physical forces can best transmute the food with the least drain upon or disturbance of the higher forces.

From the above it is plain that the student should contact the earth whenever possible. But, alas, this is not always feasible in crowded cities; for the pavements, in varying degrees according to their formation, are obstacles to the passage of the earth forces. Also the leakage from gas mains, electric conduits, sewers, etc., are all deterrents. The habits of civilization which demand that the feet, created to be the natural absorber and transmitter of these forces, shall be encased in tight impervious shoes also prevents contact with these forces. Shoes are a necessity in cities, yet everyone should find time to stand barefooted on the earth for a few moments early in the morning.[1]

---

1 This is not a requirement of the Order, but is recommended. More harm than good will result, however, if practiced only intermittently on account of the liability to take cold. Porous moccasins may be worn, and even shoes if of porous material.

CHAPTER XXIV

THE LIGHT

"And the earth was without form, and void; and darkness was upon the face of the deep. And the Spirit of God moved upon the face of the waters. And God said, Let there be light: and there was light." Genesis I, 2-3.

"Fix thy Soul's gaze upon the star whose ray thou art, the flaming star that shines within the lightless depths of ever-being, the boundless fields of the unknown." *The Voice of the Silence*, Blavatsky, Fragment II.

In *The Voice of the Silence* we read of four periods, called "modes of Truth,"[1] through which the Candidate for discipleship must pass ere his feet can be truly planted upon the Path. Until he awakens to the desirability of the spiritual life and has heard the Voice of the Divine in his heart, the candidate is passing through the first period, called in the Hindu *Ku* or the assembling of misery, or walking in darkness. When his gaze is turned toward the Star of Initiation he calls down upon himself more rapidly his past Karma. This period is called *Tu* or the assembling of temptations. In the third period he meets and conquers all temptations and wipes out all old karmic debts, which period is called *Mu*, the destruction of temptations. And only in the fourth period, called *Tau*, does he consciously enter upon the Path.

Just as the candidate requires four periods of creation through which he must pass ere he can create for himself a new life and a new world (his Path), so in

---

1 "*Ku*, suffering or misery; *Tu*, the assembling of temptations; *Mu*, their destruction; and *Tau*, the Path," p. 21.

the Creation of a planet there are four days or periods in which there is a completion of mere earth conditions (the Path of the planet) preparatory to the real purpose of evolution, which is to prepare a field (the Path) for the continued evolution of mankind.

The first creation is that of light, symbolizing the light of The Christos which breaks into the darkness of man's ignorance and sin and turns his attention toward a higher life. This light perceived in his heart is called the Star of Initiation because the first glimpse of its glory initiates him into a new world, and the memory of that flash leaves him no peace until he seeks its source. This Light shines in the darkness of the unawakened Soul and the darkness comprehendeth it not; it moves like the Spirit of God over the face of the restless waters of humanity and awakens to life that which is latent therein. The darkness is pregnant with the potencies of all things, both good and evil, which at the breaking forth of the light become energized with new life and begin their slow evolution toward perfection. As with the earth when God said, "Let there be light," so with the candidate. The instant he perceives the light of The Christ within, every hidden thing within him is energized and awakened to activity; for only by this fermentation can the evil be transmuted and evolve into good.

In the second period is created a firmament and the waters are separated from the waters. In the life of the candidate this period is passed in learning to separate his higher from his lower nature; in learning to separate the desires (symbolized by water—illusion) which drag him down from those which tend toward the higher life. By this separation he creates for himself a positive ideal toward which to strive (heaven) and recognizes the overshadowing of his

Higher Self (the firmament). The acquired meaning of the word firmament is to make firm, the true meaning being an expanse or the circle within which a definite creation takes place. In the second period the candidate creates for himself a definite circle or defines the limits of his spiritual aura within which must evolve his spiritual body, just as the earth evolves within its firmament or the limits of its auric zone.[1]

In the third period the dry land, the seas and all vegetation producing seed after its kind is created. In the candidate this is the period in which he brings forth and conquers his lower nature. He here gains the power of standing on a firm foundation (the dry land) and separating from this all that is illusory (the sea). He deliberately plants, and by the power of the Divine Will, brings forth such seeds as he chooses. Only when this is accomplished to a greater or lesser degree can he really enter the Path itself. Only when he has grasped enough of the philosophy of the workings of the Divine Law to give him a reason for the faith that is within him, a reason that cannot be shaken by doubts or sophistries, can he have a firm foundation upon which to stand.

Each pupil is passing through one of these periods of creation, but only when he has reached the fourth has he really created the Path. In ancient Temples the sacred shrine was approached by seven steps, the fourth of which was a broad terrace upon which most of the ceremonies took place. Only the few initiated priests and priestesses were permitted to ascend the higher steps; for the fourth step symbolized the Path and only those who had conquered the

---

1   See the meaning of the circle in Chapter XXXIV.

steps of approach and had created the Path could go higher. Some of you have reached this fourth step or period, while most of you are struggling upon one of the three lower, still assembling the various trials and temptations which must be met and conquered ere the Path is entered.

The trials that come to you are more than mere tests. When the gods said, "Let there be light" the light began to penetrate into the darkness—the cast-off matter of a previous world period, all that had not been transmuted into good. This is the outer darkness into which the un-profitable servant is cast,[1] which simply means that all the matter which should be the servant of its Lord (The Christ), but which fails to respond during one period of manifestation, must pass through a period of outer darkness or lie in the grave until the resurrection or the dawn of the next Manvantara.[2] In many respects the dark-ness might be compared to a compost heap into which all refuse, effete and unusable matter is cast, there to ferment in darkness until the next springtime when it can be spread upon the earth and its life-force, trans-muted by the powers of the elements, can be utilized to bring forth flowers, fruits and grains for the service and sustenance of man. This accumulated mass is dark-ness because it is composed of dead matter, incapable of reflecting light. In the same way the candidate in his past lives has left a trail of darkness composed of ef-fete emanations which he has failed to redeem. This is often poetically alluded to as the trail of the serpent. In *The Voice of The Silence*, "It is the shadow of thyself

---

1   *St. Matthew* XXV, 30.
2   A day period of the world as contrasted with a night period or *Pralaya*.

outside the Path, cast on the darkness of thy sins." Like the darkness of Chaos, it is pregnant with the germs of that which must ultimately come into the light and be redeemed by its creator, i.e., be transmuted into force that shall bring forth life more abundantly.

It was only in the fourth day that the path of the earth's evolution was really entered upon, *i.e.*, when the greater and lesser lights, the stars, the days and nights, the times and seasons were created. Only when this period was reached was the earth ready for the evolution brought over from a past world period to continue.

The loathsome, creeping things of the darkness were not created by the Light, but were all in the darkness simply awaiting the energizing force of the Light to quicken them. The Light was sent into the darkness not to stir up evil, but by the Omniscient Law, which recognizes that only by fulfilling its destiny can evil be transmuted into good. The evil weeds must grow, be uprooted, die and give their life-force back to the soil ere their power can manifest as food for man. So with the candidate. He must penetrate the darkest depths of his being and not deny, but face and recognize all he finds therein ere he can conquer. This he does through the divine power of The Christ when he says, "Let there be light." There is then created in him two great lights, the masculine force of the sun and the feminine force of the moon, the greater to rule the day, the lesser the night. The sun-force is the masculine quality of reason which gives him light, courage and power to grapple with the temptations and problems of his everyday life, while the moon-force—lesser only in that it is less apparent—is the Intuition which will illumine his darkest night and give him the power to understand the forces of his inner nature.

The instant the Star of Initiation sends down this two-fold ray into the darkness of his earth life, every creeping thing, not only in his heart, but also in his environment, comes forth. The instant he speaks the Word all this darkness filled with thought-currents of evil—powerful, malignant, deadly beyond description, but heretofore inert, asleep, quiescent—will be stirred into life, in this way precipitating his Karma upon him. In the creation of the earth it was the assembled gods (the Elohim) who spake the word, "Let there be light," and the chaotic mass out of which the new world was to evolve began its evolution. It was the offscourings, that which They themselves had left behind when They reached Godhood in previous world periods, and consequently it was Their own creation and Theirs to redeem. So with the candidate. The darkness, the evil, the temptations that assail him are his own. He has created them in ages past. And when he comes to this conscious step where, of his own free-will, he determines to create his Immortal Body, all this left over material must be purified and redeemed; for only out of it can he build his Immortal Habitation.

Try to think of a God Consciousness so comprehending this law and so recognizing the needs of the creatures of the darkness and so filled with the determination to bring good out of evil that, in speaking the Word, the full comprehension of all the steps of the evolution of the chaotic darkness, with the attendant suffering and misery through which it must pass as a result of the purifying process, was fully grasped. Moreover, having the consciousness that the light He was sending into the darkness was His very Self, His consciousness, His Soul-substance, and that all the sin and suffering that man would pass through on the road to redemption would be His own; that every

pang must be suffered with a God-like power to understand its keenest bitterness, still, in divine compassion,
seeing the end from the beginning, would nevertheless
speak the Word unfalteringly, and in speaking it take
upon Himself the whole burden of the transmutation of
the evil into good. This is the true meaning of redemption through love. For the world was not redeemed by
the crucifixion of one man—however much that man
manifested The Christ, and however much of the darkness was redeemed thereby. It is by the daily and hourly
crucifixion of the conscious power of the Godhead (The
Christ) in matter, the living in the darkness and suffering
with it until, atom by atom, the whole is transmuted by
His life-force (the symbolic "blood,") that the redemption of the world is accomplished. Every earnest Soul
who recognizes this principle and takes upon himself
the redemption of his own creations thus becomes a
redeemer to that extent, and releases The Christ from
the cross through the crucifixion of his own personality.

Do not think of The Christ as an impersonal force, a
mere law of action, but as the full consciousness of the
Godhead which is literally "wounded for our transgressions, he was bruised for our iniquities: the chastisement
of our peace was upon him; and with his stripes are we
healed,"[1] for "In him (The Christ) dwelleth all the fullness of the Godhead bodily." Some conception of this
divine sacrifice must penetrate the consciousness of every sincere follower of the Light, and in a lesser sense
he must have the same willingness to suffer and endure
with and through his creations—and for the same reason,
i.e., that Divine Compassion which "would not that any
perish, but all have eternal life." This is an effort to make
your finite minds grasp an infinite reality, but at least a

---

1 *Isaiah* LIII, 5.

faint conception of this Infinite Love and Compassion and yearning to create and redeem must be grasped ere the candidate can hope to set foot upon the Path. For this thought is the illumination given by the Star of Initiation or the Light shining in the darkness. Only the light of this star or this Divine Love can give him strength to brave "the lions in the way." The vision of the Light may be but a fleeting glimpse, but it will awaken within him a response that will forever urge him on until victory is attained.

If you carry this lesson into your own lives you will see why so many undreamed of trials and temptations are the first result of your determination to lead a spiritual life. The more powerful the Light, the more earnestly you determine to lay every corner of your life open to it, the more you let the Light shine out into the darkness of surrounding conditions, the more will the germs of unsuspected traits and temptations awaken to life and assail you and evil conditions surround you, conditions of sickness, poverty, lack of love and appreciation and many other adverse things. These conditions do not come to you to hurt you, nor are they sent by any great Being who desires to see you squirm—as a scientist might impale a beetle on a pin or cut out a frog's heart to see how long it would beat—but they come to you, their creator, to be redeemed because they were latent in your personality, and the first beams of The Christ-star penetrating the darkness awakened them to life. They are not sent to see you prove your strength by conquering them, although you grow stronger with everything you conquer, but they are the denizens of your deep, creatures of your own past evil thoughts; the devils which behold The Christ (the Light) and tremble. The word tremble is not used here with the idea of fear, but with the idea of quivering with the vibrations of the new life as it imparts a higher rate of vibration to the latent substance of evil. Hence a recognition of this fact and a determination to redeem all by the power of The Christ will transmute it into good.

Therefore do not be surprised if things assail you more than formerly. Do not expect that seeking for Spiritual Wisdom will make life easy or will mean that all your trials are over. Do not seek The Christ-life for the purpose of making your pathway in life smooth, your body free from disease or your environment free from inharmony and trial, for if you seek it for this purpose know well that you have not really spoken the creative Word and must reap bitter disappointment. These things must come, but if you are strong and determined and earnest and fearless, and keep on crying, "Let there be light," you will have the power of the Light to pass this step; for this step is the destruction or transmutation of all temptations into the strength necessary to enter consciously into the Path.

Take courage. Never say, "I cannot," for by the power of The Christ within you *can*. There is nothing in yourself or your environment that you cannot transmute into good, for all constitute the "worldly goods" given you by your Father-in-heaven, out of which you must create your Immortal Habitation. Whatsoever you put behind you and say you cannot conquer today, must pass into the outer darkness (outer, in that it is out of your present life), there to remain until you are strong enough once more to take it up and redeem it.

Your loving Father will help you. In tenderest pity he sees your struggles and your despair. But if you give up and cry "I cannot," then, in mercy, you are lifted out of the Path and another night's sleep is given you in which to gather strength—you must await the light of another day. For, know well that you must come again and take up the task again and again until all is redeemed.

It is often remarked that many reach a certain point of development and then apparently fall back. This means that they have failed in some important task and are awaiting the coming of a new day period. But "the enemies he slew in the last battle will not return to life in the next birth that will be his."

Fear not. Go forward, even though the darkness be full of life. "If thou wouldst not be slain by them, then must thou harmless make thy own creations, the children of thy thoughts, unseen, impalpable, that swarm around humankind, the progeny and heirs to man and his terrestrial spoils."[1] But if thou "Fix thy Soul's gaze upon the star whose ray thou art," it will lead thee into the Path.

Be not discouraged, for you are able and strong. You shall come forth victorious, but ask not that one drop of bitterness pass until all is transmuted; until you have drained the cup, and in its dregs have found the Jewel of Great Price, for which a man will sell all that he hath to possess. Keep on crying, "Let there be light." Create and redeem. For thereby shall you pass through the fifth and sixth periods and shall come to the seventh, when ye shall rest from your labors and the God Within shall see His creations and pronounce them good.

Just as this is true of each individual, so is it true of this Movement. And as a Movement it must pass through the same periods or stages. The trumpet blast has gone forth, "Let there be light!"

---

1   *The Voice of The Silence*, Blavatsky, Fragment III.

and all the hosts of evil are stirring into activity at the sound. The Movement must be created by the united effort of every candidate, for each is individually responsible for its success. "Wherefore take unto you the whole armour of God, that ye may be able to withstand in the evil day, and having done all, to stand . . . and above all, taking the shield of faith, wherewith ye shall be able to quench all the fiery darts of the wicked."[1]

---

1 *Ephesians* VI, 13-16.

CHAPTER XXV

THE TWO TABLES OF STONE

"And he gave unto Moses, when he had made an
end of communing with him upon Mount Sinai, two
tables of testimony, tables of stone, written with the
finger of God." *Exodus*, XXXI-18

"Therefore, the Kabalists say correctly that 'Man
becomes a stone, a plant, an animal, a man, a spirit,
and finally God,' thus accomplishing his cycle or
circuit and returning to the point from which he
started as the *Heavenly Man*."

The Secret Doctrine, Blavatsky, Vol. II, 196.

The great Law of the Universe, that which manifests
forever in man, atom and world as the law of spiritual
evolution, works forever onward and upward toward
more perfect manifestations. This great Law, or the
Flame of Divine Love burns forever, sending out its
light, its sparks and its fire-mist, which, cooling gradually, condenses into ethereal and later into what we
know as dense matter, producing the physical aspect of
planets, creatures, men. The law under which this force
of Divine Love operates is unchangeable, but its manifestations in any system of worlds are guided and varied
by the Planetary Deities or the Divine Intelligences
ruling the planets composing the system. In our solar
system these great Beings are called, in the *Bible*, the
Archangels or the Elohim[1] and in the Eastern teachings,
the Rishies.

This earth is the culminating point of this system, but in some respects the least evolved. It is the
point of greatest descent, the lowest arc of outward

---

[1] Note use of the plural in *Genesis* III, 22.

ongoing, where, having reached its lowest manifestation
in matter, the Law must turn and evolve upward. Ere the
Law can gather up the forces of the other six planets,
complete the last note in the octave of this solar system
and make it the first note of a higher octave of planetary
manifestation, there must be a great testing and balancing, both of its inhabitants and of the planet as a whole.

In the foundation of this solar system it was the force
of Saturn—as Lucifer, Star of the Morning—that was the
first to emanate from the symbolic dot in the circle and
expand into the circle itself, or the limits of manifestation during this great cycle; the circumference of which
God is the center. His is the force of inertia, of stability,
of perfect balance of the positive and negative forces,
without which a cosmic center could not manifest in matter; without which the other planetary forces could not
act; and as Cronus the Reaper his force will be the last to
be withdrawn or return to the bosom of the Infinite. It is
Saturn who says: "I am Alpha and Omega, the beginning
and the end, the first and the last."[1] In the book of Hermes
we read: "Among the Gods is none like unto him, into
whose hand are committed the kingdoms, the power and
the glory of the worlds. . . . Many names hath God given
him, names of mystery, secret and terrible. God calleth
him Satan the Adversary, because Matter opposeth Spirit,
and Time accuseth even the saints of the Lord. . . . For
Satan is the magistrate of the Justice of God (Karma): he
beareth the balance and the sword. . . . Therefore Satan
is the Minister of God, Lord of the seven mansions of
Hades (matter, our earth), the Angel of the manifested

---

1   *Revelation* XXII, 13.

worlds."[1] As the Great Tester[2] and Initiator, Saturn initiated man into the mystery of the power to create, by the
right use of which he shall eat of the Tree of Immortal
Life and become as the gods.[3] It is the perfect balancing
of its positive and negative manifestations and the right
use of this godlike power to create that is the great test
of mankind. Upon the mastering of this problem the fate
of this planet depends. "Thus 'Satan,' . . . grows into the
grandiose image of one who makes of a *terrestrial*, a
divine Man; who gives him, throughout the long cycle
of Mahakalpa, the law of the Spirit of Life, and makes
him free from the Sin of Ignorance, hence of Death."[4]

Saturn, then, is one of the Elohim who "falls"[5] from
heaven to take charge of the evolution of man on this
lowest planet, the densest field of manifestation. He it is
who becomes the Law-giver, he who writes "with the finger of God" the great Law of Divine Love upon the two
tables of stone, or man and woman, now for the first time
manifesting in separate, dense, physical bodies. He stands
upon the top of Mount Meru or Mount Sinai, the mountain of the gods, and delivers to man the Law. Those who
can behold him see that his countenance—as Lucifer, Son
of the Morning, the Herald of a new day—shines with
the light of Divinity, but for the multitude he is hidden
by the devouring fire and the clouds of smoke and they
know him only as the Tester, the Adversary. For the enlightened he is the Fire of the Lord; for the multitude, the
cloud upon the mountain. This same idea is symbolized

---

1   Quoted in *The Perfect Way*, Kingsford, Appendix XV.
2   *Job*, chapter I.
3   *Genesis*, III, 22.
4   *The Secret Doctrine*, Blavatsky, Vol. I, 220.
5   *Isaiah*, XIV, 12.

in the *Bible* by Moses receiving the Law on Mount Sinai, Mount Sin, the Mount of the Moon, or generation and regeneration. "The numbers of the name 'Moses' (345) are those of 'I Am That I Am,' (543), so that Moses and Jehovah are at one in numerical harmony."[1] But the numbers are reversed, hence Moses is but the reflection on earth of the Law-giver on high. Therefore, I Am That I Am, Moses, Mikael-Jehovah, the tribal god of the Hebrews, and Satan or Saturn are all symbols of varying aspects of the one great Law-giver.

In all philosophies and scriptures we find the term "stone" used not in a literal, but in a mystical sense. One fundamental meaning of this symbol is that power or force which is the foundation of man's manifested existence. Man is symbolized by a stone because here on this lowest of the planets he has reached his densest expression or state of consciousness, a state so dense— from the viewpoint of his Divine Consciousness—that it is like that of a stone as compared with man. The old Alchemists also used the term "stone" in a symbolic way. One meaning of the Philosopher's Stone, the Alkahest or Elixir of Life is the perfect blending of the masculine and feminine forces or the transmutation of the base principles into a perfect harmony which turns everything it touches into pure spiritual gold. Only when man had reached the point of densest materiality did the Great Law, working through Saturn or Mikael-Jehovah, make it possible for him to manifest this foundation stone of his spiritual evolution upon two separate tables. Hitherto man had been androgynous and ethereal, but because he had reached his densest state it was necessary that this "stone" be broken or that the positive and

---

1   *The Secret Doctrine*, Vol II, 568.

negative aspects of the creative force be separated in order to manifest in physical matter. For the dense animal bodies of the first *physical* race[1] (the Third Race) were able to manifest only the lower aspect of the positive force and were utterly unable to manifest the negative or feminine force.

The perfect balancing of these two forces—which Saturn demands before the Soul, on its return journey, can reach its Father's house—is the great task which humanity must fulfill in spirit and in truth. But it can be fulfilled only when the two tables of stone become one. The positive aspect of the Law is written upon the masculine table in positive, raised letters. This table has been set up in the market-place and its laws have dominated the world. The negative aspect is graven deep into the feminine table and its markings have been filled with the mire and filth of man's lusts, so that for ages he has been unable to read the writing and has imagined that the Law was written only on his own table and that the feminine table was a blank given to him as a toy, upon which, with his soiled and clumsy finger, he could trace whatever characters he desired. Sometimes he has striven to write beautiful eulogies, but in most cases lust and dominion have been his themes. And so through all the Dark Ages of man's mentality the idea prevailed that this feminine stone was man's, to use as he would. But the fires of suffering into which man has cast the negative stone is purifying its clay and is burning the divine characters into her Soul so that she knows the law of her being is Divine and is perverted only by man's refusal to recognize the writing and give her her true place by his side.

---

1   The first two Races were ethereal, not physical.

In the *Bible* we read of the stone that was rejected by the builders, but which, through the power of The Christ is to become the chief stone of the corner. But this mystic stone can not be perfected and become the cornerstone of the Temple of the New Humanity until its two halves are united, until the positive letters of the one fit into the negative characters of the other and the two are fused into one through the power of The Christ. Until this cycle in the world's history every system of religion and exoteric philosophy has rejected the feminine stone and either taught the absolute separation of the sexes—segregating women in convents and men in monasteries—or has in some way rejected woman and forced the stones to remain separate, even to the extent of denying to woman a Soul and barring her from Paradise except to minister to man's desires. The day of the fulfillment of the prophecy is now dawning, and those who can grasp the significance of the blending of the two tables of the Law have a great work to do, that the coming sixth sub-race may lay this chief corner-stone, upon which alone the Temple of Humanity can be erected by the Sixth and Seventh Great Races.

Humanity is facing its great Initiation. Mikael-Moses has brought down the two tables of stone. And it must be you, if you are ready with clean hands and a pure heart, who must set up these tables in the Holy of Holies, instead of the market-place, and read out of them the Law to the children of earth who are so eagerly waiting to learn. Individually, at the very entrance to the Path back to Eden, there confronts you the Angel of the Flaming Sword, Mikael, the great Regent of Saturn, with the two tables of the Law. He gives them to you saying "This is the Law; this the problem. Learn ye it. Work it out and teach it to the children of earth." Why is it such an enigma? Why must the cloud and the burning of the mountain hide him from your sight? Why do you let the world go on worshiping the golden calf, leaving the great problem of the Law to be solved by the few who are unafraid and who are willing to climb the Mount of Attainment and receive their great test?

The children of earth are making mock, are degrading themselves and burying the Law beneath the horrible mire of their own sensuality, because they will not read it from its two tables. Again and again have the Prophets of the Lord sought to bring the Law before the multitude. And many sincere teachers who have led their followers out of the darkness of Egypt, after wandering many years in the wilderness and laboriously climbing the mountain and receiving the dual Law, have, nevertheless, cast it out of their control and broken it. And even though they may be the means of pointing the way to the Promised Land to many followers, these teachers, like Moses, will be debarred from entering in during this incarnation.

It takes clean hands and pure hearts and brave, determined Souls to lift this banner of the Law before the world, but it must be accomplished. This is the beginning of a new cycle, when an advanced step must be taken in this old, old problem. Every Soul who is now interested in it has in ages past been among those who have tried and failed and suffered. But there must now come the strength of all the past efforts and the wisdom which the suffering has impressed upon each Soul. Many as women have had the iron of slavery driven deep into their Souls and hence find within them an inborn quality which cries out not for vengeance, but recognition, equality and readjustment. Others as men have helped trample under foot the feminine stone and striven to obliterate the writing of the finger of God, yet have found their boasted supremacy unsatisfying. They have felt the need for something more than a plaything, more than a household drudge and child-bearer, more even than an enshrined idol. The Soul knows its need of that help which can only come from the complement which God himself has supplied. For the manifestations of the Law having been separated, neither can be complete without the other. They are like children who are reading an interesting story, but who have lost the sequel. They find life an unfinished story. So the two types—all those who have reached the point of evolution where the Soul cry is heard—are ready for the readjustment and are crying out for something that shall make straight the crooked paths and lighten the great burden of misery for the world.

The natural outgrowth of these karmic conditions is unrest and dissatisfaction in marital relations. The woman-question is a burning one. Many are eager for political freedom, some few as eager to prevent it. But the political side of the question is but a bubble upon the surface of the greater question of the unification of the two tables of stone, showing that the great stream of humanity is passing over shoals which cause the bubbles to come to the surface. Only as humanity reaches into its deeper levels and its foaming waters and conflicting currents have been blended into one steady stream, can it flow in peace and power down the channels of time, watering all the land and making the desert places in life bloom as the rose. Mankind must recognize that the Law can never be fulfilled until its two tables have been cleansed from the pollution that obscures the writing and each has been given its true value and they have been fitted together and become one. Then it will be seen that neither man nor woman is superior, nor can either, by any possibility, rightfully usurp the place or perform the duties of the other; in fact, neither one can fulfill the whole Law without the harmonious blending and co-operation of the other.

Man is the positive expression of the Law on the physical-plane, but negative upon the spiritual plane. Hence, it was necessary that he dominate during those stages of evolution in which the conquering of the rude outward conditions of physical life were of prime importance to the welfare of the Race. In the united life of the family to him belongs the conditions of the outer world, the physical labor, the fighting, the providing for and protecting of the home, the execution of that which is planned by the two, in fact, all outward manifestations of the Law. True woman is positive upon the spiritual-plane, where man is negative, and negative upon the physical-plane, where man is positive. To her belongs the control of all those questions which deal with the higher life. She must use her intuition in the directing of all activities pertaining to the altruistic side of life, just as man uses his reason in worldly affairs. She should be man's moral and spiritual monitor and should be his source of inspiration and spiritual help. The two should work co-equally in all matters.

Many masculine Souls now incarnated in feminine bodies are working strenuously and with all the masculine characteristics to bring about the political freedom of woman which they were instrumental in preventing her from obtaining in the past. But it is the true feminine influence that is needed in the political arena, not masculine influence in feminine garb; for it is just as necessary there as in the home, the state and nation being but a larger family. No business or worldly affairs should be carried on without the inspiration and moral sanction of woman, and no feminine plans be carried out without man's active help and cooperation in making them positive and practical on the earth-plane. In other words, woman, while she cultivates her intuition, love, sympathy and spiritual aspiration, should have those qualities balanced by reason, logic, courage and commonsense. Man, while cultivating the positive qualities of courage, reason and executive ability, should balance them with love, sympathy and intuition. The two should blend perfectly just as Spirit penetrates matter and is the cause back of all outward evolution, yet without which outward form it could not manifest on earth. Just as both sun and water are essential to the growing plant, an excess of either bringing disaster, but the perfect blending of the two making the earth bring forth in abundance, so should the perfect blending of man and woman make this earth a fertile field for the perfect evolution of the New Humanity. Only thus can the two tables of stone fit into each other and be fused by the power of The Christ into the chief stone of the corner, upon which the fire of Divine Love may act co-equally to transmute it into pure spiritual gold.

CHAPTER XXVI

> Oh thou loving and helpful Master Jesus! Thou
> who gavest to thy disciples power to heal the sick!
> We, recognizing Thee, and realizing Thy divine
> presence within us, ask Thee to lay Thy hands upon
> us in healing Love. Cleanse us from all our sins, and
> by the divine power of Omnipotent Life, drive out
> the atoms of inharmony and disease, and fill our
> bodies full to overflowing with Life, and Love, and
> Purity.

Many pupils when they receive this prayer either
address it to a personal Jesus or refuse to use it at all
because they object to praying to a personality, be he
ever so godlike. We wish it understood, therefore, that in
this prayer we do not pray to the man Jesus but that we
recognize Him as the high Master who is at the head of
the Healing Hierarchy, ever ready to answer such a call
as this prayer sends out. Only such a call can pierce the
clouds that hide the earthly from the Divine, and make
a channel through which the divine healing forces can
reach you.

We also use the name Jesus because of its great potency, the name Jesus having been used for centuries in
connection with the thought of personal help and healing
power. "To utter a Name is not only to define a Being,
but to place it under, and condemn (obligate) it through
the emission of the Word to the influence of, one or more
Occult potencies. Things are, for every one of us, that
which it (the Word) makes them while naming them."[1]

---

1   *The Secret Doctrine*, Blavatsky, Vol I, 121.

Therefore do not hold the erroneous idea that you are to worship any personalized deity, be He ever so high, but endeavor to realize the divine Presence within you of The Christ-force which the *Bible* allegory makes a living factor in the world and which the Master Jesus personifies. Pause for one moment and try to grasp the idea that to realize the presence of the Great Healer, as in the prayer you say you do, is for the moment, while the realization lasts, to become one with the Divine. You then understand that the Real Self is not a mere personality made up of worn out and dying atoms, but is something Divine, one with God, all holy and all powerful, one with all good from eternity to eternity. This realization may be but a flash, but in that flash you have partaken of all that can be imagined of power and strength and glory. With this understanding of the prayer never repeat it without pausing at the words and realizing the Divine Presence within you, for it is not something outside yourself, but an inflow of the Divine made possible by the opening of your heart and consciousness.

If your eyes could be opened to see the effect the repetition of this prayer produces on the higher planes, the forces it brings to your aid, you would realize its beauty and its power.

When you say "lay Thy hands upon us in healing love," it is a literal adaptation of the words, "Thou hast made Thine angels Thy handmaidens, and Thy ministers a flaming sword;" for the angelic hosts minister to all pure hearts who desire their help. The hands which you ask the great Master to lay upon your head are His powers to accomplish, which powers are executed by this host of angels who have the power to carry the divine force to you. When you recite it in harmony, the angels crowd around you like flocks of doves, to ward off harmful forces and protect the germ of your physical, mental and spiritual life. For it is a spiritual battle-cry calling to your aid the angelic hosts whose joy it is to succor those who fight the good fight. The *Bible* speaks of the angels as always beholding the face of The Christ; that is, their development is such that they can see nothing on the earth-plane but The Christ-principle, or the face of The Christ, in each heart. If that face is obscured by clouds of selfishness and impurity they cannot see you, and consequently cannot bring you help. But the instant the cry for help goes up from the heart, they fly to your aid at the command of their Leader.

Angels have always been recognized, under various names, in all religions. They belong to a different evolution from humanity, although closely allied, and necessarily have different lessons to learn and different work to do. They are complementary to humanity, strong where humanity is weak; weak where humanity is strong. They stand to humanity as a true wife should stand to her husband; in fact, they may be said to represent the feminine aspect of humanity. They are the "Ministers and Stewards of the Mysteries," the "hosts of the Lord" that carry out His commands. They are the go-betweens and messengers, and have a might and a power unknown to mortal man. We must never forget the love we owe these ministering ones.

Upon the highest plane of Spirit, life is the One Life which can be nothing but perfection. The repetition of this prayer is like a projectile fired through the earth's atmosphere creating a passage through which the One Life must necessarily flow. As it passes from plane to plane it manifests upon the soul plane—the plane of creation and of redemption—as spiritual love. Thus does the Son of God (the One Life) descend from His Father to redeem the world through love. When this spiritual love reaches the plane of generation, the physical plane, its manifestation in the body is purity. Thus The Christ manifests on the spiritual plane as the One Life, on the soul-plane as Love and on the physical-plane as Purity.

This is the rationale of all healing, and a thorough recognition and realization of the presence of this spiritual life-force, and its working out in a three-fold manner, produces that harmony which is health to both mind and body. It also harmonizes conditions in your environment. Unkindness or hatred in your heart produce inharmony and sickness by condensing your aura and shutting out this force of life from you. If you send a thought of hatred toward a person you put a wall around yourself which only your own loving thoughts, and prayers such as the above, can pierce and break down, and which shuts out the life force from you and permits disease to flourish.

Whenever you desire help, physical, mental or spiritual, either for yourself or others, repeat this prayer, meditating on each word and trying to realize its true meaning on all planes of your being. Realize that there are currents of spiritual force which are potent and bring renewed life and strength to your physical body as well as peace and content to your mind and happiness and joy to your Soul. And in this prayer you are consciously invoking these forces.

As the Master Jesus gave to His disciples the power to heal the sick, and has never withdrawn that gift, so every true disciple who firmly believes this, and faithfully strives to manifest The Christ principle within him, has *now* the power, through the laying on of hands (by the summoning of the angelic hosts), to bring this One Life into manifestation, and thus dissipate ills and promote health and harmony.

CHAPTER XXVII

THE SILENCE

"But thou, when thou prayest, enter into thy closet, and when thou hast shut thy door, pray to thy Father which is in secret; and thy Father which seeth in secret shall reward thee openly." *St. Matthew* VI, 6.

We have so many inquiries from our pupils for some method by which they can strengthen their wills and hasten their spiritual growth that we desire to give a brief outline of the first stages of this process.

We cannot emphasize too strongly the fact that there is but one way to grow, i.e., according to the Law of Growth followed by Nature. "Grow as the flower grows, unconsciously, but eagerly anxious to open its soul to the air. So must you press forward to open your soul to the eternal. But it must be the eternal that draws forth your strength and beauty, not desire for growth. For in the one case you develop in the luxuriance of purity, in the other you harden by the forcible passion for personal stature."[1] In this one paragraph is contained the great secret of all growth and the student must grasp its significance and master it. Indeed, until the essence of the truth underlying the above direction has been mastered and incorporated into the consciousness, to attempt any practice calculated to unfold inner faculties is fraught with grave dangers. We begin this chapter, therefore, with the injunction to all our pupils to take the ideas contained in the above quotation and meditate upon them until they are fully understood —

---

1 *Light on the Path,* p. 5.

understood not as words merely, but as vital life experiences—ere they attempt further advance.

The student should pause here and clearly distinguish between concentration, meditation, prayer and entering the Silence. Concentration is focusing the attention upon a chosen object or idea. It is the first step toward accomplishing any given end, either in the physical, mental or higher worlds. Meditation is turning over in the mind a thought or idea that you may see it from every standpoint and grasp all its phases and relations. It is an active mental process which occupies the undercurrents of your mind even while it may be overseeing more superficial affairs. The proof that we can meditate while engaged in daily affairs is found in the fact that if we have some great joy or sorrow it will remain in the background of our consciousness no matter what we do to distract our attention from it. Apply the same principle to your spiritual life and make the attainment of that life your main thought and aim.

Prayer is an aspiration of the Soul toward the Divine. It may also be a request, not for creature comforts or physical things—answers to such prayers are but the result of mental magic—but for spiritual food, love, light, courage, etc. In fact prayer creates a magnetic line of force which unites you with the supply. Entering the Silence is an ecstatic state in which the human consciousness is transcended and, while it lasts, all sense of the personality is lost. While we teach that life itself brings to the earnest seeker all the discipline necessary to strengthen his will, and that the ruling of his life brings the most rapid spiritual growth, still it is well to have a definite time set apart each day for concentration upon the end for which he is striving.

To meditate upon the above quotation let the pupil set apart a certain time each day, preferably in the early morning—rising ten or fifteen minutes earlier if necessary—and sit in a quiet spot (in the same chair, if possible) and repeat the foregoing passage with a prayer for light and understanding, and meditate upon it. Try to picture mentally the growth of a flower. Follow every step of its unfoldment; first the tiny seed buried in the dark earth, then the force within that seed which makes it, bye and bye, burst through its confining shell. Let your mind enter into, in fact for the time being, become this flower. Dwell upon the period of darkness necessary while the seed is sending forth its thread-like feelers, groping everywhere in the dark and gathering nourishment from the earth. With unerring instinct it follows the law of its being, selecting such nutriment as will assist its growth and rejecting that which is inharmonious. Follow the seedling through every phase of its growth. At each step apply the same law to your own growth. Think of the Soul as planted in the darkness and loneliness of the material conditions of this earth, yet containing within it the possibilities of fruition—its immortal destiny.

Do not try to follow the seed through every step of its life-journey at the first sitting; but meditate day after day upon one step or stage of growth, correlating yourself with it until you are sure you have mastered its lessons and have realized their application to your own spiritual growth. Above all make the point very clear that the seed has no personal desire to grow, nor to excel some other seed, but that it is fully occupied in fulfilling the law of its being, "to open its soul to the air." When you have mastered one phase of growth you are ready to pass on to the next.

And only when you have, at least in some measure grasped all the lessons thus taught you, are you ready to enter into the Silence, where you can learn from the Divine and hear the voice of your Higher Self "the Master whom as yet thou hast not seen but whom thou feelest." For only when the flower blooms does it open its heart to the silent power of the sun and drink in the magnetic forces which could not be assimilated until the bloom unfolded. In the same way must the student open his heart to the Sun of Righteousness ere he is ready to learn from the Voice of the Silence.

Let no pupil think, however, that when, through meditation, he has reached the Silence, henceforth he has no need of meditation; for no one can enter the Silence until by meditation he has opened his heart to the influence of the Divine as the petals of the rose open to the magnetic influence of the sun. While an effort may be made at first toward its realization, later it must become a state into which you can enter at will, shutting the door of your mind on all daily affairs and finding rest, peace and communion, even in the midst of the turmoils of life. But remember that while aids, such as concentration, breathing, etc., are helpful in their proper place they do not of themselves cause spiritual growth. They are only aids. The growth must come from dwelling in the consciousness of the Divine within you and the manifesting of The Christ-force in the daily affairs of life.

When the ability to meditate has been acquired and the pupil is ready to enter the Silence, he should first spend a few moments in deep breathing, following the method called the "Complete Breath." The greatest factor in deep breathing lies in the thought held at the time. This is the difference between deep breathing as practiced for mere physical culture and for the

control of the life-currents. While the physical cultur-
ist is breathing merely for health, the occultist realizes
that much more than physical health is to be attained,
for through the power of breath combined with Will, he
can draw in the spiritual life-essence which permeates
the higher strata of the earth's atmosphere. By the act
of consciously breathing we correlate with this essence
and draw it more completely into the body.

This breath is the fundamental breath of the entire
Science of Breath, and the student must fully acquaint
himself with it, and master it perfectly before he can
hope to obtain proper results. To accomplish this requires attention, effort and persistence, but it is essential
to further the progress along this line. When fully mastered it will become automatic. Do not neglect or belittle
it because it seems simple.[1]

The following exercise will give you a clear idea of
what the Complete Breath is:

(1.) Stand or sit erect. Breathing through the nostrils, inhale steadily, first filling the lower part of the
lungs. This is accomplished by the diaphragm, which
in descending exerts a gentle pressure on the abdominal
organs, pushing forward the front walls of the abdomen.
Then fill the middle part of the lungs, lifting the chest
and upper ribs. In the final movement, the lower part of
the abdomen will be slightly drawn in, giving the lungs
support and helping to fill the highest part of the lungs.
The three movements are not separate, but continuous,
the entire chest being expanded in uniform movement.
Avoid all jerky movements, and strive to attain a steady
continuous action.

---

1 CAUTION.—Students should be careful not to overdo this, either by using
   too many counts or by taking too many breaths at one time. Best begin with
   two or three breaths and increase gradually.

(2.) Retain the breath for a few seconds, or heart beats.

(3.) Exhale slowly in the reverse order, chest first and abdomen last.

(4.) Rest the same number of counts as in (2). The rule is to inhale for a convenient number of heartbeats (6, 8 or 10), retain the breath half this number; make the exhalation the same length as the inhalation, and the rest between breaths the same number of counts as in (2).

During the inhalation hold the thought that you are breathing in the forces of love, strength, courage and purity, or any other virtues you desire; that during the pause they are filling you full to overflowing, and that during the out-breathing you are sending out help, comfort, health and love to all mankind. Think of what you need as flowing in direct from the Divine, thus making a direct line of communication over which the Divine can reach you. Dwell upon the fact that this divine force which flows through you is *not your personal force*, and therefore when you breathe out, determine that you will send out only the force of the Divine, untainted by your personality. Realize that you are thus creating a reservoir of power; that you can draw upon it in unlimited quantities, as a seed draws to itself the power of the eternal, and by assimilating it grows naturally, yet does not monopolize that power. Realize that this power will purify the vessel (the personal self, always to be looked upon as a mere channel); that you are simply filling up the vessel that it may overflow to all, as a flower sheds abroad its perfume; and that if you are thus enabled to help others *it is not because of your personal attainments* or power, but because of the power of the Divine flowing through you—because you have be-

come "a center through which The Lodge can work."[1]
Remember, therefore, that you must keep the channel
pure and free from all contaminating influences that as
little as possible of your own personality shall enter into
the good you are enabled to send forth. For a seed must
be a healthy seed or, no matter how much of the divine
force is poured into it, it will never grow. Indeed, if it
has a canker, the divine force will but hasten its decay.

It is often a help to stand before an open window,
especially one facing the East. Raise your arms in front
of you, with fingers outspread, and try to feel the force
like a tangible thing which you can grasp. As you indraw
the breath, clench your hands and draw toward your
heart, as it were hands full of force, and feel it permeating your whole body.[2] Any action such as this will help
you to realize that you are drawing in the Divine Life.
Never, under any circumstances perform this exercise
when nervous, cross or while holding any unkind or
vindictive feeling in your heart, or the consequences
will be disastrous, for you will be drawing to you more
of the same forces. If this exercise is performed in the
evening, it will be well to fix your gaze upon the stars in
such a way as to exclude all sights of earth, if possible.

After a few short breaths, sit in an easy chair (always the same one and in the same place, if possible)
or lie flat on your back with your arms outstretched in
the form of a cross. Meditate a few moments and send
up a strong aspiration of love—it should not even be
a definite thought, but a great yearning for the Divine,
and a realization that you, in your Higher Self, are

---

1   See Chapter XXXIII.
2   CAUTION—Do not take this exercise more than thee or four times at first,
    for it is a powerful heart stimulant. If you feel faint or dizzy, stop at once, lie
    down and rest, and do not try it again the same day.

the master, and in the words of *Malachi*: "If I be a master, where is my fear"[1] —then sink into the Silence.

To acquire the ability to enter the Silence properly will take time; for you will find your mind fairly bombarded by thoughts, often of a trivial nature, which you must determinately still. This may require weeks or months of practice; for as you silence thoughts on one stratum of consciousness, your mind will still be active, but in a more interior way. "Merge into one sense thy senses, if thou would'st be secure against the foe. 'Tis by that sense alone which lies concealed within the hollow of thy brain, that the steep path which leadeth to thy Master may be disclosed before thy Soul's dim eye."[2] Do not get discouraged. "Have patience, candidate, as one who fears no failure, courts no success." When you find your mind wandering, bring it back and, if necessary, repeat, "Peace, be still." Often it is a help to repeat the word Silence or repeat your given name again and again. But when you have gained the power of Silence, stop even these helps. Your mind must be like a still mountain lake, without a ripple, capable of perfectly reflecting every passing cloud. If the surface of the lake is agitated, even by a ripple, the images on its surface will be distorted; so it is with the mind. Only when you have attained to this quietude of mind can you hope to hear The Voice of the Silence without the intermixture of personality, and observe without distortion the heavenly images reflected in your brain from your Father-in-heaven.

It is important that the student school himself to think definitely and clearly of the personal guidance of his Higher self—his Father-in-heaven who is the

---

1 Malachi I, 6.
2 *The Voice of the Silence*, Blavatsky, Fragment I.

"I am I," while the personality is but the servant. Should a student attempt to enter the Silence with no definite idea as to whose voice he is listening for —who the Master is upon whom he is to fix his whole attention— and in a negative attitude, as so often happens, he is in great danger of receiving impressions from astral entities, either departed friends, elementals or powerful but perverted entities, who would deliberately mislead and deceive him and use him as a tool to further their own ends. For this reason the attitude of Soul that must always be held is one of deep humility and ardent, aspiring devotion to the Divine. There must always be the positive expectation of entering the presence of the Divine; of listening reverently for the voice of your Father-in-heaven "He that is of God heareth God's words." There must be a definite and fixed determination to listen to nothing else, and to *permit* nothing *else* to enter your aura. Have no fear, however, for "Fear, O disciple, kills the will and stays all action." "The fear of man bringeth a snare: but whoso putteth his trust in the Lord shall be safe."[1] *Dare—Do—Keep Silent.*

If two or three are entering the Silence together let no one desire to be used as spokesman for the rest, for the very desire opens a door for personality and makes possible and easy delusions from the astral plane. Let each listen only for himself, not for another. If one should speak at such a time let the others know well that if the message is true and if they are in a state of mental poise, the endorsement will be given in their own hearts. This power of distinguishing intuitively between the true and the false is often the first conscious touch between you and your Higher Self.

That the Lord, or a Divine Intelligence, does thus

---

1 *Proverbs* XXIX, 25.

guide humanity through The Voice of the Silence is amply testified to and plainly set forth in the *Bible*, both in the *Old* and *New Testaments*, as well as in all other sacred scriptures. Indeed, the *Bible* is full of allusions to those who listened to the Voice and those who refuse to listen. As we said in a former chapter[1] the *Bible* is a symposium of allegories illustrating the spiritual truths needed by the entire Fifth Race of the Red Ray. Hence, if, as plainly stated—in language so familiar as to be almost trite—the children of God were led and directed by the Voice in past ages, it is equally true today; for there has never been given to man any statement that would give him reason to believe that there had been a change in the laws of spiritual communication or that the teachings of the Master Jesus were no longer true. The Voice of God speaks today, to all who listen, as plainly as it spake to the pure in heart of old. "Trust in the Lord with all thine heart; and lean not unto thine own understanding. In all thy ways acknowledge him, and he shall direct thy paths."[2]

When Jesus told his disciples to enter into the closet and shut the door, the closet referred to the Silence, and the "door" which they were to shut was the door of the mind. The Father who seeth in secret is the Higher Self, who does not require words, but who seeth in secret, i.e., in the Silence, through vibrations of love. The open reward is the peace, comfort and spiritual upliftment which comes as the result of such communing with the Father-in-heaven.

---

1   Chapter V.
2   *Proverbs* III, 5-6.

CHAPTER XXVIII

NATURE'S MYSTIC ALPHABET

"I will meditate also of all thy work, and talk of thy doings." *Psalms*, LXXVII, 12.

"The man who is endued with this devotion and who seeth the unity of all things, perceiveth the Supreme Soul in all things and all things in the Supreme Soul" *The Bhagavad-Gita*, Chapter VI.

It is desirable that all occult students form some definite idea of the true meanings and relations of sound, number, color and form, for they stand at the foundation of all occult training. Although this theme is so stupendous that nothing more than the briefest possible outline can be attempted in this lesson, still there have been so many vandal hands digging about this foundation—disrupting, disorganizing and giving mere surface interpretations, that many a student in his bewilderment thinks the foundation is tottering. This lesson is meant to be but a hint, an incentive to deeper study. For everything in Nature has its voice which speaks in tones so positive that it cannot mislead, if we open our ears to it.

Every shade of color in Nature indicates a potency which can be measured by its wave-length and its rate of vibration, and have its tone determined. We read—"The very hairs of your head are all numbered."[1] This is literally true, for the color of the hair together with its texture, determines the number of its vibration, just as the texture of a violin string determines the number and character of its vibrations. And the vibrations of the hair, as a part of the key-

---

[1] *St. Matthew*, X, 30.

note of the body, are one indication of the character or "the measure of a man."[1]

Every flower and herb of the field, every leaf and twig of the forest, by its color and form, its odor, its environment and its manner of growing, proclaims in unmistakable language its nature, its potencies and its uses when interpreted according to the Law of Correspondences, "As above, so below." For all Nature shapes can be traced back to and analyzed into simple geometrical figures: ●, —, Δ, □, ○, just as all musical notes produce characteristic geometrical designs when made to pass through sand or other suitable material.[2] Do not think, however, that this analysis is a simple task, for very few colors stand out alone any more than there are straight lines or exact geometrical figures in Nature. We find a multiplicity of combinations of color and form, hence, to get their true meaning, they must be separated into their elements.

Only the true student who can devote much time and study to the subject can hope to penetrate far into the secrets of Nature; nevertheless we are told, "There is nothing covered, that shall not be revealed; and hid, that shall not be known." We also read, "Help Nature and work on with her; and Nature will regard thee as one of her creators and make obeisance. And she will open wide before thee the portals of her secret chambers, lay bare before thy gaze the treasures hidden in the very depths of her pure virgin bosom. Unsullied by the hand of Matter, she shows her treasures only to the eye of Spirit—the eye which never closes, the eye for which there is no veil in all her

---

1 For scientific recognition of this fact, see an article on the relation of hair to character by Charles Kassel in *The Popular Science Monthly*, September, 1912.

2 See common high-school experiment in physics—covering a metal plate with sand and vibrating it.

kingdoms."[1] This is not a chimerical dream, but an actual possibility. It is what is really meant by living close to Nature.

Sound, number and color are the three manifestations of Deity in Nature, Nature's alphabet so to speak, and these three produce a fourth, form. Loosely speaking, sound is the first letter of this Divine Alphabet, and according to the note of vibration (number) of sound is color produced—although the sound may not be audible to the human ear—and by the interaction of these three is form created. Thus is the Word or the Creative Sound made manifest, for without these three factors nothing can be produced.

That which is called the key-note of any personality is never one musical tone, but a combination of tones, a chord. There are many ways of finding this chord, but the surest is by listening in the Silence, first asking for guidance, and striving to harmonize yourself with the Divine that is within you, your Father-in-heaven, then endeavoring to silence all other activities of your mind and listen for the answer.

Many students make the mistake of selecting exterior colors and notes and surrounding themselves with them—because those colors or tones appeal to them—and imagine they belong to them. The effect of this is to hold back the development of their real key-note, for it is generally quite different from that which they imagine. The vibrations produced by the outer colors and tones focus upon the student and drown the inner. Moreover, your true color or tone is something which you must reach out for and strive to develop within you. The instant it is thus attained the next higher color or tone becomes your key-note. It may be said that man is continually playing his

1   *The Voice of the Silence*, Blavatsky, Fragment I

Psalm of Life, in the base clef of human vibrations. Hence he experiences inharmony, sickness and sorrow until he listens to and strives to sing the melody of the treble clef as sung by his Higher Self, and make his base clef but an accompaniment. When this is done the base clef gives fullness and richness to the chords and makes the melody complete.

There are three primary colors, red, yellow and blue, a trinity which may be compared to body, soul and Spirit. Each is produced by a particular tone with a definite rate of vibration (number) and wave-length. These three form the triangle, the first geometrical figure to manifest on earth. From these three emanate four other supplementary colors (the square), orange, green, indigo and violet, and by the blending and interblending of these seven, together with black and white, are all other colors produced. In numbers also the same law is operative, for by the blending of the first seven—together with 8, the number of evolution, in which the power of the numbers is evolved into a higher octave in the same way that the colors are lifted into a higher octave by the admixture of white, and 9 (black) the number of Initiation—are all numbers produced.

In the musical scale we again find this correspondence, there being seven notes, the eighth or repeated note being the point of evolution into the next octave. The sharps raise the tones while the flats deepen them. The pause or interval in which the one octave dies and the new is born is comparable to 9 in number or black in color. Although on earth this pause seems to be silence, yet in reality, upon the spiritual-plane, it is a definite tone which comprises all preceding tones and may be called the assimilation of tones, just as black swallows up all colors yet on earth is no color.

The seven colors are born from the pure white light (or no color on the physical plane), which in turn is born from darkness (black). Hence black and white in essence are one and the same thing, the two ends of the Divine Spectrum, with all the manifestations of color as vibratory steps between them. Pure white is not known on earth, what appears as white always being tinged with yellow, blue or sometimes violet. "According to the tenets of Eastern Occultism, Darkness is the one true actuality, the basis and root of Light, without which the latter could never manifest itself or even exist. Light is matter, and Darkness pure spirit. . . . Even in the mind-baffling and science-harassing Genesis, Light is created out of Darkness—'and Darkness was upon the face of the deep'—and not vice versa. 'In him (in darkness) was life; and the life was the *light* of men.'[1] " On earth all colors are swallowed up in black, for in black no colors are visible, while all colors live in white. Black and white are represented by the straight, vertical line, which after its descent to earth passes through various geometrical forms, the first of which is the triangle, composed of the three primary creative rays, their numbers being 3, 5 and 7.

Red is the key-note of physical man and his evolution, and its rate of vibration is the slowest of the three primary colors. Being the most physical, it lends its influence to all the others, yet within it are the potencies of all. It is a masculine, not a feminine color, although in a certain sense all three primary colors may be called "mother colors" in the same way that the three letters of the Hebrew alphabet— Aleph, Mem and Shin—are called "mother letters," and with much the same meaning. The Hierarchy of the Red

---

1   *The Secret Doctrine*, Blavatsky, Vol. I, p. 98.

Ray[1] is the one now manifesting on earth, and when man has evolved beyond red, in all its varied shades, he will have become something more than what is known to-day as man. Within this Red Ray, however, all the colors manifest as sub-rays, more or less tinged with red. All colors are raised to a higher vibration by the pure white light of Spirit shining through them. Hence evolution through the Red Ray is accomplished by the lightening and added brilliancy of its shades. For instance a pale rose-pink is the lightest expression of red, while the red of venous blood is its darkest.

Red is the color of the vehicle of the life-force but not of the life-force itself (Prana) which is orange. Therefore, the blood through which the life-force manifests is red. Almost everything that grows, just as it pushes up through the soil, shows a red or pink surface, which later changes to green. All red flowers, fruits, grains, vegetables and meats tend to warm and enrich the blood and strengthen the physical body. Some of the lower aspects of red are warmth, life, passion and war, while its higher aspects are strength, courage and love. The planet corresponding to the red ray is Mars; its metal iron.

Just as the Soul is the vehicle through which the Spirit manifests, so is yellow the vehicle through which the pure spiritual light manifests. Pure yellow is therefore the Soul-color, and according to its brilliancy does it show forth the overshadowing white light of Spirit. It is the messenger of the gods, for it governs the psychic powers by which the inspiration of the gods reaches the human mind. This is symbolized by the customary use of yellow or gold hangings upon the altar and gold fringe or embroidery on the altar cloth and by the flame of the sacerdotal candles; for yellow

1 See Chapter XIII.

is the vehicle of the ray of pure Spirit or the Flame. It is the color which lends to all other colors their spiritual significance. All yellow flowers and foods are vehicles through which psychic force can enter the body to strengthen the psychic currents. A free use of yellow corn-meal in the diet and corn-water as a drink frequently proves a wonderful tonic, if not a cure, for certain psychic disorders. Its planet is Mercury, and its metal also.

Blue is the truly feminine color. It is the color of the auric envelop and of the firmament which forms the blue arch of heaven, which shuts it in and protects it. It is inspiring and uplifting; for the firmament is studded with stars, which lift the thoughts above mundane things to other worlds. This is the office of blue wherever found in Nature, to inspire, uplift, soothe, calm and comfort. In all its meanings it is the opposite or complementary of red, while yellow lends its force to both. Blue being the color of the auric zone is the color of the Mother-principle which encloses, enwraps, spiritualizes. All blue flowers would have a tendency to allay fevers, cool and comfort. Its corresponding planet is Jupiter; its metals tin and aluminum.

Of the supplementary colors, orange is the color of the pranic life-force that flows in the blood. It is a cheering, warming, forceful color having for its planet the sun, the symbol of life physically and spiritually. Red and orange are the two most masculine colors, the one being the blood and the other the vital life-force in the blood. All orange flowers and foods contain an exceptional amount of life-force, and wherever orange is found in Nature it is vibrant with life-force. Its corresponding metal is gold. And because this metal absorbs and focuses the sun-force it was used to cover the roofs of many ancient temples, and for vessels used in certain sacred services. It is pertinent to the times to note that this highest metal, like the highest spiritual concepts, is now debased and used for barter.

Green is a feminine color, the middle note in Nature, F natural or *fa*, the middle principle between the material and the spiritual. When Nature strikes her true note and throws out her cheering green in the Spring it penetrates into the hearts of men and awakens in them a desire to grow, to do, to create, to accomplish. No one thinks of calling a tree spiritual, yet who can look up into the waving green branches of a noble tree and not have his Soul lifted up from Nature to Super-Nature? Green is the color of the human intellect (*lower manas*), the highest point attainable by physical man and Nature. It is the key-note of the physical plane, hence is always restful and pleasing to man. It is the color of worldly power and the success due to intellectual attainments, its lower aspects manifesting as envy, greed, etc. It is a necessary link between Nature and Super-Nature, therefore, do not despise this color or the humble works of Nature, or even a perfect animal-soul, for without its perfect functioning, there would be no stable basis upon which and through which the higher forces could act. There have been many ridiculous theories advanced as to why Nature is green, some holding that it is due to yellow sun-light pouring through blue ether, etc., but were this true everything would be green. Nature is green because green is the point or key-note in the vibratory scale to which physical Nature upon this planet responds, and to which it has evolved. Its planet is Saturn, the Binder and also the Reaper, he who limits physical manifestation and reaps from it

the seed of spiritual attainment. Saturn is the ruler of
the earth insofar as the Saturn-force must be faced and
conquered on this planet. Its metal is lead.

Indigo is by no means blue, as so many miscall it,
but is a color by itself. It represents Spiritual Mind,
the power of the spiritual plane brought to earth and
manifested through physical man, as contrasted with
human mind or intellect. It is human intellect joined to
Soul and permeated by Spirit, forming the higher triad
or incarnating Ego. While green represents the highest point to which physical Nature and the intellect of
man can reach, indigo represents this same intellect
overshadowed and inspired by something from above,
the Divine Mind. It is the power of inspiration (*higher
manas*), which enables man to project his consciousness into realms above those capable of being reached
by the intellect alone. Like its ruling planet, Venus, indigo has its two aspects. For while it always represents
Spiritual Mind, it is often submerged and held down
to worldly concerns in spite of its ability to soar into
the Universal Mind and bring to man Divine Thought.
All indigo color in Nature, if properly used, is helpful
toward the development of this god-like power of lifting
the human consciousness above that of the intellect. Its
metal is copper.

Violet is not an earthly color. True violet is not a
mixture of red and blue—although it is usually represented on earth by such a mixture—but is a color
apart which belongs altogether to the astral-plane, its
physical counterpart being but a reflection. It is said
to be ruled by the moon, yet not really by the moon,
even though moonlight contains a high percentage
of violet and ultra-violet rays, for true violet comes
from the Mystery Planet concealed from physical

sight by the corpse[1] of the old moon, which will gradually disappear during the Sixth Great Race, allowing the Mystery Planet to be revealed to the Seventh Great Race. The potency and power of violet is due to the rays of this Mystery Planet penetrating to earth and creating the astral body, the body of sensation in which the inner forces work. Where violet is found in Nature it tends to focus the astral currents and act on astral matter. In fact it has the mysterious power of holding the potency of the astral and commanding its forces. And as the astral body of all things is the pattern of the physical, the violet ray can be utilized in perfecting an astral pattern of a superior form, and in destroying harmful astral matter.[2] Violet has the power of guarding the astral, admitting the helpful and excluding the harmful astral forces. It is ruled by the moon and its metal is silver. All other colors are mixtures or shades, or rates of vibration between these seven colors, together with black and white.

Among numbers $\bigcirc$ symbolizes limitless time in eternity, unmanifested Deity. Its geometrical form is the circle from which all numbers are born.

1 is unity, creative force, life, the Father-Mother-Son, descending to earth in an undifferentiated state. Its geometrical form is ϕ, the dot within the $\odot$ or the germinal point of the mundane egg, the nucleus in the cell.

2 is separation, the Father separates from the Mother and becomes mundane. The dot cannot manifest on earth without having two dimensions, length and breadth, and two poles, positive and negative, mascu-

---

1　It is well known that our present moon is but a corpse, giving off nothing but corpse-like emanations, hence, its malefic aspects.

2　The violet and ultra-violet rays are destructive to bacterial organisms.

line and feminine. It is represented by two geometrical forms, either the straight vertical line | or the dot with two lines of force emerging from it, —•—, both forms commonly found in Nature.[1]

3 is the Trinity, sacred and divine because it is the Father, the Mother and the Son manifesting in humanity, or man and woman united in God. Its geometrical form is the triangle. Δ

4 is the completion of physical creation, the most perfect of mundane numbers as it holds within itself the power of 10. 1+2+3+4=10. Its geometrical form is the square, □, the base of the pyramid.

5 represents humanity or man, and is one of the most mystical of numbers; for man is the climax of physical evolution, the crowning point of all the lower kingdoms and the forerunner and image of God. "Man is the universally structured type. In one aspect all lower types rise toward man and are completed in him. In another aspect the specialties of type break up and distribute downward from man to form the lower kingdoms of life, as his proper base and support. Moreover, man is the only species that stands erect, with the cerebrum poised at right angles to the spine; the only species that utilizes two limbs from the function of locomotion for the exclusive service of the mind and brain; the only species whose length of the extended hands and arms is just equal to the height of the body; the only species in which the segments of the spine are the measures of the angles of the cube; the only species with a spoken language, an alphabet, a recorded history, and a prospective future."[2] 5 is also the number of the digits of man's hands. While some animals (anthropoids)

---

1   The primitive streak emerging from the nucleus in the embryo, etc.
2   *The Romance of Revelation through Natural History*. Edw. Whipple.

have five digits, still the thumb, which in man is the great factor in the usefulness of the hand, is but rudimentary, and in primitive man noticeably undeveloped. Thus the size and shape of the thumb becomes an index to the stage of man's evolution. It marks the difference between anthropos and anthropoid. Its geometrical figure is that formed by man, his two feet outspread, his arms outstretched and his head upright forming the five-pointed star ☆, the magic pentagram.

6 is man with something else added or man considered as the Lord of Creation. 6 is primarily the number of Nature. It is the number of The Christ principle, but only as it pertains to the manifestation of that Essence of Universal Power in Nature. Hence, 6 pertains to man's powers over Nature. Its geometrical figure is the interlaced triangles. The triangle pointing upward is light, signifying man's Divine nature and his ability to receive from the Divine. The one pointing downward is dark, signifying his physical nature. The two intertwined symbolize the fact that only by the perfect blending of these two natures can man attain Wisdom. Its symbol is ✡. The interlaced triangles form the foundation stone of the objective universe. Man can only attain to Wisdom as he can correlate his consciousness with Nature.

By some 6 is called the number of unrest and incompleteness. This is true in the sense that it is the unrest of Nature ever becoming, ever changing in form that the Great Creative Principle, The Christos, may manifest more fully. 6 is formed by a circle—that which is unmanifested—with a line running upward, symbolizing the unrest of a determined aspiration reaching out to and trying to manifest ever greater degrees of Divinity.

7 is the most sacred of all numbers, for it represents the point in man's evolution where he becomes more than man. Its symbol is the interlaced triangles with the dot in the center, the dot being the same germinal point or creative center found in the mundane egg which has now manifested through Nature and man. In other words, it is the perfect blending of the 4 and the 3, the human and the Divine. The 3 represents fire while 4 symbolizes the earth. Thus 3 and 4 or fire and earth must be blended by the great Mother principle water, ere creation can be perfected. This symbol is called the Seal of Solomon or Wisdom ✡ .

8 is the number of evolution or the spiral motion of cycles, the Breath of the Cosmos. Its symbol is two ciphers touching and blending ∞. 8 is also the double square, or the foundation stone with the cornerstone laid, upon which the higher life shall be erected.

9 is the number of Initiation. It is that most mysterious number which never changes. No matter how multiplied or added the sum of the resulting digits will always equal 9 *i.e.*, 9+9=18=9 or 3 x 9=27=9 etc. In it all numbers are swallowed up to emerge once more in a new cycle 10. Thus it is truly the number of initiation, for the various initiations are steps in the Soul-life. No matter how you have multiplied sensation, experiences, knowledge or attainment you cannot pass your Great Initiation until you have returned to that from which you started, just as all multiples of 9 return to 9. 9 is also 3 x 3 or the trinity of trinities, Nature, Man and God.

According to Hermetic philosophy, it stands for the Lamp of Hermes, the Mantle of Apollonius and the Staff of the Patriarchs. "Hermes has made it the number of initiation, because the initiate reigns over superstition and by superstition, and alone can advance through the darkness, leaning on his staff, enveloped in his mantle, and lighted by his lamp."[1]

In 9 we find again the cipher with which we started, but with a straight line descending from it. Later, when the Initiation is completed, this line will take its place to the right of the cipher making 10, completing the cycle and making man more than man.

All even numbers are mundane and pertain to the physical plane, while all odd numbers are Divine. They contain something which cannot be measured by the two forces, positive and negative, always operative on the physical plane. These are the principal meanings of numbers, all others must be determined by the Law of Correspondences.

The lesson to be learned from these examples of the One Law is the importance of little things, for to the occultist there are no little things. Everything that is, every thought, word and deed, has its sound, number, color and form. These letters of Nature's Mystic Alphabet are always creating—spelling out words, which words are telling the story of your life, writing it indelibly upon your countenance and upon the everlasting akashic records. Strive, therefore, to write the history of this day of life in letters of gold. Let all your colors be pure, bright and radiant; for whether you realize it or not, your colors are continually emanating from you and are implanting your history on every person and thing you come in contact with. They also bring back to you their physical results which are built into your form so that, in very truth, your physical body—as well as the spiritual, mental and astral—is the result of your thoughts. Truly is it said of man, "As he thinketh in his heart, so is he."

---

1 *Transcendental Magic*, Levi, p. 87.
   NOTE—We request our students not to ask us to give their color or key-note, for until they set to work diligently to find out for themselves it cannot be given to them. Until they have reached a stage of positiveness and have grasped some realization of how to seek within, their colors are too indistinct and changeable to be truthfully described.

CHAPTER XXIX

THE WORD

"And the Word was made flesh, and dwelt among us, (and we beheld his glory, the glory as of the only begotten of the Father,) full of grace and truth." *St. John* I, 14.

"By the word of the Lord were the heavens made; and the host of them by the breath of his mouth." *Psalms* XXXIII, 6.

As humanity advances a point is reached where there is a widespread recognition of an esoteric teaching beneath the letter of the law, and consequently many scholars are digging with vandal hands into the sacred Mysteries, and, without heeding the advice of the Sages, are flinging to the world all sorts of scholastic explanations, calculated rather to bring prestige to themselves than in any way to elucidate the Mysteries for the good of humanity. The day has passed when the majority of mankind is content to accept any translation of the *Bible* as literally true, for, like all scriptures, its teachings are given by means of parables and allegories, both the Old and New Testaments setting forth the vital truths, in symbolic language; that is, the inner and deeper truths are veiled under symbols which of themselves inculcate a complete moral code, but which are not meant to be taken literally.

From the beginning there has always existed an exoteric teaching understood by the multitude, and an esoteric teaching given only to the few whose training has fitted them to understand it. And in this cycle of spiritual unfoldment, it is advisable that a few of these Mysteries be at least partially unveiled, that the spiritual discernment of the few may lead to the knowledge of the many.

The Word is the voice of the Higher Self—The Christ within[1]—and is the personal God of each individual, because the fleeting human personality is but the shadow cast by that which is a direct Ray from the Divine—The Christ within. The sun forever keeps its appointed place in the heavens, but its rays reach and penetrate every portion of the earth. Without those rays nothing could be brought forth upon the earth, yet we do not deny that the rays are the sun although we know the sun is still in the heavens. Just so the Higher Self is a Ray from the Infinite, without which nothing spiritual can be brought forth in animal man. This Higher Self is dual: one with God, yet its earthly shadow—the human personality—is but an Emanation or Spark of the Higher Self clothed in atoms of physical matter, just as the sunbeam clothes itself in a growing plant and brings forth the perfected fruit. Thus the Higher Self is both the Father-in-heaven and The Christ within or the sun in the heavens and the sunbeam imprisoned within the fruit.

The Higher Self overshadows the personality, ever striving to guide and teach it that it may bring forth the Spiritual Man—its fruit. This guidance is accomplished in many ways; in dreams and visions, by the Still Small Voice—called by many the conscience—or, if these ways fail to impress the dense atoms of the physical brain, the personality is permitted to follow the dictates of its own rebellious animal will and learn through bitter experience to listen to and obey the dictates of the Word forever being spoken within. "Let me cease, O thou Perfectly Awakened, to remain as an Ape in the World-forest, forever ascending and descending in search of the fruits of folly."[2] Ordinarily

---

1 See the Chapter on The Wisdom Religion.
2 *Dhammapada*.

many, many lives are spent in sowing the seeds of disobedience and reaping the harvest of suffering ere the
personality will heed the guidance of the Divine.

This overshadowing Father-in-heaven is called by
some the Over-soul and by the Roman Catholic Church
the Guardian Angel whose power over the personality
is exerted through the Still Small Voice. But in reality
this Guardian is the Real Self—the God within, higher
manas and Buddhi permeated by Atma—of whom the
various personalities are but temporary garments worn
for certain occasions and for certain purposes, but all of
which are thrown off and disintegrated when the Real
Self is clothed with immortality, just as are the blossoms
when the sunbeam clothes itself in the fruit. Science has
demonstrated that the fruit is all imprisoned sunshine
and water (the Father and Mother forces—the dual aspects of the Creative Force) except a small residue of
earthy salts left behind as ash. Just so will the Word
gradually clothe itself in spiritualized matter with but a
modicum of earth.

One phase of this mystery is that as the disciple advances along the Path to Mastery, the Word becomes
manifested to the human consciousness for purposes
of revelation. Even if it be but for a momentary flash
that experience is evidence of an advanced step.
Ultimately the manifestation of the Word or the Christ-
consciousness will become continuous, as in the case of
the Master Jesus who said: "I and my Father are one,"
meaning that His personal human consciousness was so
blended with the Divine that at all times He could function in the consciousness of His Father-in-heaven. When
this point is reached the Word is consciously incarnated
in the flesh, or the fruit is perfected.

This Christ-consciousness at first may come only

in moments of extreme spiritual exaltation or ecstasy, when the human consciousness is transcended. Plotinus defines this as: "The liberation of the mind from its finite consciousness, becoming one and identified with the Infinite." By many teachers this is called Cosmic-consciousness, but Cosmic-consciousness is far more all-embracing, for it is the power to enter into and partake of the consciousness of everything in the Cosmos, from atom to God.

To one who has obtained perfect mastery over the lower personality, the Father (the Higher Self) and the Son (the personality) have become one, and the stream of Divine Wisdom flows uninterruptedly through both. Physiologically speaking, this means that by repeated victories of the Word over the flesh, through the fulfilling of the Law in many lives, the Higher Self has gradually gained increasing power over its physical vehicles and at last has built up, atom by atom, a fleshly body so spiritualized that the atoms of its physical brain readily respond to the vibrations of the Christ-consciousness, thus enabling the Word to dwell in the flesh among men, or the Son to become one with the Father. The human personality by schooling itself to listen to and obey the Inner Voice at last so stills the vibrations of the human intellect that the Word is an infallible and ever present Guide in the smallest detail of the earth life. In other words, the flesh, which has so long warred against the Spirit, has become the willing and obedient servant, eager to listen to and carry out the will of the Father on earth even as it is done in heaven.

Those who find it difficult to distinguish between the voice of the Higher Self (conscience) and the desires of the human personality can readily determine which is speaking if they will remember that when they ask in the Silence for guidance, and put themselves in a listening attitude of Soul, the reply will come either audibly or as a mental impression, but it will always come as a plain statement, clearly and concisely, requiring neither argument nor justification. The instant you begin to argue with yourself, or need to justify your decision, know well that you are not heeding the voice of your Father-in-heaven, but are following the wisdom of the human intellect or catering to the human desires. The personal self always endeavors to justify its decisions with most plausible arguments, while the Higher Self simply asserts a fact or commands.

The Word or the God within is Divine Essence or Love, for "God is love." The "lost word" in one sense, is simply the lost power of hearing the voice of the Father-in-heaven or realizing and correlating with The Christ within. The Wisdom Religion, as set forth in the Christian *Bible* while recognizing Gods, Angels, Seraphim and Cherubim and Spiritual Beings of every kind, no one would think of calling idolatrous. The recognition of all these manifestations of Deity in no way conflicts with the injunction, "Thou shalt have no other Gods before me," for it recognizes the divine unity of all. In its esoteric teaching it helps man to understand the deep, underlying meaning of this unity and to worship Divine Love, which is the God before whom alone man shall have no other and which alone he must worship in spirit and in truth. This one God he must seek and find in all things; firstly, in himself, then, by a recognition of his oneness with all that is, must find Him in all things. He must reverence, but never worship or idolize, any manifestations of Him, be they Planetary Angels, Seraphims, Devas, Avatara, Masters or what not, nor must he worship Him as his own personal God—the Word incarnate in him—but must learn to separate the Deity from His manifestations and listen to the voice of the One God—Divine Love—of which alone it is said, "I am the Lord thy God." As Epicurus said: "The Gods exist but they are not what the multitude supposes them to be. He is not an infidel or atheist who denies the existence of Gods whom the multitudes worship, but he is such who fastens on the Gods the opinions of the multitude." Only they are heathen who refuse to recognize and worship Divine Love or the Word made flesh.

Also bear in mind the creative aspect of the Word. We read much of the limitless power of the Word properly pronounced, and it is indeed all true, but before man can pronounce it he must gain the power of expressing every tone and semi-tone in Nature, for only then can the creative Word be sounded. This creative Word is continually pronounced within him by his Father-in-heaven—for it is this Word pronounced within him that is bringing forth his spiritual life—but ere he can pronounce it for himself man must become more than man.

All created things are the expression of coarser or finer vibrations, hence the Voice of Conscience (the Word), manifesting through exceedingly high and fine vibrations, finds it difficult to call forth a response from a mind given over entirely to worldly affairs and consequently attuned to a much lower rate of vibration. But if the Voice is listened for and an effort is made to follow its guidance, it has the power to create conditions in which it can manifest more plainly. Since during involution "the word of the Lord" (or Divine Law), penetrating through all the spheres, created the heavens (firmament) and the earth and thereby incorporated itself within every particle of matter com-

posing them, so, during evolution, must it evolve back
to its source, lifting up or redeeming all through which
it has manifested, thus creating a "new heaven and a
new earth, wherein dwelleth righteousness."

The creative Word manifests through Nature as tone,
color, form and number, just as a written word is composed of numbers, letters (symbols), syllables and the
meaning expressed. Hence, every tone in Nature, be
it song of bird, roar of beast, or thunder of heaven, be
it tinkle of fountain, surge of ocean or rustle of leafy
boughs, is an expression of the Word. And not a note
in Nature could be left out and the creative Word be
complete. Could man respond to and manifest his true
vibration (his key-note) in the creative Word with the
single-mindedness of Nature all would be peace, harmony and love. Man alone strikes a discordant note, not
only in himself, but also in the noises of his creations,
factory whistles, street noises, etc. And the effect of
this inharmony is impressed upon all creation so that
"Thorns also and thistles shall it bring forth to thee."

As man advances and learns to listen to the Still
Small Voice and as the Word unfolds within his heart
and manifests in his life, so will the tones of his voice
grow more tender and loving and lose their power to
wound. Thus will he become more able to comfort and
cheer, lead and command, for he then expresses more of
the creative power of the Word, until at last the Word is
made flesh and manifests continually. This is the secret
of the power of great speakers; for they express, to a
greater or lesser degree, the creative power of the Word
and literally create within the minds of their hearers that
which they wish to impress upon them.

The pronunciation of the Word is a question of

manifesting its guidance in the life; for every discord in the life produces a false note in the voice. Strive, therefore, to be absolutely true to the Word and be willing to face yourself and find and express Truth in every tone and action. Thus will you learn to take your true place and express your true key-note in the grand symphony of life.

CHAPTER XXX

ILLUMINATION

"I am the way, the truth, and the life: no man cometh unto the Father, but by me." *St. Matthew* XIV-6

"I am the Ego which is seated in the hearts of all beings; I am the beginning, the middle, and the end of all existing things."

The Bhagavad- Gita, Chapter X.

Pupils are asking continually for some formula, some prescribed "practical" thing to do to advance their spiritual evolution, complaining that they have read and studied all forms of philosophy and are now ready for something "definite." Because of this widespread demand there have sprung up on every hand those who are professing to give "practical" directions that shall lead the pupil into Illumination and give him miraculous powers.[1] On the other hand, an equally large number are writing that they have studied various systems, spent large sums of money for "advanced teachings," received the lessons of the inner section of many organizations, have passed through many mysterious degrees of various societies with high sounding titles and yet find their hunger unappeased, the net result being a mass of so-called formulas and a greater amount of discouragement. Others turn to the Wisdom Religion, supposing that it has to do with the development of psychic powers and the performance of magical rites, but in truth it has primarily to do with the development of The Christ-force within and the showing of it forth in the life. So called magic is dual. If it is the result of the recogni-

---

1 Some self-styled authorities go so far as to guarantee Adeptship for a definite sum, or publish books which they claim contain the secret of all occult Power.

tion and outward manifestation of The Christ within it is White Magic and right; if the result of seeking for power or personal stature, it becomes Black Magic and evil. Therefore, to all these classes of seekers, as well as to many other hungry hearts, we bring the old, old message, "I (The Christ Within) am the way, the truth and the life: no man cometh unto the Father, but by me."

What is it that all are thus seeking? It is so-called Illumination, yet few there be who have any realization of what this means. We have considered various phases of this Illumination in previous lessons,[1] and we will try herein to show what the real Illumination is and how it is attained. Illumination is the perfect blending of the self with the Divine or The Christ power, so that Divine Wisdom can guide every thought and act of the mortal man and the Light of Divinity can shed its radiance over the entire life.

When it is remembered that the *Bible* story of The Christ is the most complete and all-embracing narrative ever written, not of the man Jesus or even of God, but a synthetic picture of the Son of God—the emanation from the Father, The Christ-force in humanity or the Word made flesh—which symbolizes the various steps each Soul must pass through and conquer, it becomes quite plain that as this union with the Divine takes place the life of the disciple must manifest Truth. The whole mysterious transformation must be a growth similar to the gradual as-similation of the life giving constituents of the sun by the plant, until the full fruition or in-dwelling of the life-force is accomplished in the fruit. When we grasp this thought firmly we will understand that we must and shall do the works of our Father in exact proportion to our ability to

---

1 See Chapters XXIV, XXIX, etc.

make the correlation with Him, just as the plant does the works of its father, the sun—first as the blade, then the ear, then the full corn in the ear. Therefore there can be no rigid observances laid down for the attainment of perfection any more than there can be for the perfection of every individual plant. There can, however, be practices which develop the Will, awaken the Intuition and stimulate Aspiration, and there are environments which will foster spiritual growth, *i.e.*, within the ranks of any spiritual movement whose teachings satisfy your Soul-hunger, but these have been fully covered in other lessons.[1] To the average twentieth century student the effort to conquer himself is quite sufficient to develop his Will, and the only stimulant necessary is a burning, ardent seeking for a realization of The Christ-love. Illumination, however, can never be attained through the mere reading of lessons or the observance of rules. It must be the result of a vital force that comes into each life.[2] The gardener may prepare the soil, tend and water a plant, but the plant itself must assimilate the light and force of the sun and literally transmute them into living tissue within its body ere the blossom or the fruit can appear. So it is with the Illumination that each Soul is seeking. Only The Christ-force, not only talked about and in a sense realized, but literally absorbed and built into living tissue in the flesh, the mind and the Spirit, can bring about this mystical union. It is The Christ and The Christ alone who is "the Way, the Truth, and the Life."

As certain plants gather from the sun-force the power to produce poisons, so can man, by using for his own personal ends the godlike powers with which

---

1 See Chapter XXVII.
2 It is said there are as many ways of attaining illumination as there are human beings.

he can identify himself, produce evil. We do not create power, we only identify our consciousness with the Divine which is all power, just as we might attach a wire to a dynamo and obtain power. Of the Divine Self alone it is said, "All power is given unto thee in heaven and earth." This is literally true. All power is ours when we identify ourselves with the Divine, and the synthesis of all power is the ability to merge the personality into the Divine, or become one with the Father through The Christ. This gives all power because having accomplished this all things are possible. As man is endowed with free-will he can choose to take either the Right Hand Path, merge the human into the Divine and use his God-power to do the work of his Father-in-heaven, or he can graft his God-power on to the stalk of personality and, by making the intellect alone his guiding star, deliberately forswear his Father-in-heaven and become a child of evil (or the devil) and do the works of his father the devil—the concentrated force of man's wrong thoughts, acts and creations, the perverted reflection of the Good Law (the Lord) on earth. By refusing to let the light of the Divine penetrate farther than the intellect, he closes the door of his heart and allows the Light to illumine only his human brain which, without the guidance of the heart, permits evil to manifest, especially intellectual and spiritual pride, which are the most subtle and insidious of all evils.

Therefore, to teach mankind how to unfold inner faculties and how to use their power for personal ends, would be quite as reprehensible as for a gardener to propagate in a garden devoted to raising food for man, some poisonous vine which the gardener knew the very richness of the soil, the sunshine and the cultivation would cause to grow and finally either destroy the food or impregnate it with poison. This is why the inner teachings of the sacred Mysteries are given only to the few. It is no Being who gives, it is the blossom of the Soul which opens and receives the Light of Illumination, as the rose unfolds its petals to the light of the sun. If you do not receive this Light, know well that the blossoming time has not arrived for you. Had it arrived no one could withhold the Light from you.

When the divine mystery of the indwelling of The Christ has taken place in the Soul and the disciple has begun to realize in a vital, living way, that the overshadowing of his Divine Self is a real blending or indwelling, then the works of his Father will unfold within him just as the blade, the ear and the full corn in the ear unfold in the plant. Then, and then only, is he ready for the inner teaching; for he must be trained to put forth his blossoms in the manner best for humanity. Each step gained must not only show in the life, but the powers that go with that step must also manifest. *If we control one selfish trait* which before held us captive we may know that we have taken a real step upward. And the first and greatest of all magical powers to be attained by the pupil is the magical power of controlling himself, of day after day mastering the little things, with no heroics, perhaps with no one to commend him or realize that he is making any effort, yet still controlling his little tempers, his little impatiences, little acts of selfishness, his tendency to criticize and all the little, trifling things he knows are wrong, but which seem too petty to be worth mentioning.

Let no pupil ask for special lessons until these little things are in a measure conquered, for the building of these little lessons into his life is the most "practical" formula that can be given him. And if there is anyone who has thus assimilated The Christ and grown to live The Christ-life, who has gained the power of looking at the self, who has fulfilled the injunction, "Know thyself," yet who says he still lacks Illumination, let him know well that there is some hidden corner in his heart or life into which the Light is not able to penetrate, some closed door which he refuses to open. To him we would say, Look deeper and meditate in the Silence and pray for a knowledge of thyself. At the same time go forth and help to bring the Light to some other Soul, for in so doing in some part of your nature you will find that which keeps out the full radiance of The Christ-light. Let him "Learn to look intelligently into the hearts of men. Regard most earnestly your own heart. For through your own heart comes the one light which can illuminate life, and make it clear to your eyes."[1]

Occult formulas are more apt to emphasize self satisfaction and self-righteousness than to help toward self-mastery. John the Baptist had been educated in all the law of the Mysteries, had lived apart from the world in the caves of the wilderness, had fed on locusts and wild honey and had spent his life following out the most rigid formularies of the Essenees, yet Jesus said: "Verily I say unto you, Among them that are born of women there hath not risen a greater than John the Baptist: notwithstanding he that is least in the kingdom of heaven is greater than he."[2] This means that the very humblest person who has correlated with The Christ within—which is entering the kingdom of heaven—is greater than even a great intellectual teacher such as John the Baptist.

---

1 *Light on the Path*, Part II, Rules 10-12.
2 *St. Matthew*, XI, 11.

Both intellectual development and heart development *are necessary*, but if the heart is first developed and a conscious union made with The Christ within, all things are revealed unto you. This is, as it were, the shortcut to Mastery.

It is a singular fact that none of the Great Teachers— Krishna, Buddha, Jesus, etc.—ever wrote a word or were, in their day, looked upon as great intellectual teachers, but the example of Their lives lives in the world to this day, and can never die, because They made this divine correlation, literally manifesting God in the flesh. It is neither the words you speak nor the routine of your life that affects the world, but something more. It is the power of that which is "the way, the truth, and the life." In other words, both that which you teach and the example of your life must prove conclusively that it is The Christ within you that worketh through you both to will and to do.

It must not be a mere lip-service, it must be so true and so convincing that it will radiate from you rather than be a garment assumed before the world or a mere intellectual cloak that blinds your own eyes, for The Christ within you must be the Truth as well as the Way and the Life.

If there is any doubt left in regard to the Path we point out to reach this attainment we will briefly recapitulate.

Think only constructively if you desire spiritual growth.

Do cheerfully and well the duty that lies nearest.

Conquer the little faults as they show themselves.

Never let a day pass without its period of self examination, meditation and communion with the Divine.

Do unto others as ye would that others should do unto you.

Learn to love in its truest and grandest sense.

Do not criticize others, even though your criticism seems just, for to do so you must dwell mentally in the conditions you criticize.

Be not afraid to face and recognize *your own* faults.

At the same time be not discouraged.

Have perfect confidence in your power ultimately to conquer through The Christ within.

For the voice of The Christ declares, "Lo, I am with you alway, even unto the end of the world."

The following are the requirements given by a Great Teacher to those who seek Illumination:

1. Behold the Truth before you;
2. A clean life;
3. An open mind;
4. A pure heart;
5. An eager intellect;
6. An unveiled spiritual perception;
7. A brotherliness for one's co-disciple;
8. A readiness to give and receive instruction;
9. A loyal sense of duty to the Teacher;
10. A willing obedience to the behests of Truth once we have placed our confidence in and believe that Teacher to be in possession of it;
11. A courageous endurance of personal injustice;
12. A brave declaration of principles;
13. A valiant defense of those who are unjustly attacked;
14. A constant eye to the ideal of human progression and perfection which the secret science depicts.
15. These are the golden stairs up the steps of which the learner may climb to the Temple of Divine Wisdom.

All things are possible unto him who believes.

CHAPTER XXXI

THE SYMBOL OF THE SALT

"Ye are the salt of the earth: but if the salt have
lost his savor, wherewith shall it be salted? it is
thenceforth good for nothing, but to be cast out, and
to be trodden under foot of men." *St. Matthew* V, 13.

Salt plays a most important role in all life, both in
man and in Nature. It has also played its part in the
advance of civilization. The first great highways known
to history were caravan routes formed by transporting
salt from the deserts to points of civilization. Salt thus
became the great reason for communication between
different peoples, and hence the means by which civilization spread.

The use of salt marks an advance in civilization from
a wandering nomadic life, in which the people subsist
chiefly upon animal food containing a large proportion of salt, to an agricultural life in which vegetables
requiring salt for flavoring form a large proportion of
the diet. Salt in the diet is necessary for the health of
all herbivorous animals. It is a necessary constituent of
all animal tissues and of the blood. Experiments have
repeatedly proven that the heart will not beat unless
there is dissolved in the blood a certain percentage of
common salt. Its use in every-day life is as a purifier and
preservative, this being its chief function in the world.
Like the heart of man, the heart of Nature will not beat
nor will life continue without a proper proportion of salt,
for salt preserves the force which makes life possible.

Salt was one of the ingredients in the Great Work of
the old Alchemists who reduced all elements to

their mystic Sulphur, Mercury, and Salt, salt symbolizing that which purifies and preserves the life principle.
Salt is found in oceans, deserts, salt lakes, and mines, the
latter being deposits left by the evaporation of ancient
seas. But wherever salt is found the significance of its
presence is due to its purifying and preserving qualities.

The earth is a living entity, and when a portion of its
surface becomes diseased beyond repair; when weighted
down with the wickedness, crime and sin of the people
inhabiting it, that portion gives way under the load and
through great cataclysms sinks down to be covered by
the salt brine of the sea, where the putrefaction of the
mass is completed. Putrefaction is a form of digestion
or disintegration which breaks up old forms or bodies
and liberates their life-essences. These essences being
sublimed by the heat of the putrefaction rise up and certain of them combine with the various salts in solution
and are thus preserved. Others in passing up through the
brine are purified ere they pass into the regions above.
As these purified essences rise from the sea certain of
them are swept inward over the land where they are
assimilated by both vegetable and animal life, including man. In this way all the advances in intelligence,
as well as all the advances in art, science and invention brought forth for the benefit of mankind—the so
called "lost arts"—are still preserved in the thought aura
of the locality. When subsequent Races reach a corresponding stage of mental development they are able
to respond to the purified thought-forms of the former
civilizations and reproduce them as apparently "new"
ideas or inventions.

It is often noted that new ideas, new thoughts and

tendencies seem to sweep over communities in waves. They are indeed waves in the mental and even physical atmosphere, sweeping in from the sea, invigorating, stimulating and advancing all forms of life. All essences not absorbed by vegetable and animal life or utilized by man, pass into the aura of the earth as a permanent acquisition or seed for the use of future Races. The modern aeroplane is but an imperfect expression of the thought-forms left in the aura of the earth by the ancient Atlanteans, who had developed aeronautics to a far higher degree than has yet been attained in this age. There is no so-called "lost art" but will in due time be recovered or "discovered" in the same way. For every thought and act of man is imprinted upon the Akashic Records and tends to reproduce itself through the brain of the reincarnated Soul who first produced it. And when so reproduced it tends to be further perfected or redeemed, for such is the Law of Eternal Progress.

After the rise of the submerged land from beneath the brine of the sea, the waters drain off or evaporate and the purifying process is continued in the resulting deserts. Following cyclic law, when the disintegration of old forms is completed and the combination of the lower essences with the salts of the sea is accomplished, the land thus freed from its magnetic burden of impurity slowly rises above the surface, the waters evaporating and leaving behind their accumulated salt to the further action of the sun and air. Thus are formed the vast tracts of land we call deserts.

As in the body an excess of salt is injurious, so in the desert, where for ages no vegetable or animal life can exist. Yet in the fullness of time the salt is gradually disintegrated, sublimed or carried away by the action of the elements, and the land again becomes habitable. The Great Salt Lake in Utah, the desert of Sahara and the great plains of western United States are examples of different steps in this process. Thus, little by little, is the prophecy fulfilled: "The desert shall blossom as the rose."

Man passes through the same stages of purification by salt as does the earth. His youth is fresh and pure, is filled with high ideals, beautiful thoughts, and vast energy. Gradually as he reaches his maturity his pure ideals become overlaid with selfishness, dissimulation, greed and impurity, and his life becomes weighted down with the weaknesses, material desires, and impurities of the world. Then come the purifying cataclysms of sorrow and suffering in which all his boasted attainments dissolve from under him and he sinks down under the brine poured out by the salt tears that flow from his eyes. Here, as in the ocean, the salt purifies the nature and preserves the essence of good in the experiences he passes through, building it into his aura for future use. The lessons of sorrow must be well learned or they will be repeated again and again until learned. After a period of desolation when all comfort fails—comparable to a lonely desert—the paralyzing effects of sorrow gradually lessen and pass away. Then the rose that is born of suffering and watered with tears puts forth its bud and begins to open its petals in the purified and freshened soil of his heart.

Analyzed from the higher standpoint, a drop of sea water contains every constituent necessary to life, and the same constituents are found in the salt "Waters of Life" or tears. The well-known aphorism in *Light on The Path* is based upon the purifying action of salt. "Before the eyes can see they must be incapable of tears" does not mean that you must be cold or lacking in understanding and appreciation of the trials your brothers and sisters are undergoing, or that you must be lacking in sympathy; for Jesus—the type of perfected man—wept in sympathy with the sisters at Lazarus' tomb, although possessing in its fullness the power to bring Lazarus forth with a word—but it does mean that there will come a period in your life when your passions, emotions and thoughts will be so mastered and purified by the action of the salt tears—which in your present stage of development are necessary—that there will be no further need of the tears, for the salt has done its work. As in a desert, where only after the salt has been absorbed can the roses bloom, so only after the purifying and cleansing has been accomplished in your life can the roses bloom in your heart and your eyes truly see.

Many ceremonies are connected with the partaking of salt. In the Middle Ages the dish of salt was placed in the center of the long banquet-board and those who sat between the salt and the host were said to sit "above the salt." Only members of the family were permitted this honor; hence when a guest was seated above the salt he was accepted as a member of the family for the time being, and accorded all the privileges and honors due a son of the house. Those who sat "below the salt" were the squires, retainers and followers of the lord of the house and could rise above the salt only by valiant deeds. Among the Arabs to this day salt is held sacred. One with whom they have partaken of salt becomes their friend, and if by chance they partake of salt with an enemy the enmity must be forsworn.

This ceremony is called "The Covenant of Salt" and is but another remnant of the ancient ceremony which symbolized the covenant between man and his Higher Self. Traces of this symbolic meaning are found in many religions, the Roman Catholics still using salt in the baptismal service. These customs are remnants of the beautiful symbology taught the early Races by the Elder Brothers of Humanity, in which the symbolic purifying by the salt admitted the neophyte to spiritual Sonship. The self-conquering purifying and cleansing which lifted the neophyte above the salt made it possible for him to enter the higher realms and become one with his Father-in-heaven.

The first conscious step of the neophyte is a strong desire to purify his body, mind and life and preserve the divine attributes within his Soul. This step is symbolized by the effect of the salt. Each of you who is ready to make the Covenant of Salt with your Higher Self agrees to let your life be purified of all its faults both great and small through the action of salt tears, even though sorrow and suffering are necessary to accomplish this result. When you have been thoroughly salted and cleansed from earthly impurities then will you become clear crystal grains wherewith to salt the earth. Then indeed will the eyes be incapable of tears and be able to see the things of the spirit! However, this does not mean that you are to encourage mere emotionalism, or to look on the sorrowful side of life. For just as in the desert an excess of salt kills out vegetation, so giving away to excessive weeping or emotion will make a desert of your heart and life and you will remain in that state until you have conquered. You will never gain the victory until, as in the desert, the salt has been absorbed, the soil of your heart enriched by experience, and your life has brought forth its roses.

Jesus said to His initiated disciples: "Ye are the salt of the earth . . . have salt in yourselves and have peace one with another." As you start out to be the salt of the earth be not dismayed that you are such a tiny grain compared to the great world around you. Determine not to lose your savor. The little grain of salt stops not to consider if it can accomplish its mission. It simply gives forth its innate qualities in perfect confidence, for if it has not lost its savor everything it contacts must be salted. And the more it gives the more it has to give, for its crystals grow and reproduce according to their saltness. Let the light of your purified life so shine before men that they shall recognize in you the element of purification. Earnestly determine that the salt shall not lose its savor, but that you will do your duty as a grain of salt to wipe out and purify the world's misconceptions. In your daily life, like grains of salt, radiate the spiritual force which you draw from The Christ and transmute the putrefying conditions in the thought of humanity into Love and Purity.

CHAPTER XXXII

THOU SHALT NOT KILL

"Life runs its rounds of living, climbing up,
From mote, and gnat, and worm, reptile and fish,
Bird and shagged beast, man, demon, deva, God,
. . . . if one might save
Man from his curse, the whole wide world should share
The lightened horror of this ignorance
Whose shadow is chill fear, and cruelty its bitter pastime.
Light of Asia, Arnold, Book IV, p. 97.

(Note: This lesson is intended to advocate neither meat eating nor non-meat eating, but to inculcate in all that tolerance which can see others follow lines of conduct differing from their own without condemnation or a feeling of superiority.)

The command "Thou shalt not kill," is plain and distinct, with no modifying conditions, yet it is given upon the same authority as that which, in the vision of Peter, said: "Rise, Peter; kill and eat."[1] Although the vision of Peter was primarily to teach him that even though a Jew he should call no man unclean, nevertheless the Voice of God commanded him to kill, and he had to learn his lesson through his willingness to do so even though against his race prejudice.

We have explained to our pupils something of the great law of the One Life, or the Great Creative Principle sent into chaos to evolve through all forms and bring the world-stuff left over from a previous world period to perfection through physical and spiritual evolution. We have tried to picture this Great Principle as a stream of life-force animating and evolving everything through which it passes. As this is the force back of all evolution, an emanation from the Absolute

---

1 Acts, X, 13.

(which is all life), there can be no such thing as "killing" in the sense of annihilating this stream of life force. But since the above command is given, and not only in one sacred scripture but in many, it must have an important inner meaning as well as an outer.

The only sense in which man can kill is to separate any form of life from this stream of life-force, or to dam it up or refuse to permit it to manifest. A good example of such killing is given by the yogis, Brahmacharis and Bhikshus—the so-called holy mendicants of India—described in *The Light of Asia*: "Some day and night had stood with lifted arms, till—drained of blood and withered by disease—their slowly wasting joints and stiffened limbs jutted from sapless shoulders like dead forks from forest trunks."[1] Such practices prevent the One Life from manifesting through certain parts of the body, hence such parts may be said to be killed. Another form of killing is found in the various kinds of mental torture which, even in this so-called enlightened and Christian country, are assiduously followed by many who are earnestly seeking spiritual enlightenment. 'While we are wont to look upon all forms of bodily torture as horrible and revolting, many hold that Soul-torture is the only path to perfection. Such think they must make life as hard and unhappy, both for themselves and for others, as it is possible; that they must refuse to eat that which they enjoy; must starve their bodies or must scourge their mind and conscience. These are also forms of killing, because they dam up and refuse to permit the life-force to manifest in and through these conditions. Just as mind and Spirit are more important than body, so is mental and spiritual torture far more harmful and degenerating than any merely

1   Book the Fifth, p.116.

bodily torture that can be conceived of. And it has exactly the same effect, namely, to separate the tortured parts from the stream of life-giving creative force, which is The Christ or the Creative Principle of the Godhead.

The one fact which we would that we could proclaim in words of fire that all the world might comprehend is "God is Love," and love is life and growth and joy and peace and immortality. The only bar to evolution is to kill, to separate either body, mind or heart from God-Love, no matter what mistaken teaching brings this about. Just as long as the idea prevails that to be joyous and happy in life is to be far from God; just as long as love is considered a clandestine fruit, something forbidden, to be eaten only in secret and bitterly repented of later on; that to gain the pleasant things of life you must close the door on God and turn aside the stream of the vital Christ-life from you, just so long will this world be the hell it is today. The only way to cleanse the Augean stables of life's miseries is once more to turn the living waters of the rivers Alpheus and Peneus into their old and originally intended channels and let the streams of love and life and immortality flow into and through all. This was one of the fabled labors of Hercules, who symbolizes strength or power to accomplish, that God given power by which mankind can find its birthright. Through the strength gained by accepting and believing that God has sent His Son—The Christ-principle, the creative aspect of the Absolute—into chaos because His force was all that was needed to awaken seemingly dead matter into life[1] that it might evolve toward perfection, we open the flood gates and, like Hercules, turn this river of force into the stables that

---

1 See Chapter XXIV.

are filled with man's animal passions and emotions and the stables are cleansed. "Thou shalt not kill" means that you shall in no way dam up or cut off the life force.

But the question Peter had to face was: Has man the right to destroy any lower form of life, either for food, self-preservation or for purposes of hygiene? The Hindus have carried the literal interpretation of the command "Thou shalt not kill" to its extreme limits, practically sacrificing human life in preference to that of insects, and other noxious and pestiferous forms of life. Poisonous snakes, which the Hindus refuse to kill, cause the death of thousands of human beings annually; yet it is a common sight to see these same Hindus treat their domestic animals with such cruelty that a European can scarce endure the sight of their suffering. It is known that the plague, which so frequently devastates that country with its toll of millions of lives, is transmitted by rats and other rodents and is largely made possible by the unclean conditions which permit fleas, lice and other bloodsucking parasites—infesting indiscriminately the dead and the living—to flourish undisturbed; that fatal fevers are transmitted by mosquitoes, and that many other scourges of mankind can be traced to similar sources, and yet there are serious and earnest seekers after truth who ask if it is right to destroy such forms of life. There are many in this country who say they have no right to kill the disease-transmitting housefly but who will carefully exclude it from their dwellings without a thought of the suffering poor who cannot afford screens or who are too ignorant to protect their children from flies. Hence disease and death is spread among the poor by the very flies the well-meaning students have excluded from their own homes.

As to the killing of the dumb beasts your brothers,

the literal view of not killing animals for food may be a helpful step at a certain stage of spiritual growth, but later on it is well to consider a wider view of creation and the interdependence of all kingdoms; for using vegetables for food is just as much taking life as to use animals for food. Man, being a step above the lower kingdoms, owes love and helpfulness to all.

The matter of what kind of food you place in your stomach, as long as it is wholesome and satisfying, is of so little importance to spiritual growth that we give it little special attention, leaving such matters of personal preference to the common-sense of each pupil. Each one, however, is responsible for the condition of all his bodies and must give them due attention, the attention necessary to keep any high-bred animal, of which high-grade work is expected, in good physical condition.

The one essential thing is to have a strong mind in a strong body, to live in such a way that no part of body, mind or Soul is shut off from the stream of Divine Life. "Will ye, for love of soul, so loathe your flesh, so scourge and maim it, that it shall not serve to bear the spirit on, searching for home?"[1] In fact, "Thou shalt not kill" any cell, molecule or atom in any of your bodies. Hence, we do not presume to lay down set rules as to diet; for *spiritual growth is not a matter of what goes into the stomach*—else those Races which have been vegetarians for ages would be spiritual masters long ere this—*but of the devotion with which you live out the ideals of your heart.* "Not that which goeth into the mouth defileth a man; but that which cometh out of the mouth, this defileth a man."[2] If your ideal is not to eat meat, and if you find your body and mind thrive and you have gained

1 *Light of Asia*, Arnold, Book V, p. 120.
2 *St. Matthew*, XV, 12.

more strength, courage, vital force and mental power without it, then live out that ideal and find out by the results in your life if it be best *for you*. Study your fellowmen and see if a purely vegetarian diet has brought to its devotees greater health of body, vigor of mind, breadth of Soul, love, tolerance and compassion.

One of the objections frequently brought against meateating is the supposition that by eating flesh man will take on the passions of the animal. There are two points to be considered in this theory. All occult students know that the desire-body is Kama or the animal-soul, and that it leaves the body at the moment of death, hence could not in any way be taken on by eating the flesh from which it has withdrawn. The second point is the claim commonly made by vegetarians that by abstaining from meat their animal passions are lessened. The fact is that this result is attained simply because, by a decrease in their stamina and virility, their passions are temporarily masked. A perfect man must be one with all his forces in full vigor, but under perfect control. To weaken his powers to such an extent that they no longer require control is taking a step backward rather than forward, for such weakened forces are only dormant, *not mastered*, and in some life will assert themselves with all their accumulated power and demand expression. Persons who have thus weakened their powers are very apt to think they have no passions, hence permit a feeling of superiority to grow up in them. Some time in their evolution, however, they must experience the full strength of all animal desires ere they can even begin really to conquer. But this does not mean, as taught by some schools, that it is well deliberately to arouse the passions for the sake of controlling them. It does mean that each must be in full possession of all his powers and learn to master them and make them his servants; for they are steppingstones by which he must climb.

We also hear much to the effect that all Masters and Adepts were vegetarians, while the truth is that only those who have reached Mastery from non-meat-eating races were vegetarians. Right here comes in a fact we have so often reiterated, namely, that to reach Mastery each Soul must live up to the light and the conceptions of Truth as revealed to him in his own religion, nation and environment. The truth is that many, many Souls have reached Mastery through races that did eat meat, such as the Egyptians, the Norsemen, Celts, etc., and especially those who, living in a cold climate, subsisted almost entirely on meat and yet reached Mastery; all of whom are largely represented among the Masters of the Great White Lodge. Hence, the importance of a vegetarian diet in attaining Mastery cannot be very great; for we cannot believe that the Elohim, having created a planet with so many differing climates, necessitating such a variety of diets, would shut out from attaining ultimate perfection all who were placed in parts of that planet where climatic conditions made animal food a necessity for life and warmth.

It is the thought-force put into the subject that is the great factor, namely, what thoughts you hold, to what you constantly direct your mind. If you think continually of what you are *not* to eat and how you are to manage without it you are putting quite as much creative thought-force upon your food as is the glutton who thinks only of what he *is* to eat. In both cases the subject of food is taken out of its proper place—as anything wholesome that will properly nourish the body—and is given undue prominence, even worshiped, making those who worship it slaves to their stomachs, instead of looking upon food as the mere fuel that runs the engine. The mind cannot run constantly upon food and at the same time meditate on spiritual things or be filled with loving thoughts for the help of humanity. Instead you are apt to divide the world into meat eaters and non-meat eaters.

As good must evolve out of all evil, so must we gain wisdom to handle this problem, and by our thought force help make it possible for the Masters of Wisdom to use every thing and condition, no matter how apparently evil, to bring about ultimate good.

There is no such thing as death, merely various *changes in form* in the manifestation of the One Life.

Man is the result of the normal development of all the lower kingdoms; his body contains all the elements— mineral, vegetable and animal. This fact alone shows that man has absorbed and transmuted all the lower kingdoms and has thereby raised them into a higher expression of the One Life. Hence, the atoms of the mineral, vegetable and animal kingdoms which have been swallowed up by man have thereby reached the fullness of life expression, just as man must be swallowed up—and from one viewpoint be killed and absorbed—in the spiritualized Being who shall be more than man. The mineral is "killed and eaten" or absorbed from the earth, and its *form* of life expression destroyed that the vegetable may live; the vegetable is "killed and eaten" or absorbed that the animal may live, and the animal gives up its life for man just as the lower personal man gives up his life for the Spiritual Man.

Every form of life is born into the environment where its natural prey (food) is found. If you reject the teaching of the evolution of the One Life through the sacrifice of lower forms, then in despair you must agree with the dictum of certain scientists who declare the world to be but a monstrous charnel house. In each instance, however, it is the mere physical expression of the One Life that is altered, for it is not cut off from the stream of life-force, but is brought into contact with a higher and more perfect expression of that force and hence cannot be said to be "killed." It is much as though a plant, having outgrown a confining pot, was transplanted into a larger one where it would have greater freedom and could express a greater amount of the life-force; or it is like a tadpole absorbed and transmuted into a frog. This is the true meaning of the Mosaic law, "a life for a life"—exchanging a lower form of life for a higher—so commonly misinterpreted in favor of capital punishment. Jesus expressed the same truth when He said: "Except a corn of wheat fall into the ground and die, it abideth alone; but if it die, it bringeth forth much fruit."[1] For the seed must be "killed," or give up its *form* of life and be absorbed and transmuted ere the higher *form* of expression can evolve.

This is the scheme of evolution as it would be if there were no sin and no disobedience to the Law. If love prevailed evolution would be but one continued sacrifice of the lower *form* of the One Life to the next higher, that the more highly evolved form might express to a greater degree the One Life. But man's disobedience to his divine guidance has brought cruelty and suffering into the world so that all creation "groaneth and travaileth together." That is, all creation—whose end and aim is to give birth to and to bring to perfection spiritual Beings—now brings forth in pain and anguish where it should bring forth

---

1 *St. John*, XII, 24.

in joy and thanksgiving. Now everything preys upon
something instead of yielding itself a glad sacrifice to
the next higher form. If no life were taken in cruelty it
would naturally and without pain give up its life-current
that it might be turned into a higher and more advanced
channel of expression. If this did not take place evolution would cease, and the life-wave could never lift the
mineral into the vegetable kingdom, nor the vegetable
into the animal, the animal into the human or the human
into the Divine.

Through man's selfishness and unbrotherliness there
is enmity and lack of understanding between man and
all the lower kingdoms, which can only be remedied by
love and wisdom. For instance, if meat eating were abolished would that overcome enmity and cruelty? Such
changes must come from a change in man's attitude
toward life, *from within, from the heart*, and not from
any outward act or the mere abstaining from an act.

At present man is swayed mainly through his love
of gain. As long as the flesh of animals has a commercial value and commands a higher price when the
animal is improved in quality, well cared for, well fed
and sheltered, man will go on improving conditions
for the animal and thus perfecting and advancing it in
evolution far more rapidly than ages of wild life could
accomplish, even though he does this merely because
he finds it to his financial advantage. All these factors
are utilized by the Masters of Wisdom who are guiding evolution, to give a decided impetus upward to
the evolution of the animal kingdom; for the animals
must reach a state of perfection as animals ere the
wave of evolution can sweep them into the next higher
kingdom. On the other hand, if animals had no commercial value they would receive no attention from man,

would be allowed to run wild, would be cruelly hunted for sport, killed off to rid the fields of them, and many starved or frozen in winter. Thus it would take many, many more lives as animals ere they learned all the lessons and reached perfection as animals; for even the animals must learn the lesson of love and brotherhood with man and all kingdoms ere they are done with their experience as animals, and this lesson they must learn from man. The mere killing, which is but a momentary pang, does not cause a thousandth part of the suffering experienced in a wild and neglected state—the slow dying of starvation, the being torn to pieces by other animals or put to death by their own kind, as happens to the old, the sick or disabled among most animals.

Another objection to meat-eating is the brutalizing effect the killing has upon the butchers. This is indeed a serious question, but those who are butchers today are also evolving and are today a step above their former incarnations in which they may have been human butchers, *i.e.*, the executioners, inquisitors or the hired assassins so common in former ages. By the time there are no more Souls who need such an environment in which to learn their lessons and evolve there will be no more need of butchers, for the Great Law never places a Soul in an environment that is not needed for its further evolution.

In protecting himself against mosquitoes, flies and other noxious insects, man has the right to sacrifice their *form* of life. For all lower forms of life which prey upon or work injury to man are the result of man's abuse of the life-force, hence he has the right to make that life-force manifest through other *forms* which will be helpful to the Race. Therefore, when you destroy these lower forms hold the thought that their life-force shall manifest through forms that shall

be helpful and not inimical to man. It is not true brotherhood merely to drive them away from you to prey upon
your less fortunate brothers and sisters. At no point in
evolution, however, has any form of life the right to take
the life of its kind, for by so doing it could not fulfill the
Law of Compensation by raising it to a higher stage of
evolution. Nor would any form do this did not man send
forth murderous thoughts and emanations. This applies
even to the poisonous weed which chokes out the life
of the flower beside it; to the forms of life which devour
their young and their kind; for in such cases, instead of
being raised to a higher step they have to repeat the same
step again. But it does not apply to those forms of fish
and animal life which prey upon less evolved forms of
their own kind.

The whole key-note of the universe is love and as
long as man sends out the reverse of love, or inharmony,
death instead of life must result. However, the plea of
advancing evolution cannot be used to excuse or pal-
liate the taking of life for sport or vanity. Man has no
right to assume the responsibility of changing a form of
life unless conditions have proved that the sacrifice of
the lower form is necessary for the life or best good of a
higher form—mankind. To kill animals for amusement
or to kill birds for their plumage that it may add to the
vanity of woman, or to foster that state of mind which
cannot see anything beautiful or uplifting in the song
of birds or the gambols of a young animal, the sight of
which only arouses the desire to kill, is not only pushing man back to the level of wild beasts, but, because
it is not transmuted into a higher form, is retarding the
evolution of the stream of life-force, and is spreading enmity toward man among the lower kingdoms. It

also dams up love and compassion in his heart and prevents his spiritual evolution. This is killing in the full sense of the term.

Man is a free-will agent and can choose his own path. But certain it is that ultimately *love and harmony must prevail* else man fails to do his duty to the lower kingdoms by failing to put the imprint of love and brotherhood upon them, for all forms must evolve together. Man is responsible for the lower kingdoms and must do his duty by them and help them to take their next step in evolution, for he has reached a point in evolution where he must consciously become a coworker with the forces of evolution, must recognize, correlate with and begin to use the great, creative Christ Principle—which is the one Way, the Truth and the Life—by which alone evolution can reach its ultimate perfection. If man fails to do this he stops his own evolution, for he cannot expect to receive from the kingdoms above him that love and help which he withholds from the kingdoms below him.

Man will never lay down the task of aiding the lower kingdoms until all are lifted up and redeemed through Divine Love.

There is always an inner or esoteric truth beneath every phase of life, for all things work together for good, even man's mistakes being utilized. "All steps are necessary to make up the ladder. The vices of men become steps in the ladder, one by one, as they are surmounted."[1] Wisdom seeks deep into the mysteries of being for the germ of good beneath every outward seeming ere condemning anything. "Seek it (the Way) by testing all experience, by utilizing the senses, in order to understand the growth and meaning of individuality, and the beauty and obscurity of

---

1 *Light on the Path*, Part I, Rule 20.

those other divine fragments which are struggling side by side with you, and form the race to which you belong."

Do not condemn anything but cruelty, impurity and want of tolerance and brotherly love. Cultivate love and tolerance for all your brethren and avoid the thought that *your* way, or *your* view is superior or is in any way better than another's, *except for yourself.* Above all avoid the spiritual pride that results from the thought that because you do or do not eat meat, fletcherize your food, eat raw foods, follow a particular dietary or bathe in a particular fashion, you are holier than your brothers who do differently. For there is no one thing that holds back Soul-growth more, that is more subtle, or is harder to overcome, than spiritual pride.

"Thou shalt not kill" means then, that thou shalt not do anything to retard evolution on any plane, to shut away any portion of the universe from the universal love-force, to foster separateness or to retard the spread of brotherhood, harmony and unity on all planes. In *Light on the Path* we read: "Each man is to himself absolutely the way, the truth and the life," and the Master Jesus, speaking of The Christ within, said: "I am the way, the truth, and the life." These two texts have literally the same meaning. The letter "I" is formed by a straight line which geometrically represents The Christ-principle descending into matter, hence it is this life-giving force or Principle which is "the way, the truth and the life." But as each one manifests this in his life he can individually become that "I " meaning, however, not the human, personal self, which is matter, but the animating Principle of Deity manifesting through him. Therefore, from this standpoint, each one must take upon himself the responsibility of becoming "the way, the truth, and the life," not only for himself, but, by his life, his influence and example—because he stands upon what is at present the crest of the wave of evolution on this planet—for all the kingdoms below him, as well as for all his fellow beings. For the Way and the Truth is Unity or the One Life. "As above, so below."

Therefore, as to diet we lay down no set rules; we only state principles. Let each pupil take the matter of meat-eating into the Silence and find out the best way *for him* to attain the above mentioned end. And we feel sure that after he has wrestled with the question conscientiously, and has found the many differences and the many apparent contradictions which must be reconciled and blended ere this oneness with all can be even approximately attained, there will grow up in his heart such a tolerance and patience with all his fellow students—whom he can plainly see are seeking the same end—that there will be no condemnation possible. "Let not him that eateth despise him that eateth not; and let not him which eateth not judge him that eateth."[1] The instant any Soul reaches this point, where he recognizes the unity of all, and the diversity of methods by which all are seeking unity, he can but reflect in his life and conversation the illuminating power of the divine Christ Love and will then become an avenue through which this creative life-stream must flow to all humanity.

---

1 Romans, XIV, 3.

CHAPTER XXXIII

PRAYER OF CONSECRATION

The following mantra are specially given by the Masters of Wisdom as a link to bind all disciples into one great unified body. You are requested to repeat them with us morning, noon and night, keeping in mind the ideas given in the explanation below, and trying to realize their meaning in your daily life.

The power of prayers or mantra to harmonize the mind and body and bring about suitable conditions for spiritual communication has been recognized in all countries and all ages, "sound being the most potent and effectual magic agent, and the first of the keys which opens the door of communication between Mortals and Immortals."[1] "To pronounce a word is to evoke a thought, and make it present: the magnetic potency of human speech is the commencement of every manifestation in the Occult World."[2]

We, recognizing the omnipotent power of the Great Creative Force, do make most solemn covenant to present our whole selves, our bodies, our minds, our Souls, a living sacrifice to Thee.

We yield all personal desires unto the one Great Desire, to be used as instruments to create a Centre through which The Lodge can work.

Recognizing the oneess of Thy All-pervading Force, we give back to Thee, for Thy use, all that we possess, and by the power of the Living Christ demand _____ that all obstacles be removed, and Thy

1 The Secret Doctrine, Blavatsky, Vol I, 502.
2 *Ibid*, Vol. I, 121.

*work be speedily established in perfect
justice.*

These mantra, while apparently but affirmations, nevertheless contain the spirit of true prayer, for all prayer is but a recognition of the One Life, the great Universal Creative Force. This force is love in its highest conception, and it is with this conception of love, as being one with the creative energy of the Great Breath of Brahm, that we desire our students to identify themselves.

It is also the force that is meant in the passage, "For God so loved the world that He gave His only begotten Son." Just as the physical sun sends its forces into the heart of the seed, and by breaking up its confining sheath or shell utterly transforms it and causes it to grow into a plant, a flower or a tree, so this force of Divine Love pours out its power upon the immortal seed within our hearts. It is the Son of God come to earth that "whosoever believeth in Him should not perish but have everlasting life." It is that which is created from the Father-Mother-principle and sent into the world to redeem it.

A true conception of this great truth confronts every neophyte at the Threshold. He must recognize this force and correlate its inner meaning within his own heart. This is the step so often spoken of as "Know Thyself," or present yourself "a living sacrifice," your bodies, mind and Soul, *i.e.*, seek for and find this stream of divine creative energy—an unbroken thread binding and holding body, mind and Soul to the Son of the Father-Mother—for this force is the creative aspect of your Higher Self. Such a conception alone of the love principle can bring redemption.

Without this redemption, and a comprehension of what is meant by Divine Love, the student, no matter how much occult theory, fact or knowledge he may store up, will still wander in outer darkness and never find or recognize his Father's face. Once grasp this truth with Soul knowledge, not mere intellect, and you will find that you have hold of your Father's hand, and nothing can ever separate you from Him, for the Comforter has come who will abide with you forever.

Thus will you find the key that unlocks all mysteries, that overcomes sickness and conquers death, and that will ultimately place your feet upon the highest mount of attainment. This is the center that each disciple must find within his own heart, yea, within his own body, that he may realize how this creative force[1] works within himself. Having found it, let him purify the center and sanctify it to the work of the Masters, and pour out its force into the Great Center which the Masters of Wisdom are forming upon the earth-plane.

This is the only way to prepare for the coming Avatar. All who use this force wisely, with an understanding of its tremendous power and how it works in and through humanity, are doing their part to prepare a place for the Avatar to manifest. This force, verily, is God or the Devil, according to its use or misuse.

SPECIAL CONCENTRATION HOURS

We request that all pupils who earnestly desire to co-operate in this Movement or who have the success of this Order at heart, to pause for a moment each day upon the stroke of noon and send a vital

---

1 Understand clearly that we are not referring to the physical sex fluid, but to the divine creative potency of The Christ-principle.

creative thought of love to this Center, that it may be perfected in purity and power to accomplish its great mission for humanity. This should not interfere with your daily activities, for you have only to turn mentally to this Center and say, "In the name of the Living Christ may the Heart Center of *The Order of the 15* be preserved as a pure channel through which Divine Love, Life and Wisdom may manifest. May increasing power be given it to accomplish its great work for humanity."

When repeating this prayer realize that the Heart Center includes more than those personalities at the Center who are engaged in the work of the Order, for the Heart Center of every movement includes the heart-love of every member, no matter where they may be. Hence your loving thoughts directed toward helping the Order will form a magic chain uniting all true members in love. It will also create a vortex into which there will irresistibly be drawn the positive force of the Divine.

Do not try to make the time coincide with the same hour in Los Angeles. Take the time of your own locality. For as we have pupils in all parts of the world the repetition of this prayer at noon will make a continuous stream of force pouring into the Center unceasingly.

To come into close vital touch with this Order each pupil should set apart at least fifteen minutes (thirty if possible) every Sunday evening at 8:30, during which the effort should be made to correlate with the special meeting held at the Center at that time.

At that time each should repeat, either aloud or mentally, the Prayer of Consecration and the Healing Prayer, and concentrate on coming to this Center in thought, realizing that at this time the Master is in the midst of His children; that His love includes all, no matter how distant; that at this time especially He is gathering all together to bless them, and that the streams of love and healing power are going out over the lines of force which connect each pupil with this Center. Over these lines of force the pupils on their part should send their love and help and a strong will that this Movement shall lack for nothing (either spiritually or materially) to make it a powerful factor on all planes to help humanity.

While the helpful forces are sent out to all alike, nevertheless those who thus consciously correlate with them and who give of their substance—which includes their love and earnest desire to help on all planes—will receive in exact proportion to the earnestness and devotion they express, for, by their desire to become co-workers in this Movement for the upliftment of humanity, they are literally merging themselves into oneness with the streams of living force poured out by The Lodge through this Order; for their desires are creative and will bring forth after their kind.

If any find it impossible to be alone at this time let them at least send us a strong thought of loving help, even if they are in the midst of a crowd.

The Secretary would be glad to know of any experiences the pupils may have in correlating with the Center in this service.

CHAPTER XXXIV

THE MEANING OF THE SYMBOL

**"Ministers of Christ and Stewards of
the Mysteries of God."**
1 Corinthians 4 vs. 1

The symbol of an Order is its standard or flag. It symbolizes both its source, its object and its policy and sets the standard by which it must be judged. Hence it is important that persons belonging to or coming in touch with any Order or Movement should understand something of the emblem by which it is known on the higher planes.

THE SEAL

This Seal like all true symbols, has many shades of interpretation—all of which are included in the figure—and can be applied to various conditions. These shades of meaning are applications suitable to various conditions and circumstances rather than contradictions. We will take it, however, as the Seal of *The Order of the 15* and endeavor to point out not only its meaning, but also how it can be made a positive help to all who are striving to reach the goal of spiritual attainment over the Path marked out by this Order.

The Seal consists of a double triangle inscribed in a circle, with an open Eye in the center and three five pointed stars in the spaces between the sides of the triangle and the circle.

The circle represents Boundless Space and limitless Time in Eternity. It marks off the space in which creation takes place, or the circle formed by the down pouring of the Great Creative Force, in this case the circumference within which this Order is working. It is much like the circle of light projected by a magic lantern, within which the pictures are to appear. In one sense it is the circle of the Zodiac (the pathway of our solar system) from the twelve Gates or Houses of which issues the radiant light of The Christos represented as focused in the center of the Open Eye. In another sense the circle is the Ring Pass Not (the limit of the auric zone) which every true disciple should put around himself, and whose Gates (corresponding to the centers of the body) he must open and close at will to admit or exclude that which he chooses. Thus the All-seeing Eye (the Absolute) sheds its seven fold creative rays within its creations. In the case of the Ring Pass Not the Eye is the Divine Flame or The Christ-force within each heart. In this Order it is the sacred altar upon which burns the Eternal Flame of spiritual light from whose illuminating rays emanate the inspired teachings.

The Triangle symbolizes the Trinity, and is the universal symbol of Deity,[1] the three aspects of the Logos, whether taken as the Father, Son and Holy Ghost of the Christians, the Osiris, Isis and Horus of the Egyptians or the more ancient Father—Mother—Son. The apex of the triangle represents the dual creative force of the Logos, separating into its positive and negative

---

1 *The Secret Doctrine*, Blavatsky, Vol. I, p. 138.

rays; the Mother (Isis, or the Holy Ghost), and the right hand line the Father (Osiris). These two send out their forces to form the base line, Horus, the Son, The Christ-principle poured forth and raining down upon the lower world, to manifest in all kingdoms as the Great Creative Principle which shall redeem them.

As used in this seal, the Triangle is composed of two sets of lines, representing either the masculine and feminine forces or involution and evolution. The inner line, the feminine, also stands for Intuition and Love, while the outer line represents Intellect and Wisdom. The spaces between the lines represent the three planes of manifestation—physical, mental and spiritual.

Just as it is impossible to draw an equilateral triangle within a circle without leaving three spaces, so is it impossible for the Trinity to express itself within the circle of manifestation without manifesting the three worlds. Hence these three spaces symbolize the three worlds or three states of consciousness.

Within each of these three spaces there is a five pointed star, representing man with his five senses and five extremities (hands, feet, head). The symbol represents man as existing upon the three planes of manifestation and using his five senses in each of the three states of consciousness. A man using his five senses on three planes of manifestation makes the number 15. Also 1+5=6, thus announcing through the symbol that this Order is a Sixth Race movement, and that only by teaching man to use his five senses on all three planes can he prepare for the great Sixth Race. As 6 is the number of The Christ (man 5 plus Divinity 1) it symbolizes that this movement is another attempt to bring the teachings of The Christ to humanity. In other words this symbol should inspire man to stand erect, and with all his known faculties illumined by the Light of Truth, fearlessly penetrate into the mysteries of his being.

The motto of the Order is *Dare, Do, Keep Silent,* hence this must be the measure of its work. These words being placed between the double lines of the triangle show how man can conquer the three planes of consciousness. He must *Dare* to penetrate into the deeper mysteries of life; *Dare* to follow the guidance of his Father-in-heaven and *Dare* to face himself and live up to his highest ideals without regard to the opinions of his friends or enemies. He must *Do* the will of his Higher Self and manifest it in his daily life. He must *Do* with all his heart the duty that his hands find to do, the duty that lies nearest, and *Do* unto others as he would they should do unto him. He should *Keep Silent* concerning the sacred experiences of his inner life when among those who cannot understand; should *Keep Silent* concerning his own attainments, also when tempted to criticize others. *Keep Silent* also has reference to that silent hush of the physical and mental activities that must come ere the higher centers can catch and transmit the vibrations from the higher planes. These words form the triple key that will unlock for man the doors of his inner consciousness and enable him to function on all planes and master all states of consciousness.

Taking the seal in its entirety, it shows to an Initiate that this Order is put forth by The Lodge to help man, through the use of his five known senses on all planes, to unfold his higher (unknown) faculties and reach up to the Divine. Many students of the higher life are striving to unfold and use their sixth and seventh senses before they have learned to use their five known senses on all planes. If such a thing were possible it would make a gap in their evolution which nothing could bridge, and they would sooner or later find themselves plunged into the depths of error.

The whole, being inscribed in a circle representing limitless Time in Eternity, shows that the symbol is active within this cycle of manifestation; moreover that it is intended as a direct preparation for the Sixth Great Race.

HOW TO FORM A STUDY CLASS

In the study of mysticism and occultism, in addition to the careful reading and meditation upon the ideals presented, it is helpful to have a number who are interested in the same teachings organize a class and study together. The union of the auras of a number of harmonized students creates a vortex into which a strong force of enlightenment on the subject studied is naturally drawn.

Arrange to meet regularly at some convenient place, such as a member's home, in the evening if possible, as this permits both men and women to attend, and choose one of your number to read the lesson. Select a few pages of the book a week in advance of the meeting and have each member carefully study and meditate upon them during the week, making notes of the ideas that seem most important.

Begin promptly at the hour designated. Open the meeting with a period of Silence in which you still your mind, turn the current of your thoughts from the affairs of daily life and concentrate them upon some harmonizing topic announced beforehand, such as harmony, peace, light, love, understanding, etc. Have the leader read a few lines from the lesson selected and all who feel so prompted comment thereon, especially giving the new ideas that may have come to them during their study. Invite interruptions and discussion. Any questions you cannot answer send to the Superintendent of Local Centers, who will submit them to the Teacher and explanations will be returned as soon as possible. Keep a kindly but firm rein over all discussions, allowing plenty of latitude, so long as it does not stray too far away from the subject. *Studiously avoid arguments.* One should state one's interpretation of the passage under discussion and let it rest there. It will be excellent training in clear thinking to formulate your opinion as definitely as possible. Do not try to convince others or impose your views upon them. Simply state your views and grant to others the same freedom of thought and expression which you desire for yourself. Above all be cheerful and good natured and let peace, harmony and love abound, for without these conditions the study will degenerate into mere intellectual discussions and the Voice of Intuition which you are seeking to cultivate will be drowned out.

In this way meetings become intensely interesting and helpful, for the different viewpoints brought out serve to make clear phases of the subject not always in the printed lesson. Thus one lesson will often extend over three or four meetings. Strive ever to bring out the heart or Christ side in all your discussions of the lesson, not permitting the intellectual to predominate. Seek for the loving help that is contained in each lesson and always conclude by pointing it out plainly so that all can see and carry it home with them.

Let all the students strive continually to spread the Teachings wherever and whenever Wisdom inspires them, but do not seek to force them upon anyone. Have them invite their friends to the meetings, those to whom they are led to talk and who become interested, but not to be anxious about their coming, leaving them free to follow the leadings of their own hearts.

Try to send in monthly reports of the progress of your meetings and of the different members, always encouraging, however, personal correspondence direct with the Order when a student is confronted with a vital Soul problem.

If a name is chosen for the class remember that names have occult powers and the class will have to demonstrate that it can live up to the name chosen.

After the class has been working harmoniously for some time, if it is desired to expand it into a Local Center of the Order to carry on a more organized line of work, write to the Superintendent of Local Centers for further information.

ANNOUNCEMENT

"Behold, I bring unto you good tidings of great joy."

To all students of the higher life who truly desire to progress, and who wish the opportunity of coming into closer personal touch with those Masters of Wisdom, who, through all ages, have been the Teachers, Guides and Elder Brothers of humanity, there comes the following message:

In accordance with the geometrical design of the universe, a point in evolution is now reached when an advanced Order has been established upon the earth plane. This Order is not an organization in the general acceptation of the term, *nor is it connected either with the outer or inner work of any other occult organization now in existence on the physical plane.* It is a new unifying, Spiritual Movement put forth by those Great Intelligences who are the Guides and Teachers of humanity. According to its fundamental principles, only such earnest students can be admitted to full membership as have proven their devotion to humanity, and have sent out their cry for further enlightenment and help. All such persons are welcomed into this Order, and such probationary lessons will be sent them, from time to time, as will afford them an opportunity of coming into close fellowship and conscious communion with the Masters of Wisdom. Understand this point clearly: It will be *only through your own individual effort,* your attitude of Soul and the character of your subsequent life that will enable you to place yourself in personal, conscious touch with the Masters. *It depends upon no personality but your own.*

No vows or pledges are asked of Associate Students, for only those are eligible to full membership in this Order who have voluntarily given up their lives to the higher law, and have already vowed allegiance to their own Higher Self. But all who sincerely desire the help this Order offers are welcomed as Associate Students.

The teachings of this Order will not conflict with any duties of life, or with membership in other organizations, or membership in any religious denomination.

SPECIAL INFORMATION

The Order of the 15 is but one name for a great
Cosmic Order which has always existed and through
which all Souls who have reached Mastery have passed
on some plane at a certain stage of their evolution. It
has been represented upon the earth-plane at certain cyclic intervals in all ages and it has been known under
various names. Its manifestation upon the earth-plane
during the present cycle began on January 1st, 1908, in
Philadelphia, Pa., and in less than three years it encir-
cled the globe, having pupils—including Christian and
Buddhistic missionaries—in China, Japan, India and
the heart of Africa, as well as in almost every civilized
country of the globe.

THE ORDER OF THE 15

The Order of the 15 is a non-sectarian movement for
the promulgation of Christian Mysticism. It is a response
to the heart-hunger of humanity for a clearer understanding of the laws of The Christ-life. It is not put forth to
form a new sect or cult, to further divide up and separate
humanity, or to form another pigeonhole in which to
isolate a few followers, nor does it come to secure a
following for any human leader or personality. It is an
impersonal and universal unifying, Spiritual Movement,
without creed, dogma, rules or pledges. Instead of em-
phasizing the differences between its teachings and all
others, it strives to establish a platform so universal that
its pupils can find in it *some one thing* to which they
can agree, even though that one thing be not the same
for all—and thus become a link to join the best efforts

of all into one great universal effort to make Brotherhood manifest on earth. For true Brotherhood does not mean all thinking alike, but each recognizing Truth wherever found and *demonstrating* love and tolerance toward those who find a different aspect of Truth more helpful.

This Order does not ask its pupils to leave any church, society or organization in which they feel they can do their best work for humanity. It but seeks to help all to understand the workings of the great fundamental Law of Love, and thus enable them to do their own work the better, in their own way and place. It asks no one to subordinate his individuality or to follow any leader, but leaves all free to follow the Truth as revealed to them. It does not require that any of its teachings be accepted by its students because some authority says they are true, for unless a teaching appeals to the heart and rings true to a Soul it is not true to that Soul. Truth is not an abstract principle. It is that which remains as pure gold after passing through the fires of daily living and testing. Hence, no authority is enforced, except the authority of that Voice within each heart which recognizes and witnesses to Truth wherever found.

ORGANIZATIONS

All organizations and movements which receive help from the Masters of Wisdom have their own particular work to do. Whether they have succeeded in the task set before them, or whether they have failed, is clearly shown by their results, and the same rule must be applied to the work of this Order. But many students have outgrown organizations, having found them too narrow and their necessary limitations too binding. This is but a natural feature of growth and again proves the Great law, "As above, so below ;" just as the seed, when first planted, is confined in a protective sheath from which, in the process of growth, it will burst forth. Hence, an avenue of instruction and help has been put forth that is not an organization and which is not limited in its activities.

This movement is not an organization because it has no constitution or by-laws, no officers (except the Secretary), requires no pledges and no dues and does not restrict a student's activity in any society or organization. Therefore it is not antagonistic to, or a rival of, any existing organization that is helping humanity, but permits perfect freedom. It holds out the hand of Brotherhood to each and gives to all an opportunity to *prove* the ideals of Brotherhood and tolerance which they profess.

AS TO OTHER MOVEMENTS

Although we emphasized our relation to organizations in the beginning by placing the statement in italics, yet it is overlooked by many. Therefore we will restate our position more fully herewith, so that in the future there may be no question as to the significance of this Movement and its relation to all others.

We can but reiterate that while *we are not connected, in any way, with the outer or inner workings of any other organization now on the earth plane*, nevertheless we stand for Truth wherever found, our motto being, "By their fruits ye shall know them."

Under no circumstances do we criticize any. If an organization, society or movement has helped one Soul to take one step upon the Path to Mastery it has not wrought in vain.

"Whosoever shall give to drink unto one of these little ones a cup of cold water only in the name of a disciple, verily I say unto you, he shall in no wise lose his reward! . . . Inasmuch as ye have done it unto one of the least of these, my brethren, ye have done it unto me."

The fact that a teaching attracts and helps you is evidence that it contains the lessons needed by you for the step you are taking. The fact that a movement no longer appeals to you, no matter how helpful it may be to others, is evidence either that your Soul has learned the lessons that movement had for you—even though not mastered intellectually—or that the movement, no matter how beautifully conceived and launched, has become tainted with something that is not helpful, or is perhaps distinctly injurious to your physical, mental, moral or spiritual growth. Hence, to remain connected with an organization to which you no longer feel drawn, or which you have outgrown, is as detrimental to your Soul-growth as it would be for a flower to remain in a pot which had become too small for it or whose soil had become exhausted or contaminated. No vows given to any earthly organization can bind a Soul which, through natural growth, has evolved beyond them.

Each movement that aims to help humanity has its own place and its own Work. Colored blocks are necessary in the kindergarten, primers for children, text-books for the training of the mind in school and college; but when the mind has been trained it must then put that training to use in a practical way: in business, under the head of the firm or manager; in art, under a great teacher; in spiritual things, under a Master of Wisdom. But remember that, because you are no longer interested in the colored blocks or primers you once thought so beautiful, you are not to despise the children who still cling to them, or find fault with the teachers of the a-b-c's. All have their place, and the children will grow away from the blocks when they have learned their lessons, just as you have grown. And the proof that you have outgrown earthly organizations will be the love and tolerance with which you treat all your brothers and sisters who still feel the need of such methods. To rail at organizations, especially one which has helped you to reach your present state, and those who work in them, is proof that you still need their discipline. Every uplifting movement or teaching has its place and has for followers those who need its lessons.

AIMS OF THIS MOVEMENT

One of the chief objects of this Movement is to correlate advanced philosophical teachings with the orthodox Christian teachings; to form a neutral ground where both can meet and recognize Truth, and to reach the great mass of people who will not join organizations or occult societies of any kind. On this account we may disappoint many intellectual students, for our language will purposely be made simple, and the great truths which we set forth will be so stated as to appeal to minds schooled in Western religious thought. Our great object is to enable all sections of spiritual seekers—New Thought, Spiritualism, Theosophy, Christianity; in fact all lovers of Truth—to draw together at the heart center. *This is a necessary preparation for the near advent of the great Spiritual Teacher for the Western World who is soon to appear, the Avatar.* The good news of His quick coming must be given "unto all people," not merely to a few intellectual thinkers. All schools of spiritual thought need this preparation.

The great psychic awakening now sweeping over the land has brought many students to the point where

their inner faculties are unfolding. This is a point of
great danger; for here the two paths—the Right Hand
and the Left Hand—diverge. This Order may be called a
wayside House of Rest, placed at the point of divergence
of the paths, at whose door every pilgrim who knocks
finds welcome, and within rest, sympathy, understanding and encouragement, also a guide to lead him safely
past the many dangers and pitfalls that surround the
entrance to the Right Hand Path. This is a personal work
which could not be accomplished by any organization
limited by set rules.

While the teachings of this Order are those of the
Wisdom Religion, they are not theosophic in the sense
of being put forth by any of the numerous societies
promulgating such teachings, for they deal with the
Christian *Bible* quite as much as with Eastern teachings.

*One object of these teachings is to bring to the at-
tention of the world, as simply as possible, the Pearls
of Wisdom in the teachings of the Master Jesus—pearls
that have been overlaid with wordy misconceptions so
long as to be almost unrecognizable.*

As all religions, sects and creeds contain at least a
germ of Truth, our aim is to help each one to find that
germ in *his own teachings*, and to purify and develop
it into the Tree of Life in his own garden. We thus help
them to purify their conception of Truth as expressed
in their own religion.

There is a real necessity for the various presen-
tations of Truth as given to the world; for just as the
climate, flora and fauna of a country, and the language and customs of its people vary in different
parts of the world, so must Truth garb itself in habili-
ments suited to the modes of thought of the people
to whom it is given. There is a deep, occult reason

underlying this law, and St. Paul recognized it when he said, "Be ye all things unto all men." There comes a time, however, in all organized bodies giving out spiritual teachings when some student will advance as far or farther than the leaders of the organization. And since it is only natural for such leaders to assume that they are more advanced than any of their students, inharmony and dissatisfaction or even secession result.

In the development of all students a point is reached where they need the advanced, *personal* instruction, not of any leaders—who are themselves but students—but of One who has at His command all knowledge and all wisdom, *i.e.*, a Master of Wisdom.[1] It is in answer to this personal need that The Lodge of Masters has put forth *The Order of the 15* at this time. It comes as a direct response to the prayers of many, many hearts for more light, love, sympathy and *personal guidance* in the problems of their spiritual life.

As this continent is to be the home of a new Race which will ultimately perfect itself by the survival and interblending of the fittest of all the races now existing, so must its religious thought be blended and purified that it may emerge as a pure ray which has gathered into itself the force from all its sub-rays.

The Order of the 15 is put forth in an effort to awaken The Christ-love in the hearts of men, rather than to cater to the intellect or the desire for psychic powers; for only those who can correlate with The Christ-power can be gathered together to form a nucleus in which this Power can be individualized on earth. The aim of this Movement is especially to help

---

1 It is understood, of course, that the Secretary does not answer the letters or compose the teachings. He is merely the Secretary in the ordinary sense of the word.

all Christian people to find the deep, underlying, vital truths common to all religions in their own, and thus truly, and in the only way possible, prepare for an Universal Brotherhood on earth in which each Soul shall find the same vital truths spoken in his own language, *i.e.*, couched and taught in terms of the religion in which he was born.[1]

FINANCIAL OBLIGATIONS

In this present age the Masters must work through human agencies and the moment you determine to give of yourself and your worldly substance to this work you become Their recognized agent. But if you desire to help humanity through this avenue and to receive the personal training necessary to do efficient work, and have no worldly substance to give, do not hesitate on that account, for you can only give of that which you have to give.

In such an Order dues, as such, would be impossible, for there can be no price placed upon spiritual truth. But as the workers at the headquarters give their time and talents without salary, and as the expenses incident to a world-wide Movement must be provided for, it is expected that all who desire to help will voluntarily aid the work by contributions *in accordance with their ability* and the Law of exact Justice. It is a primal law of occultism that, no matter how much is set before you, you are able to assimilate only in exact ratio with the spirit of helping others which you display. If the teachings help you it will be evidence that they can help others, hence that you can best serve humanity by making it possible to spread these teachings abroad.

Of course this Movement cannot be carried on without financial support and it greatly needs such

1 See *Acts* II, 6.

support—for the Law of Justice permits humanity to be helped only to the extent that, through its own efforts, it makes it possible for the help to reach it. If you feel an inner urge to study with us, and if you find that the lessons help you, you will naturally desire to make it possible for other Souls to receive the same. Therefore, out of pure love and a desire to help others you will give as much as you can afford. Let all give according to their ability.

PRAYERS

Prayers of *The Order of Christian Mystics*

––––

PRAYER FOR LIGHT

O Christ! Light Thou within my heart
The Flame of Divine Love and Wisdom,
That I may dwell forever in the radiance of Thy countenance
And rest in the Light of Thy smile!

MORNING PRAYER

I have within me the power of the Christ!
I can conquer all that comes to me today!
I am strong enough to bear every trial
And accept every joy
And to say
Thy will be done!

HEALING PRAYER

O thou loving and helpful Master Jesus!
Thou who gavest to Thy disciples power to heal the sick!
We, recognizing Thee, and realizing Thy divine Presence with us,
Ask Thee to lay Thy hands (powers) upon us in healing Love.
Cleanse US from all OUR sins, and by the divine power of Omnipotent Life,
Drive out the atoms of inharmony and disease, and
Fill our bodies full to overflowing with Life and Love and Purity.

PRAYER OF PROTECTION

O Christ! Surround and fill me and Thy Order with the Flame of Divine Love
   and Wisdom,
That it may purify, illumine and guide us in all things.
May its Spiritual Fire form a rampart of Living Flame around me and Thy Order,
To protect us from all harm.
May it radiate to every heart, consuming all evil and intensifying
all good.
In the name of the Living Christ! Amen.

PRAYER OF DEMONSTRATION

I am a child of the Living God!
I have within me the all-creating power of the Christ!

It radiates from me and blesses all I contact.
It is my Health, my Strength, my Courage,
My Patience, my Peace, my Poise,
My Power, my Wisdom, my Understanding,
My Joy, my Inspiration, and my Abundant Supply.
Unto this great Power I entrust all my problems,
Knowing they will be solved in Love and Justice.
(Mention all problems connected with your worldly affairs, visualize each and
   conclude with the following words)
O Lord Christ! I have laid upon Thy altar all my wants and desires.
I know Thy Love, Thy Wisdom, Thy Power and Thy Graciousness.
In Thee I peacefully rest, knowing that all is well.
For Thy will is my will. Amen.

PRAYER TO THE DIVINE INDWELLER
   Come, O Lord of Life and Love and Beauty!
   Thou who art myself and yet art God!
   And dwell in this body of flesh,
   Radiating all the beauty of holiness and perfection,
   That the flesh may out-picture all that Thou art within!
   Even so, come, O Lord. Amen.

PRAYER TO THE DIVINE MOTHER
   O Divine Mother!
   Illumine me with Divine Wisdom,
   Vivify me with Divine Life and
   Purify me with Divine Love,
   That in all I think and say and do
   I may be more and more Thy child. Amen.

GRACE BEFORE MEALS
   I am a creator.
   By the power of my spiritualized Will
   I consciously gather all the forces from this food,
   And use them to create food, health, strength and harmony
   In all my bodies (physical, astral and mental).

PRAYER OF DEVOTION
   We, Thy chosen servants, to whom Thou hast given the great privilege of
   becoming co-workers with the Masters of Wisdom, ask that we may have
   Wisdom and Power and Courage and Humility to carry us through the work
   of this day.

We open our hearts that the Divine Love of the Master may fill us; that all irritation, inharmony and slothfulness may be transmuted into Love that shall draw us closer in unity to all our fellow workers both seen and unseen; that we may grow absolutely one with the force of Wisdom and Compassion that is sent forth to accomplish the great work for humanity.

Give us all things necessary, that there may be no hampering conditions.

Lead us through this day, in the name of the Divine, Everliving Christ, that the will of the Father may be done in us and through us forevermore. Amen.

PRAYER FOR WORLD HARMONY

Glory and honor and worship be unto Thee, O Lord Christ,
Thou who art the Life and Light of all mankind.
Thou art the King of Glory to whom all the peoples of the Earth should give joyful allegiance and service.
Inspire mankind with a realization of true Brotherhood.
Teach us the wisdom of peace, harmony and co-operation.
Breathe into our hearts the understanding that only as we see ourselves as parts of the one body of humanity can peace, harmony, success and plenty descend upon us.
Help us to conquer all manifestations of inharmony and evil in ourselves and in the world.
May all persons and classes and nations cease their conflicts, and unselfishly strive for peace and goodwill that the days of tribulation may be shortened.
Bless us all with the radiance of Thy Divine Love and Wisdom that we may ever worship Thee in the beauty of holiness.
In the Name of the Living Christ we ask it. Amen.

PRAYER FOR THE CHRIST POWER

O Lord Christ! Thou who hast planted within me
The Immortal Power of Spiritual Love and Life,
Help me so to correlate with Thy divine overshadowing Presence,
That all hampering conditions shall be swallowed up
In the Light of the Living Christ Power. Amen.

EVENING PRAYER

As the physical Sun
Disappears from our sight
May the Spiritual Sun
Arise in our hearts,
Illumine our minds
And shed its radiant blessing
Upon all we contact.

INDEX

www.ingramcontent.com/pod-product-compliance
Lightning Source LLC
Chambersburg PA
CBHW062144080426
42734CB00010B/1564